TANKING TO THE TOP

TANKING TO THE TOP

The Philadelphia 76ers and the
Most Audacious Process in the
History of Professional Sports

YARON WEITZMAN

GRAND CENTRAL
PUBLISHING

New York Boston

Grand Central Publishing
Hachette Book Group
1290 Avenue of the Americas, New York, NY 10104
grandcentralpublishing.com
twitter.com/grandcentralpub

First Edition: March 2020

Grand Central Publishing is a division of Hachette Book Group, Inc. The Grand Central Publishing name and logo is a trademark of Hachette Book Group, Inc.

The publisher is not responsible for websites (or their content) that are not owned by the publisher.

The Hachette Speakers Bureau provides a wide range of authors for speaking events. To find out more, go to www.hachettespeakersbureau.com or call (866) 376-6591.

This book is not associated, endorsed or sponsored by Joel Embiid, who owns a trademark registered in the U.S. for the name "The Process."

Library of Congress Cataloging-in-Publication Data
Names: Weitzman, Yaron, author.
Title: Tanking to the top: the Philadelphia 76ers and the most audacious process in the history of professional sports / by Yaron Weitzman. Description: First edition. |
New York: Grand Central Publishing, 2020. |
Includes index.
Identifiers: LCCN 2019041816 | ISBN 9781538749722 (hardcover) | ISBN 9781538749746 (ebook)
Subjects: LCSH: Philadelphia 76ers (Basketball team)—History. | Organizational change.
Classification: LCC GV885.52.P45 W44 2020 | DDC 796.323/6409748n—dc23
LC record available at https://lccn.loc.gov/2019041816

Printed in the United States of America

LSC-C

10 9 8 7 6 5 4 3 2 1

To Micole:
Thank you for trusting my process.

CONTENTS

TANKING TO THE TOP

PROLOGUE

The architect of The Process[1] had no interest in talking to me about, well, The Process. "I'm perfectly comfortable with everyone drawing their own conclusions," Sam Hinkie told me one evening. This was the second time we'd spoken over the phone. Both conversations could be best described as frivolous. "I don't have any interest or willingness to quote-unquote shape a legacy," Hinkie said. "I'm not built that way. It's just not what I want to do."

That was back in the fall of 2018, before Hinkie ceased answering nearly every one of my texts, which, of course, was his right. This was also before he began instructing friends, family, and even employees at alma maters to decline interviews with me. Also his right, and something he'd done with countless reporters before me. But frustrating nonetheless.

An example: One morning last September I called a childhood friend of his named Duane Lovett.

"I'd love to talk," Lovett told me. "Call me at two this afternoon."

When the time arrived later that day, my call went to voicemail. I texted Lovett. He responded that he was going to have to "pass on that

---

1 A Google search reveals that all profiles about said architect must begin this way.

talk." I laughed and messaged Hinkie. "I'll say this," I wrote, "I admire your relentless informing of people from your life to not speak with me." I added a smiley face at the end because I'm a serious journalist.

"You should admire the depth of our relationships," Hinkie responded.

I, however, still had a book to write, a story to tell. I still needed to illustrate who Sam Hinkie is as a person. I still needed to explain what he sought to accomplish during his two-plus years as the president of basketball operations for the National Basketball Association's Philadelphia 76ers. There's the obvious and simple answer—winning a championship—but it seemed to me that there must be more to it, or at least more to him. Few leaders in the history of sports have ever so willingly and aggressively sacrificed the present in order to chase a better future. Hinkie wasn't the first to try taking advantage of the warped incentive system found in most professional sports in which bad teams are rewarded with good draft picks, but he did take this plan to a new extreme and in doing so drove the basketball world mad. Hinkie triggered a culture war. To some fans, he and his plan—dubbed by others "The Process," as in "Trust The Process," an homage to Hinkie's belief in focusing on process over results—was the closest thing to religion they'd ever experienced. To others, he was the NBA's Bernie Madoff. He angered agents, annoyed that one of the thirty teams capable of paying their clients had essentially removed itself from the marketplace, and irritated competitors, many of whom felt Hinkie was violating the first rule of professional sports, summarized so perfectly years earlier by former New York Jets head coach Herm Edwards:

You play to win the game.

If he were to talk about his own legacy, I'm guessing Hinkie would counter that he *was* playing to win the game, but that the only game he cared about winning was the championship. Still, there was so much more I wanted to know, so much I was curious about, so much I felt I still needed to learn, and so you can imagine my excitement when, a few weeks after the quip about his deep relationships, I discovered the name of a person who I believed could provide me a more substantive answer.

In April 2016, Hinkie officially resigned from his position with the Sixers. Five months earlier, at the behest of the NBA, the team had hired Jerry Colangelo as a special adviser. Colangelo had spent nearly fifty years as an NBA executive. He was as powerful and respected as anyone within the basketball world and not a person interested in letting others dictate. Hinkie understood exactly what his arrival meant.

Hinkie resigned, and did so via letter. But this wasn't just another resignation letter. Addressed to the Sixers' equity partners—and quickly leaked to the media—it went on for thirteen pages. It featured a bullet point about a flightless bird from New Zealand called the moa. It had subsections paying homage to famous investors like Charlie Munger. It quoted Abraham Lincoln twice. That neither Lincoln quote was actually spoken by Lincoln is beside the point. (Hey, who among us *hasn't* been duped by the Internet?) More important, it offered an in-depth look into the mind of its author.

"Science is about predictions," Hinkie wrote at one point. A couple sentences later he quoted a man named Tim Urban, who, Hinkie said, "will soon be recognized as one of tomorrow's polymaths." Then, in parenthesis, came a piece of advice. "Like many of you," Hinkie wrote to the Sixers' ownership group, "he lives in New York—I'd recommend meeting him for coffee sometime."

This suggestion may not have been addressed to me, but I figured why not take Hinkie's advice? After all, I too live in New York. Also, and more to the point, Hinkie and Urban had clearly engaged in rigorous scientific and philosophical conversations. Urban, it seemed, was a man who could provide some of the answers I was desperately searching for.

But first I had to figure out who the hell Tim Urban was.

I cued up Google and discovered that Urban was the thirty-something-year-old author of a long-form blog called *Wait But Why*. One of his essays, titled "How to Pick a Career (That Actually Fits You)," was more than fifteen thousand words and featured friendly-looking graphs and charts. Another fourteen-thousand-word entry was about cryonics and why they "make sense." The posts were littered with references to Urban's relationship with Elon Musk.

I found an email address and introduced myself. A few weeks later an assistant, Alicia, replied. "We should be able to set up a quick 15-minute call for this month," she wrote. I told her that I was actually looking to follow the advice of Sam Hinkie and meet Urban for coffee.

"We stick to phone calls (or virtual coffee meetings over Skype!) as much as possible as it doesn't break up his writing flow as much," she replied, "and they're much easier to schedule ahead of time as Tim's location can be a bit unpredictable this far in advance." Not ideal, but I figured harping on whether the coffee was shared in person or virtually was the sort of thing only non-polymaths worried about. I told Alicia that Skype was great.

Two months later, on a Friday morning, I swapped my usual outfit of sweats for jeans and stopped at the Starbucks across the street from my office to pick up a caramel macchiato.

At 10:30 I called Urban on Skype and sipped from my macchiato as the app rang. No answer. I tried again. Still no answer. Finally, on my third call, he picked up. The picture was fuzzy, but he appeared to be wearing a red flannel button-down.

"Can you see me?" he asked.

"Not really."

"It's a little delayed, let me try calling you back."

He did. I answered. The picture was still delayed and fuzzy.

"Let's try one more time," he said.

He did. No change.

"How about I call you," Urban said. I gave him my number. We were now stretching the boundaries of "having coffee together."

I asked Urban how he met Hinkie. He told me that Hinkie had reached out to him a few times via email. "I know about his work, obviously," he said. "I read his long letter and think he's a pretty awesome dude." He scrolled through his computer and cued up Hinkie's first message, sent March 14, 2016. He read it out loud.

"He said that 'my name is Sam Hinkie, I've become a fan of your writing, we're headed to New York now because we play the Nets tomorrow night and I wanted to see if you possibly have any time to get together tomorrow, I'd do my best to make it interesting for you.'"

Urban doesn't follow the NBA, but he said he recognized Hinkie's name. "I knew the Sixers were doing a really creative and innovative type of rebuilding," he said. "I'm a fan." Unfortunately, he had no availability the next day. Hinkie tried again a few months later, after resigning. Once again Urban was out of town. Next, it was Urban's turn to try. He was scheduled to be in Philadelphia around October. By then Hinkie had moved to Palo Alto.

"And then he wrote back on November 1," Urban told me. He read Hinkie's message out loud. "I'll be in New York much of next week, happy to grab coffee or a meal if your schedule allows. I bet we can find a bunch to kick around."

Urban paused for a second and tapped on his keyboard.

"Oh, shoot! I never saw this and never responded." He seemed genuinely upset. "I can't believe it."

I laughed. "So you two never actually had coffee?"

"No, we never did. But I think at the time it was so imminent, it was clearly going to happen."

I was disappointed. Also a bit confused by Hinkie suggesting others do something that he himself never did. Still, it wasn't every day I got to speak with "one of tomorrow's polymaths." I figured there was still an opportunity for me to learn, to maybe gain some insight into the type of thinking Hinkie is drawn to.

I asked Urban why he believes his work appeals to Hinkie. He mentioned an idea he often writes about, which essentially boils down to inventing your own reasoning versus "copying what's normal to do, normal to think." He dived into a cooking analogy to illustrate his point. "A chef writes his own recipe, plays around with a bunch of ingredients, and fails often. But sometimes he comes up with something that's totally different and new and better than we've had before." A cook, on the other hand, "just takes the recipes that have succeeded the most, that are currently being followed, and builds everything around the recipes that have already been proven to work. That's how you protect yourself from true failure—not how you become an original. The way to actually do something great, something that really surprises people and changes things, is to be more of a science experiment and actually try stuff. That's going to lead to a lot of failure, and people who are cooks never understand the chef until the chef succeeds. But when the chef does succeed, he creates something truly transcendent."

By now he was rolling.

"Geniuses are often mocked by society before getting rewarded," he continued. "In the past they'd sometimes be executed. Society often thinks they're arrogant, when really what chefs are saying is, 'I'm more humble about what we know, about, for example, what makes a good basketball team.'"

I told Urban that boasting about one's own humility seemed sort of oxymoronic and, well, Trumpian. "But in this case it's really talking about humility," he said. "The first thing a chef says in a room full of cooks is, 'I don't know how to best do this and that's okay.'"

I texted Hinkie that night, informing him that I followed his advice and "had coffee" with Tim Urban. I also told him that Urban realized he had missed Hinkie's last email and felt awful about it.

Hinkie used his iPhone to "like" the text.

Sam Hinkie wasn't the only one who wouldn't talk to me for this project.

"The Sixers are terrified of your book," one former team employee told me in the fall. This was back when I was young and naïve and thought I was writing the NBA version of *Moneyball*, not a tale of palace intrigue more akin to *Game of Thrones*. This employee, like many of his former colleagues, had recently received a call from the team reminding him of the nondisclosure agreement he'd signed as part of his severance package.

I had notified the Sixers of my book contract over the summer, to let them know that I'd be reporting around the team and to see if they wanted to be involved. About a month later a public relations official called to notify me that the team would not be participating. This was fine, and sort of expected. I still possessed the credential that came along with my day job as an NBA reporter for Bleacher Report, which the Sixers allowed me to use throughout the 2018–2019 season. But my relationship with the team often felt strained. For one, current employees were told to stay away from me because I was writing this book. Sources were called by higher-ups and asked to strike quotes. Players were instructed not to have book-related conversations. At one point I had broached the idea of an in-depth interview with a Sixers player with whom I had a strong professional relationship.

"Sure," he said. "I'll give you an hour whenever you need."

I approached the player a couple months later about officially setting up a time.

"I'm sorry," he said. "I've been instructed not to do any interviews for the book. There's nothing I can do. They're my employer."

Officially, I had a cordial relationship with the team the rest of the year. They even helped with one or two stories. But behind the scenes the Sixers did almost everything they could to prevent me from telling this story. Only at the very end, after I sent them a list of specific questions and offered them the opportunity to comment, did they participate in any book-related discussions. These were limited to a few off-the-record conversations with Sixers public relations officials and a quick off-the-record chat with Sixers head coach Brett Brown.

I write all this to set up the context and framing of the pages ahead. For this book I conducted interviews with about 175 people. I spoke to current and former players, basketball staffers, and business employees. I spoke to these people's friends. I spoke to player agents. I spoke with opposing executives. Some individuals were willing to go on the record, but most of these interviews were conducted on background, meaning I could use the information but the sources had to remain anonymous. I discovered early on that to tell this story properly I needed sources who could speak candidly. (After I had started my reporting, I learned that the Sixers were contacting former employees to remind them of their nondisclosure agreements.) They needed to know that no stories or anecdotes would be traced back to them, which is why you won't see much direct attribution in the pages ahead.

Why no one currently affiliated with the team ever tried selling me on their version of this story, I'm still not quite sure. Something about Sam Hinkie and The Process spooks the team's ownership and management. But no matter what they do, no matter how hard they wish, The Process will always be a part of the Sixers. It hovers over the organization like a thick fog. All the drama, all the infighting between general managers and owners and CEOs and coaches and stars, all the egos and competing agendas and mysterious injuries and secret Twitter accounts can be traced back to the decision to hand the reins to Sam Hinkie in May 2013. He may be long gone, but in Philadelphia The Process lives on. This is its story.

Chapter 1

PURGATORY

Six years before hiring Sam Hinkie in 2013, the Sixers were led by another general manager who considered going down a Process-like path.

Billy King had arrived in Philadelphia a year after the Sixers had taken Allen Iverson first overall in the 1996 draft. He'd watched him grow into an MVP and seen the ways he'd energized both the city and the team. But now the time had come to move on. The Sixers were no longer winning, and Iverson's presence was doing more harm than good. In December 2006, Iverson demanded a trade. King, weary of his star's malcontent ways, was more than happy to oblige. This, he believed, was an opportunity. Iverson was still one of the league's premier scorers, still the sort of player who could fetch all sorts of different offers. Trading him would allow King to remake the Sixers any way he wanted. And what King wanted was to build through the draft.

He had two options. One was to tear everything down, to punt the rest of the 2006–2007 season, and maybe even the one after that, and to find a suitor willing to surrender draft picks and young players. This was King's opportunity to take advantage of the NBA's aspiration for parity. Every year the best college and international basketball players enter the league through a draft, whose order is determined via lottery.

The worse a team's record the previous year, the better its chances at receiving a high pick. It's a way to throw a life vest to sinking teams but also offers an incentive to lose. If King wanted to, he could gut the team, and the Sixers would likely wind up with one of the top players in the 2007 draft.

Then there was the second option. King could try threading the needle: He could target young players, and draft picks, but also try recouping a veteran or two to help keep his team afloat. This would bridge the gap between the Iverson era and whatever came next, which, in theory, would help the team's bottom line, which, in theory, would please ownership, which, in theory, would allow King to remain secure in his job.

King agonized over the choice. On December 19, the Denver Nuggets called with a take-it-or-leave it offer. King considered his options and spoke with his mentor, Hall of Fame head coach Larry Brown. Finally, he made up his mind.

That afternoon he called Iverson. "You're going to be a Denver Nugget," King told him.

Six years later, The Process was born.

———

Brown had brought King with him to Philadelphia nine years earlier. The Sixers were coming off six straight losing seasons, and the days of all-time greats like Wilt Chamberlain, Julius "Dr. J" Erving, Moses Malone, and Charles Barkley captivating fans while donning Sixers uniforms were long gone. Sixteen years had passed since the team's last NBA title. One of the NBA's most iconic franchises had somehow faded into an afterthought.

But now there was a hope. The Sixers possessed a young, transcendent star in Allen Iverson. A once-in-a-generation talent, Iverson was a fierce and fearless not-even-six-foot jitterbug who could impose his will in a game typically governed by giants. On the floor, Iverson was a spectacle. But he was also more than that. He was brash. He didn't care for authority. The ink blanketing his black skin was as much a part of his uniform as his Sixers jersey. He'd stroll into press conferences with his hair braided into cornrows and pants so baggy that you couldn't make out the outlines of his skinny legs. Players around the league followed his lead. Almost single-handedly, Iverson merged the worlds of hip-hop and the NBA. Mostly as a reaction to him, and in an attempt to soothe its spooked corporate (i.e., white) partners, the NBA instituted a dress code in 2005, banning players from showing up to league events in hats, do-rags, large jewelry, or pretty much any article of clothing or accessory that looked lifted from a rap video.

Iverson had played just two seasons at Georgetown University before being drafted first overall by the Sixers in 1996. He was named Rookie of the Year in 1997, even though his Sixers won just 22 games, at the time the third-worst mark in franchise history. It was the beginning of a trend that would follow Iverson throughout his career: individual accomplishments not always translating into team success.

The team's new owners at Comcast Spectacor—a subsidiary of Comcast run by chairman Ed Snider—were unwilling to accept such results. The losing especially irked new team president Pat Croce, who was in the midst of launching a massive rebranding project meant to "modernize" the team. He'd soon unveil a new logo, with the team's name written in gold blocks as opposed to the traditional blue and red, and have the Sixers wearing black uniforms on the road. But he knew winning was what mattered most and that turning the Sixers into a winner meant pairing Iverson with the right coach.

Enter Brown, a former collegiate point guard who as a coach had led the University of Kansas to a title in 1988. Brown had spent the previous decade bouncing around the NBA. He was considered one of the shrewdest, and sternest, coaches in the league. Croce believed Brown possessed the acumen and demeanor to both connect with Iverson as a person and harness all his electrifying talent.

At times, the partnership flourished. The two men had more in common than most knew. Like Iverson, Brown was raised by a single mom. Like Iverson, the 5-foot-9 Brown had thrived on the court despite being undersized. Like Iverson, Brown's fire was fueled by a compulsive need to win, no matter the cost.

But the stretches of harmony grew shorter as the years went by.

One problem? Iverson knew just one way to play: at full speed, with the ball in his hands. Everything ran through him; his teammates were left to fight for the scraps. There were other issues, too. Iverson often showed up to practices late and smelling of booze. He barely lifted weights or tended to his rail-thin 165-pound frame. He asked out of games. He often loafed on defense. His shoulders occasionally sank when teammates held the ball. He hoisted ill-advised shots, causing the veins in a seething Brown's forehead to pop. He sometimes hurled curses at Brown when the coach removed him from the game. The root of the warfare was that strain of DNA that all competitors possess. "Larry and Allen had the same goal in mind, they just didn't realize it then," King said. This led to constant bickering, with many exchanges growing heated. Neither man was shy about taking shots at the other in the press. "It was like being on a roller-coaster ride," former Sixers forward Aaron McKie said. "You knew there were going to be some things going on and some things being said in the media."

In December 1999, during the third quarter of what would be a double-digit loss to the Detroit Pistons, Brown pulled Iverson—and the four other starters—and benched them for the remainder of the game. In the locker room afterward, with Brown standing just ten feet away, a smoldering Iverson addressed reporters.

"I've never been done like that in my career," he said, adding, "If that's the way it is, something needs to happen. Something's got to give."

Two days later, Croce bounded into a practice and summoned Iverson and Brown into a conference room in the Philadelphia College of Osteopathic Medicine, the team's makeshift training facility. Both men issued me-or-him directives to the Sixers president. Desperate, Croce prayed that a group therapy session could keep him from having to blow up his core.

Brown and Iverson aired their grievances. "You could hear them yelling, 'The hell with you' at each other," McKie said. He and the rest of his teammates had cut short their pre-practice stretching and sidled over to the thin wall separating the gym from the conference room. "We all had our ear to it, listening," McKie said. "We did not think it was going to end well."

Inside, Iverson and Brown sat at opposite ends of the table. Iverson condemned Brown for describing the team as a family one moment and excoriating Iverson in the press the next. Brown explained how difficult it was to position himself as the team's leader with Iverson often undermining him. Croce pointed out to Brown the similarities between how he, as a coach, was treating Iverson and how police had derided Iverson when he was running around the projects of Hampton, Virginia. That last point in particular struck Brown.

The two promised to be better, to listen to each other more. Iverson walked across the room. The two men embraced.

"And they came out and it was like everything was okay," McKie said. "Allen came out and clapped his hands and was, like, 'I'm ready to go.'"

Three months later in Miami, Iverson called Brown to tell him that he wouldn't be able to make it to that morning's practice. A night out in Miami had left him hungover and unable to climb out of bed. A few months later the Sixers fell in the second round of the playoffs to Brown's former team, the Pacers, for the second straight year.

That summer, Brown and Croce, frustrated and angry and feeling betrayed, decided the time had come. They found a taker for Iverson: the Pistons. It was a complex, four-team deal. The Sixers would receive a package featuring All-Stars Eddie Jones and Glen Rice, along with veterans Dale Ellis and reserve power forward Jerome Williams. But the deal fell through when Matt Geiger, a Sixers reserve center who'd be headed to Detroit, refused to waive his trade kicker, making it impossible for the Pistons to complete the trade.[1]

For now, Iverson would remain a Sixer.

In a few months, Croce and Brown would be thankful that he was.

———

Fifty-five seconds remained in overtime and the Sixers led the defending champion Lakers by two. The 18,997 fans in attendance at Los

---

1 A stipulation in his contract that he'd receive a 15 percent raise if ever traded. The raise would have lifted the Pistons over the NBA's salary cap.

Angeles' Staples Center rose to their feet. Iverson caught the ball on the right wing just inside the three-point arch, turned toward the rim, and crouched so that his gaze could meet that of Tyronn Lue, the Laker tasked with guarding him.

It had been a magical year in Philadelphia. The Sixers kicked off the 2000–2001 season by reeling off 10 straight wins. "Allen came back after that failed trade and had a burning desire to prove everybody wrong," said one member of the team's front office. Also, after years of tinkering, Brown and King, who by then had climbed the ranks to general manager, had surrounded Iverson with the ideal roster. "Billy did a great job of bringing in the right type of players, tough, hard-nosed guys who wouldn't be affected by anything Allen did or said," the front office person said. The Sixers' hot start emboldened King and before the trade deadline he acquired the perfect Iverson wingman—the 7-foot-2 Dikembe Mutombo, one of the greatest interior defenders in NBA history.

With Mutombo, who would later be named Defensive Player of the Year, manning the back line; McKie, who would later be named Sixth Man of the Year, commanding the bench; Brown, who would later be named Coach of the Year, drawing up schemes; and of course Iverson, who would later be named the season's Most Valuable Player, leading it all, the Sixers went on to win 56 games, their most since 1985, and ended their NBA Finals drought.

"The building was really just on fire that year," said the team's longtime trainer, Lenny Currier. The Sixers entered the Finals as heavy underdogs. They may have boasted the NBA's MVP, but the Lakers had Kobe Bryant and Shaquille O'Neal, and were being coached by Phil Jackson. These were future legends, first-ballot Hall of Famers, at the height of their powers. Yet here were the Sixers, and here was Iverson, ready to snatch a Game 1 victory in overtime on the Lakers' home floor.

Iverson clutched the ball with both hands. He stared at Lue. He lowered the ball to his knees and took one hard dribble right, dropping his chest below his waist. With Lue on his left hip and lunging toward the ball, Iverson planted his right foot, somehow halting all that force driving toward the court's baseline. It was like a driver spotting a stop sign at the last moment and slamming on the brakes. He smoothly bounced the ball back toward his left hip. For years, Iverson had viciously cut down opponents with his violent crossover, yet never before had he seemed so cold-blooded. He gathered, rose above a stumbling Lue, and drained a jumper, giving the Sixers a four-point lead. The crowd moaned. Lue, who had fallen to the floor, peered up. Iverson looked down, lifted his right leg, and slowly stepped over his vanquished opponent.

The Sixers, thanks to Iverson's 48-point performance, upset the Lakers that night. They'd fail to capture another victory that series and would fall in five games. But, for the first time in years, they appeared to be on the brink of something special.

"It took us a while to get there," McKie said. "We had to pay our dues, and when we finally got there we were like, 'Man, we're going to be there again next year.'"

The game—the Sixers' final home contest of the season, Fan Appreciation night—would be starting any moment, yet Iverson was nowhere to be found.

It didn't matter that he'd be sitting out due to a lingering ankle injury that had plagued him for most of this 2005–2006 season. The injury was the problem. The saga had begun around March, when the Sixers discovered that Iverson was skipping rehab sessions. In April, Iverson told reporters he'd be shutting himself down for the remainder of the season. The Sixers learned of the decision in the press.

By this point, King, then team president, had begun contemplating breaking up his core. The Sixers never did make it back to the Finals. They fell in the playoffs' early round in consecutive years and then watched as Brown bolted for Detroit, taking the Sixers' chances with him.

"There was just something about him that made us function differently. If you talk to any of the guys that played for him, everybody says the same thing. It's, 'Oh man, I was so happy to see him leave,'" McKie said. "And a month or two or a year later they say, 'Man, I miss that guy.' Just the detail, the accountability. He has a presence and essence about him, and everybody doesn't have that. When he spoke, because of the level of basketball acumen he had, the knowledge and all the players that he coached and all the coaches that he coached, he commanded your attention. So when he stepped in the room, he had a presence about him, and that was on top of him being a great X's-and-O's guy."

King cycled through three coaches over the next year-plus—Randy Ayers, Chris Ford, and Jim O'Brien—before settling on Maurice Cheeks, a former All-Star who had served as an assistant under Brown. The heralded group of veterans that King had surrounded Iverson with in 2001 had mostly moved on. Iverson's supporting cast now featured a crop of undeveloped prospects and overpaid, underperforming veterans, such as former All-Star Chris Webber. The Sixers were also about to miss the playoffs for the second time in three seasons.

At 7:07—seven minutes after tip-off—Iverson finally showed up. He refused to put on a Sixers uniform and join his teammates on the bench.

King was livid.

"I got a team that sucks," he told reporters. "I got a lot of fucking work to do. Am I pissed off? You're damn right I am. Is that what you wanted to hear? You've fucking heard it."

"Shit will change," he added later.

King started shopping Iverson that summer. The Celtics came in with a proposal. The Denver Nuggets offered Andre Miller (one of the league's better point guards), Marcus Camby (one of its top defensive centers), and a first-round pick. King was ready to say yes and brought the deal to Snider. Snider told him to hold off. He was in the early stages of negotiations with Charles Kushner, a real estate magnate from New Jersey[2] who was interested in buying the team. The conversations between Snider's Comcast Spectacor and Kushner, who was wrapping up a fourteen-month prison term for tax evasion, witness tampering, and illegal campaign donations, eventually stalled.

---

2 And, yes, and the father of Donald Trump's future son-in-law.

But once again the Sixers, after vowing to trade him, would begin the following season with Iverson on the roster.

This time, there'd be no magical run.

They dropped 11 of their first 16 games. "By then we were no longer winning and it was clear Allen didn't want to be here," a Sixers assistant coach from that time said. In December, the Sixers traveled to Chicago to take on the Bulls. After the third quarter, with the Sixers down by double digits, Iverson told Cheeks that his back was hurting. He retreated to the locker room and never returned. King sat behind the bench that night. He witnessed the entire episode.

"I knew before the season we probably should have traded him," he said. "After that game I knew it was time, for all our sakes. Allen wanted to win, and we weren't going to get to the top of the East in the near term with that group."

After the game, King confronted Iverson. "Do you want to be traded?" he yelled.

"Yeah!" Iverson shot back.

The Sixers ordered Iverson to stay away from the team. Two days later, Snider confirmed the Sixers' intentions, telling reporters, "We're going to trade him. At a certain point, you have to come to grips with the fact that it's not working. He wants out and we're ready to accommodate him."

The offers came flying in. The Nuggets were still interested. The Minnesota Timberwolves called. King tried prying away a tantalizing twenty-one-year-old named Shaun Livingston from the Los Angeles Clippers. There were negotiations with the Boston Celtics. King considered hunting for a package of veterans. But he and ownership decided that rebuilding was the proper path. They liked their current core of prospects. There was Andre Iguodala, a third-year wing who was both a tenacious defender and a relentless attacker. There was Kyle Korver, a deadeye shooter in his fourth year. They thought Willie Green, a fourth-year guard, had flashed signs of growth.

"We decided it was best to try resetting the books, get some picks, and start building through the draft," King said. He also wanted a veteran or two to help mentor his younger players. In mid-December, about two weeks after the clash in Chicago, the Nuggets called with a proposal, similar to the one from the summer: Miller, veteran big man Joe Smith, and two first-round picks. The deal offered King everything he wanted. Not only would he have three first-round selections in the upcoming draft, but Miller was the perfect point guard to bridge these two Sixers eras. He was a brilliant passer. He read the floor like a coach. He could help facilitate the development of players like Iguodala and Korver and also allow management to properly evaluate just how good the team's young players were. All of which was great. But it was the upcoming draft that would determine the Sixers' future. And by placing that future in the steady hands of a savvy floor general like Miller, King had sentenced the Sixers to nearly a decade in NBA purgatory.

———

That March, King traveled to Allen Fieldhouse, home to the University of Kansas's basketball team. Alongside dozens of other NBA scouts and executives, he watched a Texas freshman named Kevin Durant light up the Kansas Jayhawks, the No. 3–ranked team in the country. Durant drilled fadeaway jumpers and threw down breakaway dunks. He uncorked smooth jumpers from what seemed like half-court. Durant was considered the second-best prospect in the country—Greg Oden, an ambidextrous seven-foot brute out of Ohio State, was ranked No. 1—but he was unlike any college player King had ever seen.

At halftime, after Durant had amassed 25 points, King took out his cell phone and dialed up Snider.

"I could bring this guy back to Philly tomorrow and he'd be starting for us and be our best player on the floor," King told him.[3]

There was just one problem: The Sixers were winning too many games.

The night before King's trip to Kansas, the Sixers had knocked off

---

3   For what it's worth, and for you skeptics who will say, "Well of course Billy King says he wanted to draft Kevin Durant," this was confirmed by another source as well.

the Grizzlies in overtime for their third straight win. They'd win their next four games as well, bumping their record up to 25–38, despite going 5–18 before the Iverson trade. They weren't competing for a title, but they weren't losing enough games to receive one of the draft's top picks either.

"Andre [Miller] really helped out young guys and he really made the players around him better," the assistant coach said. "He was really good for that group. Probably too good." At one point Cheeks even approached King in his office and asked whether management preferred that he "focus on development," teamspeak for "bench our better players so that we can lose games."

"Ed Snider doesn't want you to lose," King told Cheeks. "And if you do that, you're going to lose the locker room, and we don't want that." As Comcast Spectacor chief operating officer Peter Luukko would say years later, "Our organization is never the type to say, 'Let's just lose this year.' For one, you're never guaranteed that things are going to get better. But it's not in the makeup of our culture."

King dreamed of landing Durant. He made clear to his front office over the next few months that the Texas freshman would be the top player listed on the team's draft board. But Durant wasn't the class's only promising prospect. There was Oden, and also Joakim Noah and Al Horford, a pair of seven-foot teammates who the previous year had led Florida to an NCAA championship.[4] All the Sixers had to do was finish toward the bottom of the standings. Instead they finished 35–47 and were awarded the draft's 12th pick. There, they selected a versatile 6-foot-8 freshman out of Georgia Tech named Thaddeus Young, who would go on to have a successful, ten-plus-year career as a role player.

Durant, drafted second by the Seattle SuperSonics, would go on to become an MVP and all-time great.

---

4   They'd go on to win that year's as well.

The Sixers began the following season by dropping 12 of their first 17 games. In December, a frustrated Snider fired King. "We have a good plan in place, but we needed a fresh approach in the leadership of the franchise," he explained at the time.

For years, Snider—who adored hockey and had also founded the National Hockey League Philadelphia Flyers in the mid-1960s—ran the Sixers with a hands-off approach. He'd sit in the war room during drafts, speak with King nearly every day, and offer his thoughts on potential signings and deals. "But he'd always say that the decision was mine to make," King said.

King loved working for Snider. He considered him an ideal owner. King was allowed to buy draft picks and, early in his tenure, was even urged by Snider to bolster the team's scouting department. Snider's one preference was that the Sixers remain below the NBA's luxury tax threshold, which forced teams to pay one dollar to the league for every dollar of player payroll that crossed over the line, a pot that would then be redistributed to smaller-market teams. "But even that was flexible," King said.

Around the time of the Iverson deal, Snider and, more specifically, the analysts at the publicly traded company he represented, began wondering whether the Sixers were worthy of such an investment. Attendance had dipped from an average of 20,560 per game during the 2001–2002 season to 14,843 in 2006–2007. And according to *Forbes*, their operating income had plummeted too.

"When Comcast purchased the Sixers, it was more to bring more content into the arena, which they owned, to have more games, more dates in there. Basketball just wasn't Ed's focus," said Salvatore Galatioto, a sports business banker who was friends with Snider. "Comcast is a media company who viewed this as media content value and only worried about whether the team was profitable. It's not that Comcast didn't want to win a championship, but they're a huge corporation, they couldn't view it that way."

In other words, the mandate had changed. A slow rebuild was no longer an option. And a championship, while nice, was no longer the primary goal.

Snider tapped Ed Stefanski, a longtime NBA executive, to serve as general manager. His directive was to chase a playoff spot, but not by mortgaging the team's future. Comcast owned the Wachovia Center. It wanted fans coming out to games. With Iverson now in Denver, Cheeks put Miller and Iguodala at the center of his offense and the Sixers returned to the playoffs. They lost in the first round—again to the Pistons—but that summer inked Elton Brand, a 6-foot-9 two-time All-Star who had missed the majority of the previous season due to a ruptured left Achilles tendon, to a five-year, $82 million deal.

Once again, expectations in Philadelphia were high, which is why Stefanski fired Cheeks after the Sixers' 9–14 start to the 2008–2009 season. Cheeks was replaced on an interim basis by assistant general manager Tony DiLeo. DiLeo led the Sixers to the playoffs, where they fell in the first round, which was followed by the hiring of former New Jersey Nets head coach Eddie Jordan, which precipitated a disaster of a season in which the Sixers won just 27 games, which led to Jordan's firing that April, which led to the tabbing of longtime NBA executive Rod Thorn to serve as team president above Stefanski, and the hiring of longtime head coach Doug Collins, a man venerated for his basketball wisdom but also known for wearing out his welcome after two to three seasons.

Thanks to Snider's edict, the present had become the priority. Long-term consequences were no longer taken into account.

"It was difficult to be consistent with that much change," said Willie Green, who played for six different head coaches over seven seasons in Philadelphia. "You try to take something from every coach and apply it to your game, but it's difficult having to keep learning new systems and philosophies. It's hard to be consistent like that, especially for young players."

By then, the Sixers had amassed an impressive collection of up-and-coming players. Jrue Holiday, whom they stole with the 17th pick in the 2009 draft, was on his way to becoming an All-Star. Thaddeus Young was a double-figure scorer. Lou Williams, a 2005 second-round pick, was on his way to becoming a two-time Sixth Man of the Year award winner. Evan Turner would never live up to his billing as the No. 2 pick in the 2010 draft, but he'd go on to play more than ten years in the NBA. And then there was Iguodala, who by then had grown into a versatile and athletic defensive force who, while not a lead scorer, could create off the dribble and puncture defenses with his pinpoint passing.

The core of a winner was there. All the Sixers had to do was tweak along the edges.

Ownership, however, remained an obstacle. Comcast continued shopping the team even after the talks with Kushner fell through. More problematic was its refusal to build the Sixers a training facility. Instead the team was forced to rent space at the Philadelphia College of Osteopathic Medicine, known as PCOM.

"That place was a dump," said one former Sixers executive. "It was worse than a high school gym."

It wasn't just the layout—a locker room in the basement with coach and executive offices on the third floor—that was problematic. It was that the Sixers, an NBA team boasting professional athletes being paid millions of dollars to perform, were forced to share the facility with medical students. The Sixers were granted certain practice hours, but players who wanted to shoot either before or after the team's designated time would often arrive and find the court occupied by an intramural basketball game. If it were, say, eleven o'clock at night, a player would have to notify security in advance. Sometimes a gym supervisor would (politely) kick Sixers players off if a different group of students had previously reserved the court.

"You could never get in when you wanted to or stay until you wanted to," said Thad Young. "I had to do a lot of my shooting at different places. I would have a friend of mine at Villanova get me in there."

The Sixers executives begged Snider to upgrade the team's facilities. Comcast nearly obliged. Then the Great Recession of 2008 drowned the world's economy. The Sixers were stuck, and in more ways than one. They ranked 23rd in home attendance in 2009, 26th in 2010, and 25th in 2011—despite playing in the country's fifth-largest metro area. They were irrelevant and mediocre and trapped in NBA limbo. Nearly five years had passed since they had dealt Iverson, and still they were no closer to ending their championship drought.

Even worse, Snider seemed to be at a loss.

"I have to be honest with you—if Flyers fans only came out when they thought we could win a championship, we wouldn't be the strong organization we are today," he said at the time. "They love to watch hockey. I don't know what the situation is with basketball. We don't have a large, loyal following."

Yet to some keen observers there was a foundation of something greater in place. Better yet, the Sixers, given their market and the rich basketball history in Philadelphia, presented an intriguing buy-low opportunity. Perhaps there was a way to salvage the franchise. Perhaps all it needed was an injection of new blood.

Chapter 2

THE BUYOUT

Josh Harris had amassed a fortune of $1.45 billion by following a simple principle. "Buying good companies with bad balance sheets," is how he once put it to a Bloomberg reporter. "We seek to buy when the world appears to be very, very cheap." It wasn't an original strategy. But only a handful of people in the history of modern finance have possessed Harris's skill for spotting when to buy low.

A Wharton graduate raised in suburban Maryland, Harris was introduced to this approach in the late 1980s while at the investment bank of Drexel Burnham Lambert, where he worked as a financial analyst for two years. The firm was led by a man named Michael Milken. Known as the "Junk Bond King," Milken had pioneered a new form of finance. Under his stewardship, Drexel created a marketplace to buy and sell bonds issued by poorly rated companies. These businesses, desperate to get their hands on any cash, would pay out higher-than-usual interest rates to bond owners, potential bounty that enticed buyers to roll the dice.

In 1989, Milken, as part of a wide-ranging SEC investigation into Drexel, was indicted for racketeering and securities fraud. It turned out parts of his empire were built upon corruption and deceit. Drexel filed for bankruptcy. Milken served two years in prison.

By then Harris had left the bank to enroll in Harvard's MBA

program. In 1990, he joined a group of Drexel alumni—led by Marc Rowan and Leon Black, the latter of whom was the former head of Drexel's mergers and acquisitions department—who had decided to set up their own shop. They called it Apollo Advisers. Over the next twenty years, Apollo (which would later change its name to Apollo Global Management) grew into one of the largest and most successful private equity firms in the world. The firm's playbook was an evolution of what the ex–Drexel employees had learned under Milken. They specialized in spotting value where others saw junk.

The primary tool for private equity firms had always been the leveraged buyout, many of which in the late 1980s were financed using the junk bond model pioneered by Drexel. In these sorts of deals, the PE firm seeks out a flailing business, takes out heaps of debt to help finance an acquisition, and purchases a majority stake of the business (sometimes without the business's approval). In theory, the combination of a cash injection along with the PE firm's expertise helps turn the company around. But these transactions often wind up resembling the type made infamous by Michael Douglas's Gordon Gekko character in the Oliver Stone movie *Wall Street.*

"They care about the future of their PE firms but not about the viability of the companies they buy," wrote *New York Post* reporter Josh Kosman in his book *The Buyout of America: How Private Equity Is Destroying Jobs and Killing the American Economy.*[1]

For one, PE firms typically saddle the acquired company with the financing debt. (It's sort of like the process everyday people go through when buying a house, with the key difference being that it's the purchased business—i.e., "the house"—that gets billed for the mortgage.) The acquisition is often followed by major cuts to help pay the debts and shine the company up for a potential resale. Perhaps layoffs. Or slashing employee benefits. Occasionally these tactics are needed in order to save the company, as was the case when Apollo, along with the investment firm Metropoulos & Co., spent $186 million to purchase a chunk of a bankrupt Hostess Brands in 2013. Less than

---

1   A Sixers spokesperson said this is not true of Harris.

four years later, Hostess was sold in a deal that valued the company at $2.3 billion, though Apollo forced it to shut down multiple factories before doing so.

Where Apollo and Harris truly separated themselves, though, was in realizing how to leverage their grasp of debt into savvy takeovers. Rather than buying the stock of a public company, Apollo could acquire the debt of a troubled one for a steep discount, perhaps 50 cents on the dollar. If all the purchased company needed to turn around was that cash injection, then Apollo would make a killing. If the purchased company continued to flail and eventually filed for bankruptcy, Apollo, as a creditor, would be at the front of the line to take over the company and profit off its turnaround.

"These guys [Apollo] are putting money to work where others are too afraid or not as sophisticated," said Sujeet Indap, a reporter for the *Financial Times* who's spent years covering Apollo. "They're very clever at finding stuff that's out of favor and stuff that's undervalued and being one step ahead of everyone else."

There were bumps along the way. In 2006 Apollo purchased Linens 'n Things for $1.3 billion, only to see it file for bankruptcy two years later. Around the same time, Apollo, along with another firm named TPG Capital, agreed to put down $17.1 billion in cash, along with $10.7 billion in assumed debt, and took over Harrah's Entertainment (later renamed Caesars Entertainment Corporation). At the time this was the seventh-largest leveraged buyout in American history. It was also executed right as the Great Recession was sinking the world economy.

Soon after, according to a report from the *Financial Times*, Harrah's was on the hook for nearly $2 billion in annual interest payments. In response, Apollo sold off portions of the more profitable arms of Harrah's (intellectual property, Las Vegas locations like Planet Hollywood and Bally's) to other entities controlled by...Apollo and TPG. Harris (officially a senior managing director at the firm) wasn't the point man on the Harrah's transactions, but this sort of dealing fit snugly with his business ethos.

Harris had helped build Apollo's empire by ruthlessly hunting every opening and advantage. "He's tenacious," said Mark Epley, a onetime co-head of global financial sponsors at Nomura Securities, the banking subsidiary of Nomura Holdings, which worked extensively with Harris and Apollo. "If you make a mistake or don't deliver, you're going to get bitch-slapped by him." Everyone who knows or has worked with Harris, a physically unassuming 5-foot-8 former college wrestler, has a story illustrating his zeal. Running marathons. Waking up at 5:30 a.m. during ski vacations to squeeze in some work. Bowling over a summer intern during an Apollo intracompany soccer game. More telling, though, are the relationships Harris has cultivated in the political world. He's donated hundreds of thousands of dollars to various campaigns, mostly Republican, and watched the 2014 Super Bowl in a suite with then–New Jersey governor Chris Christie. He developed a close relationship with Donald Trump's son-in-law, Jared Kushner, and in 2017, according to the *New York Times*, floated Kushner's real estate firm an unusually large $184 million loan to help refinance a Chicago skyscraper. He's also advised the Trump administration on infrastructure policies.

But there's no debating Harris's skillset. Or, as Epley put it, his capacity "for just getting shit done. Which, in private equity, is probably the most difficult part."

The best example of this came around 2007, when Apollo began buying up chunks of debt belonging to LyondellBasell, a floundering multinational chemical company. As the global recession hit, LyondellBasell plunged further. Apollo, with Harris at the lead, kept scooping up more and more of its debt, reaching about $2 billion worth of investments, even as the company declared bankruptcy in January 2009. But LyondellBasell eventually rallied, giving Apollo the opportunity to trade the purchased debts for equity.[2]

Post-bankruptcy, LyondellBasell's stock soared. Apollo wound up clearing about $12 billion in profit, at the time the largest private equity windfall ever.

In March 2011, Apollo went public and raised $565.4 million in its

---

2   According to a report from Bloomberg, declaring bankruptcy also allowed LyondellBasell to skirt nearly $5 billion in fines issued by U.S. Environmental Protection Agency as punishment for allegedly polluting an eighty-mile stretch of Michigan's Kalamazoo River.

initial public offering, an amount pegging the firm's value at around $7 billion. Harris had reached the top of Wall Street. It was time to apply his skillset to a new field.

––––––––––

It was the spring of 2010 and Ed Stefanski, the general manager of the Sixers, needed a head coach. This was nothing new for the Sixers, who had cycled through six head coaches in the previous seven seasons, the latest being Eddie Jordan, whom Stefanski fired in April, just ten months after hiring him.

Jordan's tenure derailed the Sixers' progress. He clashed with Elton Brand, a former All-Star and the team's highest-paid player. He tried forcing his pet system (the Princeton offense) onto the team, despite the scheme not being a good fit for the Sixers roster. Under Jordan, the Sixers went just 27–55, their worst record in thirteen seasons.

Stefanski believed the Sixers' young but talented roster was better than that. He was also aware that ownership—Comcast Spectacor, with chairman Ed Snider running point—was dismayed by the team's recent financials. He knew he needed a coach who could instantly transform the Sixers into a playoff contender.

Doug Collins had been drafted first overall by the Sixers in 1973. He played eight seasons before a series of leg and foot injuries forced him to retire. He shifted into coaching after that. He spent three years leading the Bulls,[3] another three in Detroit, and another two in Washington.

Collins was an old-school taskmaster who worked his players hard and wasn't shy about raising his voice. He specialized in orchestrating quick turnarounds. The Bulls won 30 games the season before Collins's arrival and 40 in their first season with him. The Pistons went from 28 wins to 46, the Wizards from 19 to 37. Collins's teams defended well, took care of the ball, and controlled the pace. He also

––––––––––

3 Where he coached Michael Jordan before being replaced by Phil Jackson in the summer of 1989. He would coach Jordan again more than a decade later in Washington.

had a knack for harnessing the potential of young players, something that the Sixers, who were building around former first-round picks like Andre Iguodala and Jrue Holiday, as well as the No. 2 pick in that summer's draft, Evan Turner, desperately needed.

Stefanski knew that Collins wouldn't last more than three years. He never did. His style wore players down. But Stefanski also knew he couldn't afford to worry about the future. The present was what mattered.

He hired Collins in May 2010. The Sixers got off to an ugly 3–13 start but turned things around. They finished the season with 41 wins, good enough for a playoff berth. They became a top-10 defense.[4] Holiday nearly doubled his scoring average (14 points per game). Iguodala posted the best passing numbers of his career (6.3 assists per game). "Doug is up there with your top basketball minds," said former Sixers forward Aaron McKie, who was an assistant coach under Collins. "In terms of X's and O's and getting guys ready to play, few people were better."

But the Sixers still averaged less than 14,751 fans a game that season, the fifth-worst mark in the NBA, and were still losing money. A .500 season wasn't enough to convince Comcast that the business was one worth holding on to—especially considering that it owned the team's exclusive television rights, the Sixers' most valuable asset, for the paltry price of just $12 million per year. Also hurting the Sixers' case was the fact that starting in the 2011–2012 season the team would be paying rent to Comcast Spectacor for the right to play in the Wells Fargo Center (as the Wachovia Center had been renamed in 2010). The only building revenues they'd collect would be those basketball-related.

In early 2011, Snider called up Salvatore Galatioto, the New York–based sports business banker. The two men had known each other for years, and, at Comcast's request, had previously broached the possibility of selling the Sixers. Galatioto, who specialized in facilitating the sales of professional sports teams, had shared who he believed might

---

4 Based on points per 100 possessions.

be interested in the team and how much Comcast could get. Marc Lasry, a billionaire hedge fund manager, had raised the possibility with Comcast about five years earlier. "But they wanted us to assume all the liabilities," Lasry said. "We would have been losing $30 million a year."

This time, Snider told Galatioto, the situation was different. Comcast had made up its mind. It was time to cut bait.

Galatioto, who maintained a database of people interested in buying sports teams and with the means to do so, began making calls. He found a few potential buyers and pitched them to Comcast, the company that owned the Sixers' television rights through 2029.

"They wanted someone who had a vision and plan to turn the team around," Galatioto said.

Galatioto knew two people who were keenly interested in breaking into professional sports: Josh Harris and David Blitzer, the latter a fellow Wharton graduate and senior executive at the private equity firm Blackstone. Galatioto kept in touch with both men regularly and knew that the Sixers—a big-market team, close to their New York homes, with a built-in fan base, and history—were exactly what they were looking for.

Harris enjoyed basketball. He was a competition junkie who, as a kid growing up in the 1970s, had attended Washington Bullets games with his father (an orthodontist who moonlighted as a comic opera performer). But Harris was far from a die-hard. For him, it was about the math. He was intrigued by the idea of running a business that, for the most part, operated in a universe independent of the stock market. "It's a very unique asset class, different from anything else you own," Galatioto said.

Harris and Blitzer were also aware that the NBA's league-wide media contract would soon be expiring, and that the league's next TV deal could double in size. At the time, the NBA was collecting $930 million per year from its national TV partners—an amount that was split among the NBA's thirty teams. But that deal was negotiated before DVR and on-demand options shook up the television land-scape. Viewers were now avoiding commercials, making sports one of the few events fans feel compelled to watch live and therefore a golden commodity. Experts were estimating that the NBA's next TV deal would fall somewhere around $2 billion.

Galatioto set up meetings between Harris, Blitzer, and Comcast. "They told Comcast that they were going to build a winner," Galatioto said. Comcast liked what it heard and loved that both Harris and Blitzer were capable of buying the team without financing. "The whole thing was pretty smooth," Galatioto said. "Harris's group was clearly well organized."

On July 13, the *New York Times* ran the news of the sale under the headline "Private Equity Princes Reach Deal for 76ers." The Sixers cost Harris and Blitzer about $280 million, $45 million less than the Detroit Pistons had sold for a month earlier and $170 million less than the Golden State Warriors had fetched the previous November. Harris and Blitzer then sold off minority shares to nearly a dozen other individuals, a group including former NBA player agent and Sacramento Kings executive Jason Levien; a Goldman Sachs executive named David Heller; another private equity magnate and Wharton graduate named Art Wrubel; Adam Aron, the CEO of Vail Resorts; and even Philadelphia native Will Smith.

The ownership charter stated that title of managing partner—a.k.a. head honcho—would rotate from Harris to Blitzer after three years.[5] Aron would be the team's CEO. Rod Thorn, who had been hired by the previous regime as president of basketball operations, would stay on in that same role. Stefanski, whose contract was up in a year, would be let go. (Harris and Co. didn't want to pay both Stefanski and Thorn, and getting rid of Thorn, whose contract ran longer than Stefanski's, would have cost more.)

"We're lucky enough to buy the third most winning franchise in basketball history. We are getting a storied franchise at a time where we were able to get what we think is an appropriate deal for the team," Harris said, in his typical drowsy monotone, three months

---

5   Blackstone, however, wasn't keen on the idea of one of its top executives officially running *another* business in Philadelphia. It told Blitzer that being the Sixers' "managing partner" was a no-go. Harris would wind up retaining the title of managing partner permanently.

later at a press conference announcing the sale. "We think we are able to participate in breathing new life into the team. The team has been less connected with its fans and as a result was not generating revenue and selling tickets as we think we can do. It wasn't realizing its potential."

Harris was upfront from the start. Yeah, he was competitive and wanted to win. But this wasn't an example of a Philly kid doing right by his hometown, or of a basketball fanatic fulfilling his lifelong dream.

"This," Harris added, "is a really exciting business opportunity."

———

The Sixers were coming off their most exciting stretch in years. They'd finished the regular season (shortened due to a summer lockout) four games over .500 and snagged the Eastern Conference's final playoff spot. They defeated the Bulls in the first round, becoming just the fifth eighth seed in NBA history to upset a No. 1, and came within one win of knocking off a loaded Boston Celtics squad in the second round. Attendance—thanks to the team's performance and owner-ship's decision to slash ticket prices, in some instances by as much as 50 percent—had soared to 17,502 per game, the 14th best number in the NBA.

But Harris, Blitzer, and Heller, the minority owner enlisted to help oversee the team's basketball operations, were wary of buying into what they believed to be fool's gold. They knew the only reason the Sixers advanced out of the first round was because the Bulls had lost two of their best players, Derrick Rose and Joakim Noah, to injuries. They also recognized that they lacked the one thing nearly every title team in NBA history possessed: a true superstar.

First they had to shore up their front office. Collins had spent the year trying to consolidate power and after the season had convinced Harris to demote the seventy-one-year-old Thorn to the role of adviser. In June, Harris flew to San Antonio to woo Danny Ferry, a former player who'd spent five years as general manager of the Cleveland Cavaliers and who at the time was working as the Spurs' vice presi-dent of basketball operations. The Spurs had made the playoffs for fifteen straight years and won three titles over that span. They were widely regarded as the best-run organization in the NBA. "I want the Spurs model," Harris told Ferry. He had Collins's blessing too. Ferry considered the offer but took one from the Atlanta Hawks instead.

The Sixers drew up a new list of candidates. In the meantime, there was a more pressing matter at hand.

The Orlando Magic were looking to trade Dwight Howard, a dominant center and one of the league's most exciting players. Howard was set to become a free agent the following summer and had no desire to remain in Orlando. He wanted to play in Brooklyn for the Nets or Los Angeles for the Lakers, and the Magic figured it was best to acquiesce so that they could at least receive some players or draft picks in return.

The simplest deal would have been flipping Howard to the Lakers in exchange for Andrew Bynum. An All-Star center who was still just twenty-four years old, Bynum would have been the perfect player for the Magic to rebuild around. But he too was scheduled to become a free agent in a year, and he refused to give Orlando a long-term commitment. The risk of watching the player they received in exchange for Howard bolt one year later wasn't one the Magic were willing to take. They instead began searching for additional trade partners to help facilitate the deal. The Sixers were a perfect fit. They had a talented crop of young players. Also, Bynum had grown up in central New Jersey, just an hour north of Philadelphia. His agent, David Lee, spoke to Tony DiLeo, a longtime Sixers coach and executive who was serving as the team's top decision maker. Lee told DiLeo that Bynum wouldn't make any promises, nor sign any extensions,[6] but that Philadelphia was certainly a city where he'd be happy to remain long-term.

Bynum was exactly the type of player the Sixers had been searching for. He was a seven-foot, 285-pound force, both overpowering and graceful, the rare center who could dunk on an opponent one possession and flip a soft baby hook over him the next. Bynum had

---

6   Bynum's options were to sign a three-year, $60 million extension before the season or wait to become a free agent after and be eligible for a five-year, $102 million deal.

helped the Lakers win two titles and was coming off the best season of his career (18.7 points and 11.8 rebounds per game). He was a star, one who could catapult the Sixers up toward the top of the Eastern Conference standings and into title contention. "We felt Bynum was a transcendent player," Thorn said. The only question was Bynum's health. He'd missed a chunk of games in each of the previous five seasons due to a series of knee injuries.

The Sixers consulted with their own medical staff, as well as some outside doctors. Ownership received pressure from two of the most powerful voices inside the organization. Collins, then sixty-one, wasn't keen on the idea of a slow rebuild and loathed Nikola Vučević, their 2011 first-round pick and a player whom the Sixers would need to include in the deal. Aron, the team's newly appointed CEO, had sold himself as the man capable of revitalizing the Sixers' business operations and believed Bynum could be the face of those efforts.

On August 10, 2012, the Sixers, in a deal negotiated by senior vice president Tony DiLeo, agreed to a four-team, twelve-player trade. The Sixers received Bynum and veteran guard Jason Richardson in exchange for Vučević, Moe Harkless (their 2012 first-round pick), and a conditional first-round pick, all of whom went to Orlando, along with Iguodala, who went to Denver. The price was steep, but to the Sixers, the chance to hook one of the league's transcendent young stars made the deal a no-brainer.

Five days later, the Sixers held a press conference at the National Constitution Center on Independence Mall to introduce Bynum to the city. Fifteen hundred fans showed up to greet their new savior. Bynum, wearing a generic white Sixers T-shirt, sat next to a giddy Harris and fielded questions from local reporters.

"I just thought I was coming home, I was super excited," Bynum said when asked what his initial reaction was to the deal. Fans screamed, "I love you!" Bynum was asked whether he could see himself playing in Philadelphia long-term.

"To be honest, man, my first experience here has been so great that I'm leaning toward making this my home," Bynum said. A boisterous cheer broke out. "I'm not a guy who wants to be all around and have a lot of teams under my belt," he continued. "But that's really the answer. I'm really looking forward to making this my home."

"Where do I sign?" responded Josh Harris, wearing a dark suit and slime-green tie. Big-time deals were nothing new to him, but this—the euphoria sweeping over Philadelphia, a type of civic joy that only a local sports team can shower an entire city in—was completely new.

A large smile stretched across Harris's face.

One Saturday, about three months after the party celebrating his arrival, Andrew Bynum went bowling.

The 2012–2013 season was a few weeks old and Bynum had yet to take the floor. An injury to his right knee—officially deemed a "bruise"—was taking longer than expected to heal. Bynum had traveled to Germany in late September to undergo an experimental procedure (Orthokine therapy injections, which involve removing a patient's own blood, "centrifuging it down," and then reinjecting it back into the painful area). He'd done so on the advice of his former Lakers teammate Kobe Bryant, who had undergone the same procedure the previous off-season and seen it save and revive his career.

Bynum returned to the United States in late fall. In October he received a series of preventative lubricating injections. Around this time he also developed a bone bruise on his right knee, which sidelined him indefinitely. Before a mid-November win over the Utah Jazz, he provided local reporters with an update.

"I had a little bit of a setback. Just working through some issues with the right knee, I kind of have a mirror thing going on with the left knee," he said. "I don't know what's going on. The doctors are saying it's a weakened cartilage state, so we kind of wait, I guess. We can't do anything. I just have to wait for the cartilage to get strong."

Soon after, ESPN.com published an update. The setback, according to reporters Brian Windhorst and Chris Broussard, had occurred while Bynum was...bowling?

The next week Bynum stood before local reporters once again. He'd grown out his hair into an afro and wore a pink polo shirt under a dark jacket.

"I think it happened bowling, to be honest," he said. His face twisted into an embarrassed smile. "I don't think anyone could have told me I couldn't do that. You know I was doing squatting and lower back training."

Bynum was asked how he managed to hurt his other knee while bowling. "I didn't twist it, fall or nothing," he said. He was adamant that it felt fine afterward. Only later did he realize that his left knee had swelled in size. He sounded perplexed.

"We're trying to figure out what's going on," he said.

Bynum spent the next five months rehabbing but never made it back to the court. His absence, combined with the loss of the players surrendered in the trade, was too much for the Sixers to sustain. Also, as Stefanski had predicted, Collins's intensity had begun grating on the players. He'd yell and curse and scream. He once stopped a practice for ten minutes to berate second-year big man Lavoy Allen for not inbounding the ball correctly and, in front of the team, accused him of "pouting because I wasn't playing, which was not the case," Allen said. Collins also refused to consult the plethora of advanced metrics that were becoming more accessible across the league. "My analytics are here and here," he once said, while pointing to his head and gut. He publicly called out his players and tried laying the blame of the Bynum trade at the feet of DiLeo, who had since been promoted to GM.

"We made a huge deal. And we have nobody playing as part of that deal," he complained to reporters following a late-season loss to a terrible Magic team. "How many teams can give up Andre Iguodala, Moe Harkless, and Nik Vučević, and have nothing in return playing? That's tough to overcome, right? That's just the facts. I'm not looking for any out. But that's the facts. Nik Vučević had 19 rebounds tonight. [Sixers center] Spencer [Hawes] had one. I think Lavoy [Allen] had two."

The Sixers finished the season 34–48, missing the playoffs once again. The Bynum miscalculation left ownership feeling disillusioned with the direction of the franchise. It didn't matter that it was Harris who had been most excited by the deal, or that he'd been the one who handed the keys to Collins. "That was a turning point for him and his group," said a member of that team's front office. "That changed their mindset."

Embarrassed and emboldened, Harris slowly began modernizing the front office. The previous summer he'd interviewed three data-savvy executives—Tom Penn, a lawyer and former assistant general manager for the Portland Trail Blazers; Mike Zarren, the assistant general manager for the Boston Celtics; and Sam Hinkie, a little-known Houston Rockets executive with an MBA from Stanford—but wanted to learn more about the NBA business before making dramatic changes. In November, the Sixers hired Aaron Barzilai, an MIT graduate who had previously conducted research for DiLeo, to serve as their first ever director of analytics. He was a part of the regularly scheduled meetings between the front office and ownership and presented on topics ranging from the upcoming free agency market to the trajectory of teams that draft in the lottery. "We like how you speak our language," the owners told Barzilai, who had previously worked as a management consultant. Barzilai would also check in about once a week with Heller, who, retired from Goldman Sachs, had the most time on his hands and seemed most interested in the day-to-day details of the team's basketball operations. "He was clearly doing a lot of research and on top of all the advanced stats and things like that," Barzilai said.

After the season, Collins announced that he was stepping down and would be retiring. At the press conference, Harris was asked whether he regretted the Bynum deal. "If I had to make that decision again, I'd make it again. Things don't always work out, you just make good decisions and over time they work out," he said, a process-over-results response that would foreshadow his upcoming decisions. "In the world of business, to be successful, you make decisions. You take risks and then you live with the outcome." Around that time, ownership notified Thorn, DiLeo, and Courtney Witte, a longtime executive, that it wished to meet with them regularly. The group understood exactly what these meetings were. They were being granted the opportunity to sell themselves as the right people to lead the Sixers into the future. That summer, Thorn, DiLeo, and Witte met with ownership about a half dozen times in Manhattan, usually at Harris's forty-third-floor Apollo office. The room overlooked Central Park and was decorated with business awards and pictures of Harris at various races. Over gourmet meals cooked up by an Apollo chef, the trio would spend hours fielding all sorts of questions from Harris, Blitzer, and Heller. Ownership was adamant about bolstering the team's analytics department, and Heller's actions—he'd pop into the team offices in Philadelphia about once a week—and line of questioning left Thorn, DiLeo, and Witte believing that he was interested in playing the role of shadow general manager.

Thorn, DiLeo, and Witte explained their personal and collective track records. They broke down how they viewed the Sixers' current roster, and how they'd plan on moving forward. Ownership seemed to like what it heard, though it was hard to read the socially awkward Harris. He'd often toss out financial jargon ("optionality" was a favorite of his) that the basketball lifers would have to look up on the train ride home.

Toward the end of April, Harris notified DiLeo that he'd be receiving a new contract offer to become the Sixers' permanent general manager. Excited, he began mapping out a strategy for the upcoming draft, which was less than two months away.

Then, one afternoon, about two and a half weeks later, Harris called DiLeo again.

"We're going to be going in a different direction," he told him.

It would be one that would change the Sixers forever.

Chapter 3

"HE SPOKE STANFORD"

In 1977, Charley Casserly was offered what he considered to be a dream job: an internship with the National Football League's Washington Redskins. Casserly at the time was a twenty-eight-year-old high school football coach. It didn't matter that the job was unpaid, with no promise of a future, and that he'd have to live in an $8-a-night YMCA to make the math work. This was his chance to break into the NFL, to learn from a legend like George Allen, the Redskins' Hall of Fame head coach.

Twenty-seven years later, Casserly was sitting in an executive office at the facility of the NFL's Houston Texans. That original Redskins gig had changed his life. He'd climbed the ranks all the way up to general manager, a position he held in D.C. for ten years. Now here he was, in the spring of 2004, wrapping up his second season as the Texans' GM, scanning letters asking *him* for an internship. He yearned to do for someone else what Allen had done for him.

One letter stood out above the others. The candidate, a twenty-six-year-old named Sam Hinkie, hadn't played college football or coached at any level. He'd briefly interned for the San Francisco 49ers, but his résumé looked more like one you'd find on the desk of a hedge fund executive. Hinkie had graduated from Oklahoma University with a degree in business administration in finance and all sorts of impressive-sounding accolades ("Outstanding Senior in the Price College of Business"). After college he had taken a job with Bain & Company, one of the largest and most prestigious management consulting agencies in the world. He left that job for one with a major private equity firm in Australia, then returned to the United States to get an MBA from Stanford's business school. He now had a year left to go before graduating and was looking for a summer internship.

Casserly scheduled an interview with Hinkie. He loved what he heard. Most of Hinkie's time as an intern that summer was devoted to analyzing the draft. "The good ones, though, typically take those simple things and come back with them expanded," Casserly said. "Sam was like that. It didn't take long for me to figure out he was the smartest person in the building."

Hinkie provided data illustrating that, historically, there were certain positions (linebacker and safety) where good players could be found later in the draft. This sort of information was helpful, but there was one project in particular that left Casserly in awe. For years, most NFL teams had based draft trades off a chart developed in the late 1980s by former Dallas Cowboys head coach Jimmy Johnson. The chart assigned a point value to each pick. The No. 1 pick, for example, was considered to be worth 3,000 points; the No. 10 pick, 1,300 points; No. 100, 100 points. Say you want to trade up for the No. 1 pick? Any team working off this chart would expect 3,000 points worth of picks in return.

One day, Hinkie came to Casserly with a discovery. He had deconstructed some of the information and believed that the chart was assigning points based off historical Pro Bowl appearances, which were subjective. Hinkie's point was that if the rest of the league was working off a chart built on such a flimsy foundation, then ignoring its math could present the Texans with some market inefficiencies to exploit.

After the summer, Casserly kept Hinkie on as a consultant and leaned on some of his data in the lead-up to the 2005 NFL draft. Hinkie told him he was aching to work in sports and was hoping the Texans would have an opening for him after he graduated. He even pitched a new position: statistical analysis for head coach Dom Capers's staff.

"I loved Sam, but we had no spots and that role was just something that wasn't going to happen in our building," Casserly said.

Hinkie wasn't one to give up. Perhaps an NFL career wasn't in his future, but that didn't mean he couldn't try a different sport, one that had provided some of the best moments of his life but also comforted him during the worst.

————

It was a cool, breezy Oklahoma morning in January 1989 when the sound of a gunshot rang out from inside the home.

The house belonged to Ron and Sarita Hinkie, who had just moved in. Ron had recently received a promotion, allowing him to rejoin his family in the town where he grew up. A longtime Halliburton employee—he got his start painting company equipment in the 1970s—Ron had spent the previous decade toiling on offshore oil rigs off the coasts of Sicily, Denmark, and the Netherlands, where Sam, the youngest of his two children, was born. His family had moved to Easley, South Carolina, seven years earlier, but Ron's time there had been limited.

That was now all set to change. Ron had returned to Marlow, a tiny, nearly all-white oil town seventy miles south of Oklahoma City, and brought his wife and two kids—seventeen-year-old Bill and ten-year-old Sam—with him.

The morning, the second-to-last Friday of the month, began like most. Then, at around 10:30 in the morning, Bill, wearing nothing but shorts, picked up a 12-gauge shotgun, pointed it at his own face, and pulled the trigger.

Later that day, a man by the name of John Smith came by the Hinkie home to console the family. John's son, J.J., had grown close to Sam. Smith sat with Sarita and Ron for about an hour before looking for his son's friend. He found Sam in his bedroom, traumatized.

"Do you want to come with me?" Smith asked.

He brought him back to his house and out to the family's court. J.J. came out too. They stayed out there for rest of the day and into the night.

"It got me out of a situation that no ten-year-old wants to be in," Hinkie said years later, "and allowed me to kind of find this refuge in a game I loved at a time I really needed it."[1]

———————

His career with the Texans over, Hinkie figured he'd try another Houston professional sports team. He sent a letter to George Postolos, the CEO of the NBA's Rockets. Impressed with what he saw, Postolos knocked on the door of Carroll Dawson, the Rockets' GM, and told him to take a look. Dawson, too, was intrigued. He was different from the majority of his fellow scouts and coaches who dedicated their lives to visiting all sorts of gyms all across the globe. These men—and they were almost all men—felt that no math equation provided by an outsider could help quantify what it was they, as trained basketball lifers, could see with their own eyes.

Dawson knew better. Years earlier he'd witnessed how beneficial even rudimentary statistical analysis could be. In his first season as a Rockets assistant coach, back in 1980, he and the team's head coach, Del Harris, had a question they wanted answered. They were curious about the difference in their offense between the possessions in which star center Moses Malone touched the ball and those when he didn't. They wanted hard data. Dawson began charting every Malone touch from the sidelines. He'd mark down if Malone shot or passed (and who that pass was to and where on the floor that player stood) and if the Rockets scored or came up empty.

"And we figured out we were a hell of a lot better off if Moses touched the ball 100 times down the floor,"[2] Dawson said.

---

1   Hinkie has never spoken publicly about his brother. This story, told during an interview on the *Invest Like the Best* podcast with Patrick O'Shaughnessy, was in response to the question "What was the kindest thing anybody has ever done for you?" He described the incident as "a real tragedy in our family that was hard" but didn't delve into more detail.

2   It's worth noting that since the NBA, in 2013, began keeping tabs of how many times each player touches the ball, no player has averaged more than 98.8 (Charlotte Hornets point guard Kemba Walker during the 2013–2014 season).

In 1981, after finishing with a disappointing record of 40–42 and barely sneaking into the playoffs, the Rockets, armed with Dawson's statistical analysis, upped Malone's minutes and force-fed him the ball. The strategy worked. The Rockets upset the defending champion Lakers and made the Finals (where they lost in six games to Larry Bird's Boston Celtics) for the first time in franchise history.

Looking over Hinkie's résumé twenty-four years later, Dawson thought back to that magical 1981 run. Like Casserly one year earlier, he was impressed with what he was reading, and he liked the idea of bringing someone with a different background into the front office. "We basically had all former players," he said. Dawson hired Hinkie as a "special assistant to the general manager" in the summer of 2005. For Hinkie, it was the perfect gig, even if it meant flying from Stanford to Houston one day a week. He could help with draft research and analysis and suggest changes to on-court strategy as well. It was similar to the type of role he'd pitched to Casserly. Dawson didn't always take Hinkie's advice—Hinkie wanted the Rockets to shoot more three-pointers; Dawson didn't believe the strategy was a good fit with the team's personnel—but he was always open to his thoughts.

"He spoke Stanford and I spoke basketball, but we got along great," Dawson said. "He was smart, but didn't talk down to people. It's really hard when you're smart to be just one of the guys, but he pulled that off really well."

———

Most kids spend their childhoods watching cartoons, reading comic books, and goofing around with friends. Hinkie was different. He was singularly focused, interested in figuring out "what it took to get to the top," he once wrote, "how hard you had to work and how even when you got to the top, you had to keep working."

He overachieved in everything. He was valedictorian and president of his high school class all four years. As a senior he was voted Most Likely to Succeed. His high school biology teacher would make him special tests. He was the basketball team's point guard and, despite being just 5-foot-9 and 145 pounds, one of the football team's safeties. By his senior year he was squatting close to 500 pounds.

"He couldn't have just walked out on the court or field and competed with other kids at the time without putting in the behind-the-scenes dirty work," Kenny Ridley, his basketball coach, said.

Hinkie enjoyed football, but basketball was his true love. He worked on his game whenever and wherever he could. He honed his ball handling by dribbling down Marlow's streets and tried boosting his vertical leap by working out in Jumpsoles shoes. He'd attend all sorts of summer camps. "Basketball was a pretty important part of my life," he said. He kept a key to the high school gym so that he could shoot whenever he had the time and by college was good enough to walk onto a Division I team. But he knew that would likely have led to him spending his life as a college coach. Hinkie had greater aspirations. He enrolled in the University of Oklahoma Price College of Business and signed up for all sorts of fancy committees and classes: the Student Business Association, the Management and Marketing Club, the Student Advisory Board of the JCPenney Leadership Program, Student Congress, the Price College of Business President's Round-table. In school he became obsessed with weighing future possibilities instead of solely focusing on present realities, a way of thinking that would quickly grow into a personal credo, one to be applied to all facets of his life. While at Oklahoma, Hinkie took out a classmate named Alison Burness. Upon coming home that night he told friends that he'd found the woman he wanted to spend the rest of his life with, and not because he was some lovestruck college kid who had been swept off his feet.

"The reason I thought I wanted to marry her was all about the long view and all about what that could mean," Hinkie said. "[I was thinking], 'This could be a great life. This could be an amazing partner to spend your life with,' and all those things. The thing I was thinking about was not what the next twelve or eighteen months would be like, but what life would be like in our fifties, sixties, and seventies."

A year after meeting Burness, Hinkie took her to Paris and proposed on a bench beside the Arc de Triomphe.

After college, Hinkie tried his hand in finance. He excelled, but it didn't take long for him to realize that the world of professional sports was where he wanted to make his career. Not as a part of an organization, though. No, his intention, he once told the University of Oklahoma's *Price Magazine*, was always "to lead." He applied to Harvard and Stanford's MBA programs, and was accepted to both. He chose Stanford because of the school's close relationships with NFL teams.

———

In 2007, Hinkie, just twenty-nine, was promoted to Rockets vice president, making him the youngest person in NBA history to hold that title.

He'd impressed his bosses during his two years with the team. But the catalyst for the promotion was the Rockets' decision to replace the retiring Dawson with assistant GM Daryl Morey. Like Hinkie, Morey had a background in business and revered statistics. He had studied computer science at Northwestern, received an MBA from MIT, and worked for a consulting firm before getting a job with the Boston Celtics. Afterward he founded the MIT Sloan Sports Analytics Conference.

"They formed a really close bond and saw things similarly," said Jeff Van Gundy, the Rockets' coach at the time.

In Morey, who would later be profiled by Michael Lewis in the *New York Times Magazine* and billed as the NBA's answer to Billy Beane of *Moneyball*, Hinkie had finally found his rabbi, despite the two sharing little in common. Morey was gregarious and jovial, optimistic and open. Hinkie was serious, guarded, and, as he would say years later, "I come from a worldview that everything we do sucks." Hinkie was religious and sentimental (he'd somehow purchased a piece from the bench in Paris where he proposed to his wife); Morey was not. Hinkie loved country music; Morey would taunt him that country was the one musical genre that had never produced anything worthwhile. But they bonded over their intellectual leanings, and it didn't take long for them to revamp the Rockets' front office. They relied on statistical analysis, sure, and more so than almost all their peers. But the foundation of the makeover was deeper. Hinkie and Morey both craved information and had no qualms questioning previous norms. *Because that's how we've always done things* was never an acceptable explanation.

Hinkie and Morey were also firm believers in basketball philosophies that would help trigger a revolution in the way the game was played and evaluated. They loved threes. They thought traditional stats measured defense poorly. What they really believed, though, was that running an NBA team was about asking the right questions, studying the right data, leveraging that information into gaining a competitive advantage—and basing every decision off that approach. It was about having a process and trusting that over the results. "Separating the difference between randomness and skill is critical," is how Hinkie once explained it. Hinkie enjoyed running Monte Carlo simulations on the NBA season, his way of attempting to sift out the outcomes that owed themselves to luck.

"I don't even care if [the shot] goes in or not. I'm all about, 'Should it go in?'" Hinkie once said. "I can live with randomness. I mean, if it's a close game in the end, yeah, I'm just like anyone else. But I just want us to play the odds all the time."

But claiming principles and sticking to them are two different things. Even Morey wavered occasionally, especially at the beginning of his tenure. It was in these moments that the more resolute Hinkie nudged him back toward their shared views.

In the lead-up to the 2006 draft, just a few months after Morey was hired by the Rockets as Dawson's assistant so that he could be groomed for a season before taking over, Houston received a call from the Memphis Grizzlies. They wanted the Rockets' pick—No. 8 overall—and were willing to part with Shane Battier to acquire it.

Battier was an unremarkable 6-foot-8 forward out of Duke entering his sixth NBA season. He had barely averaged 10 points per game for his career. He couldn't run very fast and he didn't jump very high.

What he did do, though, was help his team win games. The Grizzlies won 23 games the season before Battier arrived; by his third season they were a 50-win team. Battier wasn't the primary catalyst for this jump. But the data was clear. The Grizzlies were significantly better with him on the court.

The Rockets' front office was split on whether to do the deal. Morey himself was unsure. On the one hand, Battier was the perfect piece for his team. The Rockets were led by two All-Stars in Yao Ming and Tracy McGrady. The goal was to win a championship, and what they needed to get there were players to help along the edges of the roster. In other words, players like Battier.

On the other hand, Morey was new to the job, and trading a No. 8 pick—a slot that often yields high-upside young players—for a seemingly run-of-the-mill veteran with a dreary game was a big risk.

The back-and-forth irked Hinkie. "We either believe in the stuff we're doing or we don't," he yelled in his Oklahoma accent during one meeting debating the deal.

Moved by Hinkie's conviction, Morey pressed the Rockets to do the deal. With Battier harassing opposing scorers and knocking down three-pointers and boxing out and spacing the floor and making the extra pass, the Rockets jumped from 34 wins to 52, and then to 55 the season after that, at one point even winning 22 games in a row.

"Sam's advocacy for that deal really pushed it through," Morey said.

Recurring injuries to McGrady and Yao derailed Houston's championship hopes. The Rockets traded a diminished McGrady to the Knicks in 2010. Yao retired the next year. The losses dropped the Rockets into the middle of the Western Conference standings, and left Morey and Hinkie searching for new ways to build a contender. The two would discuss, often over late-night table tennis games at the team facility, the best paths toward achieving that goal. Outright tanking was not an option that team owner Leslie Alexander was willing to tolerate. That meant a high draft pick was likely out of the picture, which meant Morey and Hinkie needed to discover a way to sign or trade for a star.

And so the Rockets spent three seasons building up a treasure chest of assets. One day, they figured, a top-10 player would come on the market. When that day arrived, they'd be ready to pounce.

———

In the spring of 2013, Hinkie met Sixers managing chairman Josh Harris and the team's No. 2 owner, David Blitzer, in Manhattan for dinner. The Sixers had interviewed Hinkie the previous summer, when ownership was unsure whether it wanted to promote assistant general manager Tony DiLeo or hire someone from the outside. They elected to keep DiLeo, who had helped negotiate the deal to acquire Lakers star center Andrew Bynum, a move that at the time thrilled ownership.

Nearly a year later, the Sixers were coming off a disappointing 34-win campaign. Injuries sidelined Bynum all season; his career was now in jeopardy. Ownership was embarrassed and frustrated—and no longer content operating in the background. Harris and Blitzer kept thinking back to Hinkie, and how he had cautioned them during their talks the previous summer. Their focus on the present, he had said, was sending them down a dangerous path. The warning had turned prescient, and now ownership was interested in hearing Hinkie's vision for rebuilding their team.

Hinkie, brown hair parted to the side like an accountant, arrived at the restaurant carrying a laptop. The answer was inside. A few months earlier, in late October and just three days before the start of the regular season, the Rockets had traded for Oklahoma City Thunder guard James Harden. A former third overall pick, Harden was a twenty-three-year-old guard and reigning Sixth Man of the Year. But his contract was set to expire, and he was requesting a raise. His new deal would have pushed the Thunder's payroll above the luxury tax line, a no-no for team ownership.

This was the opportunity for which Morey and Hinkie had prepared. Armed with more assets than any other suitor, the Rockets were able to pry Harden away and immediately signed him to a five-year, $80 million extension. That season, Harden upped his scoring from 16.8 points per game to 25.9. He also made his first All-Star team and led the Rockets back to the playoffs.

Hinkie opened up his laptop and cued up a PowerPoint file featuring all sorts of diagrams and arrows—graphics to demonstrate, step by step, how the Rockets had collected the pieces (guards Kevin Martin and Jeremy Lamb, two first-round picks, and a second-round pick) required to pull off the Harden trade.

"The big message was, through a variety of actions and things and circumstances, not any one person's fault, the crops have been eaten, your future ability to nourish yourself is impaired," Hinkie later said of his back-and-forth with Sixers ownership. "You are a long way away."

Hinkie didn't care that the Sixers were just a year removed from coming within one game of the Eastern Conference Finals, or that the roster featured some nice young players. He'd spent years studying the history of the league. "He watches more basketball than anyone I know," Morey said. He knew that champions almost always boasted multiple stars. It's what makes team building in basketball so challenging. There are only five players on the court at a time. Everyone plays both offense and defense. There's no limit on how many times a player can touch the ball. In no sport does one player have more influence over the outcome, and in no sport is the amount of available players capable of leading their team to a championship so limited. And so to Hinkie, there was nothing more important than hooking that first big fish. He believed that a team that secured one could quickly attract another. But, he'd say often, acquiring that first star was "the most challenging part."

Hinkie presented his information to Sixers ownership during the interview process. "I suggested that if you really want to build a team that competes deep in May and June, then you have to ask: How have other teams like that been built?" he recalled a few years later.

Harris and his partners assured Hinkie that, yes, a championship was the goal. Also, they were familiar with this equation. Even before hiring Hinkie, they had commissioned Aaron Barzilai, the team's director of basketball analytics, to research the different paths toward obtaining a superstar. "They basically wanted to know how often teams that get good draft picks succeed in winning a championship," Barzilai recalled.

Hinkie and the Sixers went back and forth for about a month. Hinkie questioned the owners more than they questioned him. He wanted to ensure that his goals and their goals were aligned, that Harris and Co. were fully on board with and committed to his rebuilding plan. He asked the owners why they had originally decided to buy an NBA team, and then why they had pulled the trigger at that time, and why they had specifically bought the Sixers, and what their expectations were going forward, and what was it they truly wanted. It was Hinkie at his best, both charming—which he could be when he wanted to—and curious, interesting, and interested.

On May 14, 2013, just a few weeks after telling DiLeo that he'd be receiving a new contract to serve as Sixers GM, and just three days after Harris had called DiLeo to notify him that ownership had changed its mind, the Sixers held a press conference. The thirty-six-year-old Sam Hinkie was being named president of basketball operations and general manager. Speaking to the Philadelphia press and the team's fans for the first time, he did his best to explain his operating philosophy.

"We talk a lot about process—not outcome," he said.

Chapter 4

THE LONGEST LENS

No event is more important to NBA general managers than the draft. Every June, each team spends a night huddled in its so-called war room (a conference room in which the sharpest object is a pen) mapping out its future. Draft night offers hope, but also risk. Tab the right player, make the right trade, and glory will follow. Choose poorly—an incredibly likely option given that the whole endeavor is centered on predicting how a bunch of kids will translate when dropped into a man's world—and it might take your team close to a decade to recover, and by the time it does someone else will have taken your job.

NBA teams typically spend a year, if not more, planning for the draft. Sam Hinkie had just forty-four days.

"We were very much behind the eight-ball from just doing all the work," said one former member of the team's front office.

Two days after being officially introduced, Hinkie met the Sixers' top player evaluators in Chicago for the pre-draft combine, a league-organized event where most of that year's top prospects work out in front of all thirty teams. The scouts and executives, some of whom had been with the team for more than ten years, and all of whom were close with Tony DiLeo, were anxious. All they knew about Hinkie was that he was the guy who'd always show up at games in a blue blazer (he owned twenty-five of them, all the same color and all size 40 regular, his Steve Jobsian way of reducing decision fatigue) and that he had spent the previous eight years as one of the chief analytics guys for the Houston Rockets, one of the league's most quantitative-driven teams. Did that mean their jobs were in jeopardy? It was like a bunch of yellow cab drivers learning that an Uber executive was their new boss. Making matters more complicated, DiLeo's older brother, Frank, was still employed by the team as a scout. The group yearned for some sort of reassurance—or at least an update—and thought they'd receive one in Chicago. Hinkie didn't see why such a talk was necessary. "Proceed as usual," was the message he passed along.

"No one really knew where they stood," a member of the front office said. "The scouts, but also the training and administrative staff. Everyone was kind of unsure what was going on and there were all these radically different expectations from what we were all used to. There was a lot of tension in the air. Everything felt very unresolved."

A couple weeks later, and after much goading, Hinkie finally met with his basketball staff at PCOM to address their concerns. He began the meeting by complimenting the group's recent draft record. In the nine years prior to Hinkie's hiring, the Sixers had nabbed two All-Stars (Andre Iguodala and Jrue Holiday), two starting-caliber players (Thaddeus Young and Thabo Sefolosha), a blossoming young center (Nikola Vučević), and a prolific bench scorer (Lou Williams, whom they had scooped up in the draft's second round). "I respect what you've done here," Hinkie told the group.

But, he added, the way the Sixers attacked the draft was about to change. For years, the team's scouts had mostly dictated selections. "That was one piece of advice Mr. Snider"—the team's previous owner—"always gave me," recalled Billy King. "He'd say, 'Let the scouts run the draft. They see the players more than you.' And I listened to him. I'd make a decision if it was close, but our scouts and their board led things."

This was not how Hinkie planned on operating. It's not that he didn't value his scouts' opinions. "But," he told them, "even the best are going to miss often." Draft night would no longer be about simply selecting the best player on the board. "I want as many swings at the plate as I can get," he said. It's a phrase he'd employ often over the next few years. To him, the math was simple. He'd spent years studying the rosters of NBA champions. He knew that five teams had combined to win twenty of the previous twenty-three NBA titles. He knew that these teams had monopolized the NBA championship trophy because they boasted multiple all-time greats, players like Jordan, Olajuwon, Kobe, Shaq, Wade, and LeBron. He also knew that, typically, these players spent the majority of their careers playing for the teams that had originally drafted them[1]—and in those rare cases where they changed teams, it was usually to link up with a star somewhere else. And Hinkie knew that these types of players were typically selected early in the draft.

He also knew that the draft was closer to crapshoot than science, and so if the best chance to win was by acquiring a superstar, and if the best chance to acquire a superstar was by landing a high draft pick, then his best chance at succeeding would be by acquiring as many high draft picks as possible.

"We will not bat a thousand on every single draft pick. We also have them by the bushelful, in part, because of that," he'd explain a couple years later. "We don't have any hubris that we will get them all right. We're not certain that we have an enormous edge over anybody else. In some cases, we might not have an edge at all."

Hinkie spent the next six weeks amassing information from every possible source. The Sixers owned the 11th pick, but prep wasn't limited to players who'd likely be available at that spot. Hinkie doled out video assignments on dozens of prospects. He requested that his scouts pay close attention to more granular details—not, for example, whether a player turned the ball over frequently but instead whether his turnovers came off the dribble or when passing out of the post. Notes were

---

1   This would change a bit over the coming years, mostly thanks to a revolution sparked by LeBron James. His decision (no pun intended) to "take his talents" from the Cleveland Cavaliers to the Miami Heat three years earlier, and to do so on national TV, altered the NBA landscape. But the age of NBA stars feeling fully empowered to demand trades, sign short-term deals, and turn the NBA into a game of musical chairs—meaning stars *could* be acquired outside the draft—was still a few years away.

to be submitted in bullet points. "And he read and commented on every report," one Sixers scout said. "That's not something that usually happens." Hinkie had Aaron Barzilai compile lists of advanced stats like points per possessions, true shooting percentage, and rebounding rate. These numbers, along with a summary of the scouting reports and medical notes, were compiled onto a PDF and printed out. Hinkie was particular about every detail, from the statistics chosen, to the format, to the font color (he preferred dark blue).

"He'd say things like, 'Can we go from a ten-point font to an eight and a half?'" said one former colleague. "Or maybe, 'Can we move this three pixels to the right?'"

Hinkie had no problem utilizing the skills of the holdovers. But he never disclosed to them how all the information they were collecting was influencing his thinking. He believed that keeping other teams in the dark about his intentions could be leveraged into an advantage (the less people in the know, the more likely his intentions would remain secret). Also, as one former colleague put it, "Sam didn't know any of us." In other words, he wasn't sure who he could trust to not get chatty with a friend from an opposing team.

Still, most of the evaluators, holdovers from the previous Sixers regime, were worried about their job security. They were eager to prove themselves to their new boss, and also wanted to help him navigate what would be his first draft at the helm.

"But Sam wanted to tear the whole thing down," one colleague said. "He didn't need our help for that."

———

One evening the week of the draft, Hinkie called the team's top evaluators into a third-floor conference room at PCOM for one final pre-draft meeting. Courtney Witte, the team's director of player personnel, attended. So did Vince Rozman, the team's scouting coordinator. A bunch of scouts had come in as well. Rod Thorn, too.

Thorn, then seventy-two years old, had been in and around the NBA since being drafted in 1963. He'd spent the previous thirty-five years as one of the league's most respected executives. The Sixers hired him to serve as their president of basketball operations in 2010. Thorn planned on retiring in a few months, but he'd told ownership he'd stay on in a consulting role to aid Hinkie with the transition. In theory, this meant he would be advising Hinkie about the upcoming draft.

There was just one problem.

"Nobody knew what was going on except Sachin," one member of the front office said. "He and Sam spent the whole week leading up to the draft locked in Sam's office barely speaking to anyone."

Sachin was Sachin Gupta, a thirty-two-year-old MIT graduate who was in the midst of receiving his MBA from Stanford University's Graduate School of Business. Gupta had worked alongside Hinkie in Houston—a job he landed after meeting Daryl Morey, a fellow MIT graduate and the Rockets' general manager. Gupta was working as a software engineer at ESPN at the time, where he'd been introduced to a treasure chest of numbers, including NBA play-by-play data and the Player Efficiency Rating (PER) metric invented by John Hollinger, who'd go on to become the vice president of basketball operations for the Memphis Grizzlies. Gupta also built ESPN's trade machine, an online tool where fans constructed fake trades between teams and could see if the NBA's Collective Bargaining Agreement (a complex document, featuring terms like "trade kicker" and "Bird rights" that can cause dizziness in the most ardent NBA followers) deemed them kosher.

"And he built that in less than a week," recalled Chris Ramsay, Gupta's boss at ESPN.

The trade machine became a sensation among NBA fans. More important to Gupta, it forced him to become schooled in the league's CBA. His skills made him an ideal fit for Morey's Rockets front office. There, Gupta and Hinkie spent years sitting side by side, talking strategy, about both on-court performance (they were particularly interested in toying around with play-by-play data being captured by new, high-tech cameras) and how to build a championship team. They grew close, and when Hinkie got the Sixers job, he brought Gupta along with him (officially as a consultant; Gupta was still completing his MBA) to serve as his right-hand man.

That evening's draft prep meeting lasted a couple of hours.

Afterward, Hinkie and Gupta retreated into Hinkie's office and closed the door. It was about 8 p.m. Thorn and the scouts chatted about the draft and shared league gossip. One hour passed. Some of the staff headed to their respective offices to watch more film. "We were just really bored," one of the scouts recalled. Another hour passed. Hinkie remained in his office with the door closed, working the phones and putting the finishing touches on his player rankings. Another hour passed. It was apparent to Thorn, whose upcoming retirement likely left Hinkie dubious about enlisting his help, and to everyone else present, that Hinkie no longer had a use for their services. But he was still their new boss and they were worried about losing their jobs. No one wanted to leave without being officially dismissed.

Thorn found the behavior insulting. He'd been around the NBA longer than Hinkie had been alive, with a long and impressive résumé (he had drafted Michael Jordan while with the Chicago Bulls in 1983). And yet here he was being treated like an intern.

"Rod was going apeshit," recalled one person who was in the room. Around midnight, he retired to his office and began packing up. One of the scouts popped his head in and spotted Thorn folding a Sixers sweatshirt.

"Do you want it?" Thorn asked.

"Yeah," the scout said.

Thorn told him it was his. Hearing this back-and-forth, another member of the front office came darting in.

"What else you giving away?" he asked.

"I got an idea," Thorn said. His office was littered with all sorts of mementos he didn't want to bring home. "Let's play a game." He called the group back into the conference room across from Hinkie's office and, from the head of the table, began tossing out trivia questions. *What year did I get drafted? What were the most points per game Allen Iverson averaged in a season? How many games did Gene Shue*—a former Sixers head coach who was one of the team's scouts at the time—*win in 1977?* Whoever called out the correct answer first, or was closest to the right answer, received the souvenir. There was a chunk of the Hershey Sports Arena gym floor that Wilt Chamberlain scored 100 points on fifty-one years earlier. A blue Sixers windbreaker. Some jerseys and autographs. At one point Thorn brought out an $180 bottle of Silver Oak wine that, he had forgotten, was given to him by Witte as a birthday gift. Witte, dismayed to see his gift unopened and on the verge of being passed along to someone else, sat there silently.

The game went on for more than an hour. The group filled PCOM's third floor with shouting and laughter.

Finally, a confused Hinkie, dressed in slacks and an open-collared dress shirt, emerged from his office.

"You guys are still here?" he asked. He told the group they were free to go home.

———

The first pick shocked everyone, including the player himself.

"I'm just as surprised as anyone else," Anthony Bennett told reporters at Brooklyn's Barclays Center after being drafted by the Cleveland Cavaliers. Bennett, an athletic 6-foot-8 forward, had put up solid numbers during his lone season at UNLV, but few prognosticators pegged him as the No. 1 pick. Most analysts and scouts believed a bouncy 6-foot-11 center out of Kentucky named Nerlens Noel to be the draft's top prospect. Noel—who'd been ranked No. 1 in his high school class one year earlier—was leading the country in blocks per game before landing awkwardly during a February contest and tearing the ACL in his left knee. The injury cost him the rest of the season and he'd spent the months leading up to the draft rehabbing eight hours a day at a clinic in Alabama. He appeared to be recovering well. But it was unlikely he'd be cleared to return during the upcoming NBA season. Some teams wondered how a prospect whose game was predicated on athleticism would bounce back from such a serious injury.

Hinkie transformed his PCOM office into the team's command center. He, Gupta, Witte, Thorn, Harris, Blitzer, and Heller crowded around the small circular table across from Hinkie's desk. Hinkie handed them dark three-ring binders that he said were not to leave the room. Inside were all sorts of numbers and graphs and notes, compiled to guide the team's draft. The goal was no longer to simply select the best player on the board. It was to spot value, to project which players were worthy of which selections and pounce at the right time.

Meanwhile, the rest of the basketball operations staff followed on a TV outside Hinkie's office.

"None of us had any idea what was going to happen," one recalled.

Hinkie continued working the phones. The next four players—Indiana guard Victor Oladipo, Georgetown forward Otto Porter, Indiana center Cody Zeller, and Maryland center Alex Len—came off the board, gifting Hinkie an opportunity. Noel, who he had deemed worthy of the No. 2 pick, was still available. Hinkie thought Noel had the chance to grow into an elite NBA center. He loved how Noel could protect the rim, a skill Hinkie believed to be "at a premium" in the NBA. He knew the ACL tear presented a risk, but that it was also thanks to the injury that the Sixers were able to grab Noel. And while Hinkie never gave others the impression that he had targeted Noel *because* he'd be out for the year, that Noel was slated to miss the entire 2013–2014 season, which would likely boost the Sixers' draft lottery odds, offered a nice bonus.

This was Hinkie's chance to pull the Sixers out of purgatory. He knew Andrew Bynum—the talented center the Sixers had traded for the previous year only to see him miss the entire season due to a series of knee maladies—wasn't returning, and that without Bynum his roster had no chance of competing for a title. Swings at the plate were what Hinkie wanted, and the New Orleans Pelicans, desperate to surround their twenty-year-old franchise center, Anthony Davis, with proven talent, were prepared to hand Hinkie a couple more.

All Hinkie had to do was part with his team's best player.

Since being drafted by the Sixers in 2009, Jrue Holiday had grown into one of the NBA's better point guards. He was a tenacious defender, prolific distributor, and solid scorer. He had played a key role in leading the Sixers to within one game of the Eastern Conference Finals a year earlier and was rewarded the previous November with a four-year, $41 million extension that was set to begin the following season. All of this made him the Sixers' most valuable trade asset. Holiday was good, young, and signed at a reasonable rate for four more years. Had the Sixers been ready to compete, Hinkie would have been happy to keep him. But with no chance of contending within that four-year window, flipping him for more swings at the plate made more sense.

Hinkie and the Pelicans general manager, Dell Demps, discussed the deal and officially agreed to terms. New Orleans would draft Noel and send him to Philadelphia in exchange for Holiday and the 42nd pick. The Sixers would also receive the Pelicans' 2014 first-round pick, as long as it didn't fall within the top five. The protection made the deal dicey, but Hinkie and Gupta were confident the Pelicans would be bad enough to make the pick valuable while also not quite good enough to avoid finishing the following season with one of the league's five worst records.

Hinkie believed his ability to wield the "longest lens in the room"—a favorite phrase of his—gave him an edge over his competition. He wasn't worried about how many games he'd win the following season. By shooting for a target five, or seven, or even ten years down the road, he'd be free to operate in a way distinct from his competitors. While everyone else was fighting over the present, Hinkie would be alone cobbling together assets for the future and leveraging his lack of a timeline into an advantage.

The Pelicans drafted Noel sixth. A few minutes later ESPN announced the trade, stunning the Sixers employees seated outside Hinkie's office. Holiday was shocked too. He thought he'd wear a Sixers uniform for the rest of his career. "Normally you're kind of given a heads-up that something like that could happen," his agent, Tony Dutt, said. "But I think they knew it was something different that they had to keep to themselves." Instead, Holiday and Dutt heard about the deal from Demps, who earlier that day had notified Dutt that he and the Sixers were in negotiations. This was the first time Hinkie would be accused of dismissing the feelings of a Sixers player. It wouldn't be the last.

Hinkie wasn't done dealing. He was intent on drafting a point guard out of Syracuse named Michael Carter-Williams. Hinkie loved that Carter-Williams boasted so many qualities that couldn't be taught. At 6-foot-6, he was a good three to four inches taller than most point guards, allowing him to zip pinpoint passes through gaps his peers couldn't even see. "I told all the NBA teams that asked that Michael had a ton of potential because of his size, quickness, and passing," said Syracuse head coach Jim Boeheim. But there were still questions surrounding Carter-Williams. He was one of the worst shooters in the draft. He'd also been busted the previous December for shoplifting a bathrobe and gloves at a Syracuse Lord & Taylor. Some teams were scared off. Not Hinkie. No prospect was perfect, especially ones picked outside the top 10. And anyway, a crooked jump shot was the sort of flaw that could be fixed with the combination of tutelage and hard work. Carter-Williams fell to 11, where the Sixers scooped him up.

Hinkie stayed on the phones. "The guy tried to trade for every pick," a confounded Thorn told colleagues afterward. "I've never seen anything like that." Sometimes, the door to his office would swing open and the scouts seated outside would catch a glimpse of Hinkie pressing one phone to each ear.

The first round came to an end. The Sixers' next pick was early in the second. Hinkie kept working. He knew many teams considered second-round picks expendable. He felt otherwise. Sure, it was rare to see a player drafted in the second round stick in the league for more than a few years. But all Hinkie was looking for was assets and swings at the plate. Not only could second-round picks be used as currency in future trades, but players drafted in that round weren't entitled to guaranteed contracts. This meant that if any did hit, they'd likely be locked into a team-friendly deal.

The Sixers tabbed a Georgia Tech forward named Glen Rice Jr. at No. 35. They immediately traded him to the Washington Wizards for picks No. 38 and 54, and drafted South Dakota State guard Nate Wolters at 38, whom they then traded to the Milwaukee Bucks in exchange for another 2014 second-round pick and Providence forward Ricky Ledo, whom they then traded to the Dallas Mavericks in exchange for another 2014 second-round pick before drafting an Oregon big man named Arsalan Kazemi at No. 54.

"The owners loved it," recalled one member of the front office. "They watched Sam work the phones the entire night and thought it was the greatest thing they'd ever seen."

The night was a huge success. There was no question the Sixers would fail to match their 34-win total from the previous season. But it was clear that the organization finally recognized the dangers of residing in NBA purgatory.

"The exact status quo," Hinkie told reporters after the draft, "wasn't going to get it done."

The night foreshadowed everything that would come to pass within and around the Sixers over the next three years. Trading a good present for the chance of a better future. Tabbing a young, talented center as the savior. Disrespecting veterans. Marginalizing agents.

The seeds were planted. The Process had begun.

Chapter 5

"WHO THE HELL IS BRETT BROWN?"

Sam Hinkie's first off-season at the helm was nearly complete. He'd spent draft night uprooting the Sixers' foundation, dealing their best player for a nineteen-year-old with a torn ACL.

The next few months were spent tearing down nearly everything that remained.

Andrew Bynum, the Sixers' marquee acquisition just one year earlier, was allowed to walk in free agency without so much as a contract offer. So were other veterans like Nick Young and Dorell Wright. It was clear what path the Sixers were heading down. They were planning to sacrifice the present in order to chase a brighter future. Hinkie figured the best way to escape the hamster wheel of NBA mediocrity was to just jump right off, consequences be damned. It might hurt a bit, but the reward of breaking out of NBA purgatory was worth the cost.

Losing, in other words, would be tolerated. Winning, for the time being, would not be a concern.

All Hinkie needed now was to find a head coach open to being a part of his plan.

Bob Brown was a man of rules, a small-town high school basketball coach straight out of central casting. Short and portly with a round face, he believed in discipline and order. He was a member of the New England Basketball Hall of Fame, the kind of high school coach who didn't allow his players to grow their hair long. Who forbade tattoos. Who required his students to wear hats when walking out of the gym and into the cold Maine night. He spent fifty-two years coaching basketball at various high schools and colleges in the New England area, winning four state titles. "An absolute legend in Maine" is how longtime NBA head coach Steve Clifford, a fellow native of the state and former assistant and colleague of Brown's, described him.

Brett Brown, Bob's bushy-haired son and his starting point guard, was not a man of rules. He enjoyed pranking friends. He was the kind of kid who, from the passenger seat of his high school buddy's pickup truck, would lean over and honk the horn when driving by a group of girls, then duck below the window, framing his friend.

Bob and Brett occasionally clashed. Bob once threw Brett out of a practice. "We ruined many of my mother's dinners," Brett said. "It's my nature to be a little bit challenging, and at times combative, so you jump through the hoops with him at practice, and then you'd come home and I'd say, 'Well, I don't agree with you. What are you going to do, suspend me from the dinner table?'" But basketball was a language they both spoke. Like his father, Brett loved the game. He loved the work. The strategy. The cheerleaders (he dated one at South Portland High School). During the winter, he'd wake up before school, pull the family car out of the unheated garage attached to the four-bedroom home, and use the space to work on ball handling and defensive slides. Brett was named All-State twice during his high school career and as a senior led his father's team to a 29–0 record and state title.

"[My dad] was a very hard taskmaster, just a real sort of old-school disciplinarian," Brett said. "But playing for him was just something you wouldn't trade for anything."

It helped that Bob's preferred style suited Brett's game. Bob liked his teams to play fast. He wanted his offense to move the ball and his defense to force turnovers. Brett was a 5-foot-10, lightning-quick guard who could dribble circles around opponents. Eventually, he caught the eye of a twenty-six-year-old New York native named Rick Pitino. Wrapping up his first year as the head coach at Boston University, Pitino was looking for a point guard who could help him rebuild the BU basketball program. He wanted his team to press and trap and run, and that wasn't the only similarity he shared with Brett's dad.

Pitino, who years later would be inducted into the Basketball Hall of Fame, was intense, strict, and, well, a bit nuts. "He came in trying to change the culture," said Glenn Consor, BU's starting point guard when Pitino took over. Pitino knew he wasn't exactly inheriting a group of high flyers or sweet shooters (BU had amassed just 17 wins in the two years prior to his arrival), so he figured instead he'd try out-conditioning his opponents. The Terriers practiced twice a day and three times on Sunday—Pitino's way of keeping his players out of the local bars. Tape blanketed all the gym's windows and clocks. As a punishment for mistakes, players were forced to spend a minute holding a brick in each hand while sliding in a defensive stance across the gym floor. He'd force the team to hit 170 layups in four minutes—a rate that translated to about one make every 1.5 seconds. Failure to do so would result in laps. He'd yell. He'd scream. He'd curse. He'd insult.

Brown arrived on campus in the fall of 1979. "He is a very intelligent backcourt player with outstanding quickness," Pitino wrote of Brown in his scouting report at that time. "He should fit right in with our fast break style of play." Practices began soon after. One day, following one particularly grueling session, Consor found Brown in the showers, nearly collapsed, leaning on a wall.

"I don't know if I can do this anymore," he told Consor.

Consor talked Brown off the ledge. Brown kept working. He grew more comfortable, which allowed his skillset to shine. "His knowledge of the game was advanced," Consor recalled. "He was super quick and could handle the ball and knew how to play point guard really well."

He also quickly established himself as one of the team clowns. "The best thing he did was keep everyone's spirits up during hard times," Consor said. Brown particularly enjoyed pranking his teammate and suitemate Gary Plummer. He'd eat the homemade sweet potato pies sent to Plummer by his mother—and then deny doing so, even when Plummer spotted the orange crumbs dotting Brown's mouth. Once, he and another former teammate were out with Plummer at a bar in Kenmore Square, about a half mile from campus. It was past midnight and time to go home, but Boston's "T" had stopped running. The group had no money. Brown went searching for a cab willing to drive them for free. He found one—and then asked the driver if he'd be willing to go along with a prank.

Plummer climbed into the car. Brown leaned over. "When we stop, get out and run as fast as you can," he whispered.

Plummer was terrified. "I'm a 6-foot-9 black man in Boston," he shot back. "I'm the one who's gonna get screwed."

The cab stopped at a light close to the dorms. Brown and the third teammate leapt out and ran. Plummer took five quick steps, stopped, and turned around.

"I'm sorry," he told the driver. "I promise I'll get you back."

Brown, a few feet away, burst out laughing.

Brown occasionally poked at Pitino too. One time he showed up at 5:59 p.m. for a bus scheduled to depart at 6:00—fourteen minutes late in Pitino's world—and after a game the next night was forced to race the team bus back to the hotel. But Pitino also appreciated his work ethic, verve, and thirst for knowledge, and despite the clowning around, he saw Brown for what he was. "Brett was always like a sponge, always asking questions and trying to get better," Consor said.

Brown was named team captain before his junior year and as a senior led BU to the NCAA tournament for the first time since 1959. He finished his collegiate career second in school history in assists. After graduating he stayed at the university for a year to work as a graduate assistant before leaving in 1985 to take a sales job with AT&T. The telecommunications industry was exploding at the time and the gregarious Brown was earning "more than I ever could have imagined." He'd grown up in small-town Maine, raised by two teachers who earned around $60,000 combined. Now he was clearing six figures and owned multiple properties and he hadn't even turned twenty-five. Yet, for a reason he couldn't quite pinpoint, something still seemed to be missing in his life.

"It was sort of a stage for me where I was lost," he said. "I did not know really what I wanted to do."

So he did what lost college grads tend to do: He quit his job, packed his bags, and booked a one-way ticket to the other end of the globe.

———

Brown backpacked through Oceania for more than a year. He bounced between campsites in Fiji, Tahiti, New Zealand, and Australia. He fished and drank beer and hunted abalone with a knife. "You just peel them off, put them in the mesh net, pan-fry them in some olive oil—delicious," he recalled.

But now he needed a job. He'd met a girl. Well, he'd met lots of girls, but this one was special. "I could have a laugh with her, have a beer with her. It was just good fun," he said. Her name was Anna. She was the daughter of a farmer and living along the Great Barrier Reef, near the Great Keppel Island campsite where Brown was staying. It didn't take long for him to discover that something about her was different. He couldn't imagine leaving her behind.

Basketball was just starting to grow popular in the region. Maybe, Brown thought, there was a local team that could use a coach. An intermediary introduced him to the owners of a team in Auckland, New Zealand. Brown convinced Pitino, who was then serving as an assistant coach for the New York Knicks, to write him a letter of recommendation. Only after being named the team's head coach, at the age of twenty-seven, did Brown realize, "I really didn't know what I was doing."

So he leaned on the lessons he'd learned from the men who had coached him. His team wouldn't be the most talented but his players would be disciplined and in shape. He found that he enjoyed coaching, and thought he could make it a career. He reached out to Lindsay Gaze—the head coach of the National Basketball League's Melbourne Tigers and one of Australia's most accomplished head coaches—shared his background, and laid out his simple pitch. "I'll coach anybody that'll listen," Brown told him. Twelve-year-olds, adults, assistants. "It's all fine by me." All he wanted was to be a part of Gaze's program and to get a job across the Tasman Sea so that he could be closer to Anna.

Gaze accepted Brown's proposal. Brown came to Melbourne, got married, and spent three years as an assistant for the Tigers, where he also coached the program's Under-16, Under-18, and Under-20 teams, and worked in its marketing department. The Bulleen Boomers, who played in a second-tier league, hired him in the spring of 1992 to be their head coach. Then, that November, he received his big break: The North Melbourne Giants, one of the Tigers' competitors, made the thirty-one-year-old Brown the youngest head coach in the NBL.

Under Brown, the Giants became one of the league's top teams. His players, some of whom he was younger than, loved him. He was upbeat. He kept things simple. He had a great Boston accent that they could all mock. "He had this sense of humor and passion that really appealed to us," said Paul Maley, who played for Brown in Melbourne. "He was fun, but he also just lived and ate and breathed basketball."

Even early on, Brown displayed a knack for player development. He preached process over results. ("If we lose with the shots that you guys are missing, I quit," he'd tell his team during cold streaks.) He had Paul Rees, a 6-foot-9 center, simultaneously dribble two balls up and down the court. He encouraged all his players to work on their outside shooting. He even taught concepts that wouldn't trickle into the NBA for another twenty years.

"Any shot with a toe on the three-point line is the worst in the game," he'd repeatedly say, the point being that if you're going to shoot from that far, you'd better make it worth three points.

But as the years ticked by, Brown's demeanor began to change. "He was capable of flying off the handle," Rees said. He'd grow emotional and fiery and seemed to be having less fun. He'd sometimes smash his whiteboard after a loss. The Giants struggled financially, and in 1998 they began losing more than they won, too. The players got younger. They repeatedly blew double-digit leads.

"He'd put pressure on everyone, say, 'We're not going to let this happen again,'" Maley said. "I didn't think it was the right approach for that group of guys. It was a noticeable change in his style."

One night, after yet another loss, Brown fired curses at his players, hurled his whiteboard against a wall, its pieces falling to the tiled locker room floor, and stormed out. The tantrum hurt his players. Maley, one of the team's elder statesmen, rose up and spoke out.

The next morning, Brown called Maley into his office.

"You don't agree with me, Paul?" he asked.

"I don't," Maley responded. He told Brown the group was tight, that they needed pressure relieved, not added.

Brown thought about it. He approached Maley at practice the next day. He told him he appreciated the back-and-forth, but he would stick with his approach.

"This is a group of professionals," he said. "They need to be held accountable."

The Giants finished that season 9–21. Hemorrhaging cash, they merged that off-season with another NBL franchise. There was no longer a team for Brown to coach. By that point he was ready to move on, and being granted the freedom to explore new jobs would wind up being one of the most fortuitous events of his life.

In the summer of 2002, the San Antonio Spurs were preparing to move into a new 37,800-square-foot practice facility. Located on the Northwest Side of San Antonio, the building featured every amenity a professional sports team could want: two full-sized basketball courts, a state-of-the-art weight room, a therapy room, a players' lounge, office space for coaches and team personnel. The Spurs were ecstatic. For years they'd shuttled between various local colleges and athletic centers. Finally they were getting a home of their own.

The new facility would also allow the Spurs to devote more time to player development. To do so, though, the team needed a coach to lead the program. R. C. Buford, the Spurs' general manager, knew just the guy.

Years earlier, Buford had traveled to an Australian basketball camp organized by two of the country's top coaches: Brett Brown and Lindsey Gaze. Brown and Buford hit it off, and in 1998, upon the folding of North Melbourne, Brown had an idea. He called Buford and shared his story—how he'd grown up in Maine, played for Pitino, won a championship in Australia. But now he was out of a job. He wasn't desperate for work. The previous owners of North Melbourne had agreed to honor his contract. What he was, though, was interested in spending some time around an NBA team, and he wanted to know: would Buford and the Spurs be open to hosting him for the year? He asked Bruce Lindberg, a fellow Maine basketball coach who was close with both Buford and Spurs head coach Gregg Popovich, to reach out on his behalf.

"I had heard good things from people back east about him and checked him out a little bit," Popovich said. "I thought that would be a good addition, just to see what I could learn from him, that kind of thing. As soon as he got there, we started putting it together, the way we wanted to run the program. We became fast friends and never changed since then."

Brown worked as an unpaid assistant for a year. He took notes and helped out during practices and sat behind the bench during games. The Spurs won their first ever championship that June. Soon after, Brown returned to Australia to coach the Sydney Kings. Then, in 2002, he received a call from Buford. The Spurs were moving into a new practice facility and looking to hire a director of player development—was Brown interested in the job?

This was Brown's dream gig. It offered a good contract, autonomy, security, and the opportunity to learn from the brilliant Popovich and the revered Spurs. Also, the position would free him from all the additional responsibilities that get heaped upon head coaches and allow him to devote all his focus to working with players, the thing he enjoyed most.

Brown accepted Buford's offer. It didn't take long for him to impress the players he was brought in to improve.

"People loved the fact that he worked so hard," said Bruce Bowen, a longtime Spurs wing. He and Brown spent countless hours together. "And anytime I called he'd be right there," Bowen said. "It didn't matter if it was midnight. He would never send a film guy or someone like that. And he'd get creative with me in our drills." The players loved how earnest Brown was. They loved how excited he'd get about their success. They loved how every year he handed out CDs of Christmas music around the holidays.[1] Tim Duncan, the team's star, got a kick out of Brown's accent—he described it as "Bostralian." Manu Ginóbili, a second-round pick who, with Brown's help, grew into a two-time All-Star, described Brown as one of his "favorite people, not coaches" in the NBA. George Hill, a Spurs first-round pick, appreciated the way Brown worked. "He wasn't just standing and rebounding," Hill said. "He'd get out on the floor, move around, hit us. It was great."

But it was the connection with Popovich that influenced Brown the most. Brown was drawn to Popovich's pass-happy offense and competitive drive. He admired the way he held players and his staff accountable, how he didn't accept mistakes but balanced his authoritarian streak by making it clear that he truly cared for those who played and worked for him, a combination of attributes that helped propel the Spurs to four championships while Brown was in San Antonio. Most of all, Brown learned from Popovich the importance of building a barrier between the job and everything else in his life.

"[He] reminded me of what's most important," Brown said. "Care for your family. Do your job. Don't get distracted by the noise."

The two men shared off-court interests too. They loved talking politics. Popovich graduated from the U.S Air Force Academy and spent time in eastern Turkey as an intelligence officer. Brown's time in the South Pacific had sparked an interest in foreign policy. Popovich was an oenophile. Brown was more of a beer guy, but he was more than happy to crack open a bottle of red.

In 2007, the Spurs promoted Brown to assistant coach. Scouting and game planning were added to his plate, though player development

---

1   Everyone except, that is, Nick Van Exel. Van Exel, a one-time All-Star, had been in the NBA for twelve years when he signed with the Spurs in 2005. A black Wisconsin kid raised by a single mom, he did not share much in common with Brown. That December, Brown tried giving him one of his Christmas mixes. Van Exel refused to take it. "I don't have anything to play that on, Coach," he said. Brown was confused. Van Exel had made more than $70 million throughout his career and routinely rolled up to practice in a Mercedes-Benz or BMW. How could he not have a car with a CD player, or at least a Discman? The answer, according to Bowen: "Nick wasn't trying to hear any Christmas music from Brett Brown."

remained his primary area of expertise. Two years later, the Australian national team, for which he'd previously served as an assistant, tabbed him as their head coach. The experience changed him. He never thought the NBA would give him that sort of shot. But then he led Australia to the 2012 Olympic quarterfinals, a finish that impressed NBA observers, and for the first time in nearly a decade Brown began to consider that, just maybe, there was a future for him as an NBA head coach. He loved everything about player development—from the on-court work to the lack of stress to the security that came with the job. And he and his family were happy in San Antonio. But the opportunity to become an NBA head coach—to build a program and lead a team, and also receive a nice pay bump—would be too good to pass up.

"The Australia gig changed things for him," said John Welch, a longtime NBA assistant coach and friend of Brown's. "It opened his eyes to the possibilities that existed."

In June 2013, Brown's phone rang. It was Sam Hinkie, the Sixers' recently hired president of basketball operations. He wanted to know if Brown was interested in filling his coaching vacancy.

Brown, then fifty-two, his once-bushy brown hair thin and cut shorter and a little gray, boasted every attribute Hinkie was looking for. The Sixers would be filling their roster with players young and raw—Brown was a skilled and enthusiastic player development coach. The Sixers would likely lose most of their upcoming games—Brown's friends described him as "relentlessly positive." The Sixers were trying to build a program—Brown had spent more than a decade working for a Spurs team that had achieved this very goal.

Brown told Hinkie he was interested. But he also had a request. His Spurs were trying to repeat as champions and were in the midst of a tight series with the Miami Heat in the NBA Finals.

"I want to be talked to last," he said. "Do whatever you need to do with your interview process, speak to who you want to speak to, I just want to go last."

Hinkie, in no rush, agreed. He knew this would be one of the most consequential decisions of his Sixers tenure. And it's not like Brown was the only candidate he was considering. Hinkie had asked his staff to submit names of coaches they thought he should consider. The list featured almost two dozen. Inside the organization some began to wonder, only half-jokingly, whether Hinkie was just trying to gather as much information as possible from his competitors.

Hinkie interviewed around a dozen coaches throughout the summer. "He was really confident about the position the Sixers were in and had unwavering faith that they were going to succeed," said Adrian Griffin, an assistant coach at the time for the Chicago Bulls who interviewed for the job. "His attitude to me was, 'We're going to turn this around and build something special, and you're going to want to be a part of it.'"

Griffin met with Hinkie in Las Vegas in July 2013, during the NBA's annual Summer League. Hinkie handed him an iPad and quizzed him on various in-game scenarios. He asked how Griffin would handle a disagreement with management. He wanted to know how he would discipline a player who broke team rules, or arrived at a practice hungover from the previous night. The meeting lasted an hour. "On the dime," Griffin said. "Exactly as long as he had said it would."

Brown met with Hinkie in Houston. "I was pretty candid with Brett throughout the process, about the challenges ahead," Hinkie said. "There has to be trust." Brown thought the interview went well, but he didn't hear again from the Sixers until late July, about a month later. He and three other coaches—Boston Celtics assistant coach Jay Larranaga, Atlanta Hawks assistant Kenny Atkinson, and Sixers assistant Michael Curry—were invited to come to Manhattan and meet with Hinkie and the team's owners.

Brown impressed them all, and while in a Chevy Suburban on his way to LaGuardia Airport, he received a call from Hinkie offering him the job. Brown respected Hinkie's background. He appreciated his analytical approach and bought into his plan. He liked the idea of returning to the Northeast. He was excited that the team was building a new training center and that he'd be able to have input into the plans.

He was eager to work for an ownership group with deep pockets. But he was also wary. He'd been around awhile and seen too many examples of franchises talking about an enduring rebuild, only to reverse course and cast out the head coach as the sacrificial lamb. And anyway, this wasn't a job Brown *needed*. He was happy in San Antonio. Also, Popovich's top lieutenant, Mike Budenholzer, was leaving the bench to become the head coach of the Atlanta Hawks. If Brown returned, he'd be promoted to lead assistant, a job that no doubt would lead to future head coach offers.

"I needed to feel good and secure," Brown said, "that the ownership group was committed and had a plan, and Sam was going to be the architect of that plan, capable of delivering that plan."

He told Hinkie he needed a four-year deal. The Sixers were led by a group of owners with backgrounds in private equity who were not used to doling out high salaries to companies they were in the midst of stripping down. They balked at the proposal.

Brown held his position, removing himself from consideration. He called Popovich, who told him how great his life would be if he returned to the Spurs. For a day, it looked like the team would be moving in a different direction. The season was getting close. Training camp was just about a month away and the Sixers needed a coach.

But they also recognized that Brown was the perfect leader for the journey they were about to embark on. He had every attribute they were looking for, and he'd spent more than a decade learning from the Spurs, an organization Harris was infatuated with.

One day later the Sixers called him back to offer that fourth year.

The move shocked the holdovers from the previous regime. "Who the hell is Brett Brown?" was a common reaction, both in the Sixers front office, including among staffers who had spent years accumulating files on potential head coaching candidates, and across much of the NBA. Many viewed Brown as a "workout guy," and were stunned that the Sixers would choose a coach who in the NBA had never been more than a No. 2 assistant. Hinkie wasn't concerned. "He's the perfect coach to get us through these first few years," he told a colleague.

The Sixers called a press conference for August 14 to announce the hire. Brown arrived early that day and walked around the team's practice facility. He offered thoughts about the office's layout and smiles to his new colleagues.

"He was so enthusiastic," analytics director Aaron Barzilai said.

Later that day, Brown and Hinkie took seats behind a table draped in a black cloth. A baby blue banner adorned with the logos of the Sixers and the cable provider Xfinity hung behind them. For about forty-five minutes, the two men fielded questions—about Brown's background, about Hinkie's decision to hire him, about the new direction of the team. Both men wore black suits and dark ties; sitting next to each other, they looked like a pair of personal injury lawyers filming a commercial. Hinkie's responses, as usual, were methodical and monotone. He repeatedly folded and unfolded his arms and, with his eyes glancing around the room, often looked bored. Brown, on the other hand, was enthusiastic and expressive. He talked about how thrilled he was to be in Philadelphia, and how his team was going to run and play hard, and how he wouldn't have left the NBA heaven that was San Antonio if he didn't believe, truly believe, that Hinkie and the Sixers were about to do something special, and how special it would be to do so for the championship-starved city of Philadelphia.

At one point, in the middle of one of his typically verbose responses, Brown, excited, posed a question to his audience:

"Can you imagine if we can get this thing right?"

Chapter 6

"EVERYONE IN THE CITY IS GOING TO HATE ME"

Jason Richardson was sitting at home watching the 2013 draft when he saw the news flash across his TV screen: The Sixers—*his* Sixers—were trading Jrue Holiday, just twenty-three years old and already the team's best player, for a...draft pick?

The deal shocked Richardson. Thirty-two years old, he recognized that he was no longer the young, high-flying, 20-plus-points per game scorer that he once was and that his time in the NBA was winding down. But he wasn't interested in spending his final days in the league playing for a tanking team.

Richardson fired off a couple of text messages. "I don't know what's going on here," he wrote to Holiday. Another was to his manager, Paisley Benaza. He told her he was worried about his future. Benaza researched Sam Hinkie, the Sixers' new general manager. She learned that he didn't particularly enjoy dealing with agents or managers.

"You should speak with him in person and ask him these questions," she told Richardson.

In September, a few weeks before training camp, Richardson and Benaza met Hinkie in his PCOM office. Hinkie came out from behind his desk, set up three chairs in a circle, and laid out his plan.

"He was very candid about what the strategy was," Benaza said. "It was clear that this was tanking."

But, Hinkie clarified, he wasn't solely interested in constructing a team to lose games. Yeah, the Sixers would be running a young, inexperienced team onto the court. But, he said, he also planned on investing in player development in a way the Sixers never had. "He said he wanted to give the players everything," Benaza recalled.

The team was going to build a new training facility, one where the players wouldn't have to worry about tripping over med school student intramural games. They'd start utilizing technology to better track players' on-court performances. Not only would analytics be employed, but the numbers and what they meant would also be explained to the players.

"You could tell how excited he was," Benaza said. "It was definitely a 'This is my dream job,' kid-in-the-candy-store type of thing."

True to form, it was Hinkie who asked the majority of the questions. He wanted to know how Richardson believed a team could build a winning culture, and how it could best support its players, and what examples from his career he could share.

The three met for nearly an hour. As Richardson was walking out, Hinkie asked if he had any good local restaurant recommendations.

"I need one that will be open late and let me use the back door," Hinkie said. "Everyone in the city is going to hate me."

Richardson and Benaza laughed.

"But it will all be worth it," Hinkie said.

———

The Sixers had a little over a month to assemble a coaching staff for Brett Brown. Most NBA observers assumed they would surround him with a group of veteran assistants and maybe one person with experience as a head coach. That's how teams with first-time head coaches typically operated.

Hinkie wasn't concerned with conventional wisdom. And anyway, player development was his priority, not winning games.

Two of the coaches hired by Hinkie and Brown—Lloyd Pierce and Chad Iske—were known as experts in this area. A third, Greg Foster, was a former NBA big man who was coaching at the college level and, just ten years removed from his playing days, was still nimble enough to join players on the court. A fourth, Billy Lange, was an energetic forty-one-year-old Villanova assistant.[1] The lone outlier was Vance Walberg, a longtime high school and college coach who broke into the NBA the previous season. Walberg was known for pioneering the "dribble-drive" offense, an attack predicated on spreading a defense thin and attacking its holes, exactly the sort of fast-paced, attacking offense Hinkie—and Brown—believed to be most effective. Both men knew the Sixers didn't possess the players to win many games in the present, but that didn't mean they couldn't begin implementing the schemes they believed would produce wins once the talent arrived. Brown was upfront with all of them.

"He explained it all," Foster said. "But he also explained why he thought it was an exciting opportunity. We were going to be on the ground floor of something."

As he prepared for his first season at the helm, Brown leaned heavily on his Spurs background and the pedigree that came with being associated with one of the NBA's most revered franchises. "He did a lot of things that [Spurs head coach Gregg Popovich] did," Walberg said. "He wanted to bring that culture and offense, and just make a few tweaks." Brown also did his best to invoke the Spurs name whenever possible. He'd bring up war stories during film sessions. He'd mention Duncan during practices. He'd begin each day with quick discussions about current events, just like Popovich did with the Spurs. The players, many of whom were young and receiving their first taste of the NBA, ate it all up. "We all had big eyes and were ready to listen because he came from the Spurs," said Tony Wroten, a guard acquired by the Sixers in August. "He coached Tim Duncan. He was with Pop. He had championships."

The Sixers opened training camp in late September. Brown's primary focus was fitness. His practices resembled college workouts. He was energetic and enthusiastic but also tough. "If you messed up,

---

1   He also hired a bunch of younger intern and player development coaches who in upcoming years would be tasked with coaching Brown's middle school son. Excited to be in and around the NBA, none had any issues with the request.

he'd let you know, but then he'd come back with a positive message," Richardson said. He'd force players to pass conditioning tests. He'd have Lange and Foster put players through college-style drills. It was all about developing skills and teaching the game.

The Sixers dropped their final four preseason games, all by double digits.

"You have six NBA players and then you have a bunch of guys who are fighting for spots and want to be seen and need an opportunity," was how Brown assessed his team at the time. Oddsmakers, who in their preseason over/under totals predicted the Sixers would win a league-worst 17 games, agreed. "The challenge is harder than I thought," Brown told reporters before the start of the regular season. "We were grounded and realistic coming in. But having lived and breathed it, you can see it a little bit more intimately for what it really is."

On the last Wednesday in October, the Sixers welcomed the Miami Heat to Philadelphia for their regular-season opener. The Heat were the defending champions. They boasted a lineup full of future Hall of Famers: LeBron James, Chris Bosh, Dwyane Wade (who was out that night). The Sixers were starting a trio of mediocre veterans (Evan Turner, Spencer Hawes, and Thaddeus Young), a rookie point guard in Michael Carter-Williams, and a journeyman forward named James Anderson. Clash of the Titans this was not. The Sixers, though, managed to open the game with a 19–0 run. Wells Fargo Center was booming. Carter-Williams, making his NBA debut, was brilliant. His handle was smooth. He was quick and fast and athletic. One possession he'd strip a Heat ball handler and charge down the floor for a dunk. On the next he'd contest on a shot, grab the ball, and fire a pinpoint cross-court pass.

The outburst awoke the Heat. They charged back in the second half and took an eight-point lead with just six minutes remaining.

That's when Carter-Williams took over. He hit Hawes under the hoop for an easy two and then found him again, this time for a three. Down one, with just over two minutes left, the Sixers stripped Heat point guard Mario Chalmers and Carter-Williams hit Hawes again, this time for a streaking layup, to put Philly ahead. With 27.5 seconds left and the Sixers clinging to that one-point lead, Carter-Williams soared high above the basket following a Heat miss, corralled the ball, was fouled, and then knocked down one of two free throws, putting the Sixers ahead by two. Eighteen seconds later he splashed another two free throws to seal the win. He finished the night with a video-game-like stat line: 22 points, 12 assists, nine steals, and seven rebounds, one of the greatest rookie debuts in the history of the game.

"What a debut for Michael Carter-Williams!" shouted Sixers broadcaster Marc Zumoff on the telecast as the final buzzer sounded. "Simply amazing." Hall of Fame point guard Magic Johnson tweeted his praise.[2]

Brown and his players were ecstatic, and even more so after winning their next two games. Nobody—not analysts, not fans, not Brown, certainly not Hinkie—expected a 3–0 start. The Sixers were running and moving the ball and shooting lots of threes, and then running some more. All those preseason conditioning drills were paying off. Everything that former head coach Doug Collins—an old-school type who directed his teams to play slowly, take care of the ball, and shoot twos over threes deep—seemed to preach, Brett Brown seemed to scratch. "We were really excited," third-year center Lavoy Allen said. The players knew better than to read into early season results. But they couldn't help but feel a tinge of optimism or keep from wondering, *What if?*

———

Such flights of fancy didn't last long.

Things got ugly fast. The Sixers started the year 4–2 before losing 26 of their next 30 games. With the season slipping away, Brown was approached by his assistants. They wanted to know if Hinkie would be willing to bolster the roster.

"This is what we've got, this is the plan," Brown told them. "We're going to stay with it."

The losses tortured Brown. He knew before he took the job what

———

2 We'd learn a few years later that this wasn't exactly the compliment we all once thought.

he was getting into, but expecting failure and experiencing it are two different things. Sometimes after games he'd call Popovich, looking for a pick-me-up. Sometimes Harris would come by Brown's office to pick his brain and offer some reassurance. Brown would listen, then meet with his coaches, or take them out for dinner (he'd always pick up the bill). He did his best to keep his frustrations bottled up, especially in front of his players. The day after losses he often came in toting an uplifting quote. He knew that his ability to remain positive was one of the reasons he had been hired.

"At night the losses hurt," Walberg said. "But the next morning Brett was always right back at it. To me that was, by far, the most impressive thing about him."

That got harder and harder as the season inched along. The Sixers went all of February without winning a single game. They were 15–43 at the end of the month, and in a flurry of deals prior to the league's February 20 trade deadline, Hinkie had gutted the roster even more. Allen and Turner were shipped to the Indiana Pacers. Hawes was sent to the Cavaliers. In return for three of his best players the Sixers received...four second-round picks, plus an NBA Development League forward named Earl Clark. Hinkie filled the open roster spots with cheap free agents.

"It was like a college team," Brandon Davies, a rookie big man, said. "We had so many young guys trying to make a name for themselves and there were so many guys coming in and out, it was hard to develop chemistry." NBA rosters are allowed to carry fifteen players. Most teams see, maybe, eighteen suit up for them in one season. The Sixers in Hinkie's first year had twenty-eight come and go. Six of them were originally signed to minimum, ten-day contracts. Twelve had spent time in the NBA Development League. Some were acquired and then cut before ever putting on a Sixers uniform. Some would arrive the day of the game, meet Brown for the first time, and a few hours later take the floor with the starters.

"The turnstile," Foster said, "made it really hard to build relationships with the guys."

Brown did his best to remind himself that the Sixers' priorities were long-term. He focused his energy on areas like player development. He worked with Lance Pearson, an assistant coach from a small Kentucky college with undergraduate degrees in mathematics, computer science, and philosophy, and a PhD in cognitive and neural systems, on laying the foundation for the future. Pearson, about 6-foot-4 with long hair, broad shoulders, and a thick Kentucky accent, had been hired late in the summer after applying for the job online. His résumé mentioned that he'd developed a tracking program to aid and enhance basketball scouting. It was exactly the sort of technology and thinking Hinkie appreciated. To him, traditional coaching and advanced analytics were part of the same equation, not competing ideals. That's where Pearson came in. Instead of sticking him in a basement office, Hinkie made him a part of Brown's staff. And Brown, Pearson said, "was open to anything that could give him an edge."

One of Pearson's primary projects was to chart games—but not in a traditional sense. The Sixers weren't interested in the outcomes; they were interested in tracking the actions that led to the outcomes. They knew that, statistically, a team could get cleaner looks at the basket if it pushed the ball, so Pearson tracked how quickly Sixers players ran up the floor. He tracked passes deflected. He tracked shots contested.

"It wasn't about things directly tied to winning and losing, because we knew that wouldn't have a lot of payoff," Pearson said. "We wanted to develop a culture so that when we did get the talent, everything was in place stylistically."

During games, Pearson and a staff of nearly a dozen, all armed with laptops, would set up in the players' lounge at PCOM. They'd follow the action on the four TVs hanging on the walls, shout out results, and mark them down. Each player would receive a grade for the game. The results would be cut up and packaged, with video clips to accompany each merit. The grades would be posted for the players the next morning.

"You could score 40 or 50 points and still someone would say how you didn't box out enough or that you didn't get enough deflections," said Tony Wroten, a second-year point guard. "We weren't being shown highlights of points."

Wroten never scored 40 or 50, but, in averaging 13 points per game, he was a pleasant surprise. One morning, after a particularly impressive performance—"One of the best games of my life," he said—he arrived at PCOM smiling, expecting plaudits and pats on the back. Then he was handed his grade for the previous evening, a D.

"I thought it was a typo," Wroten said. The coaches sat down with him and explained why his grade was so low. They had clips of missed box-outs, of not sprinting up the floor. "It made sense after they showed me the reasons," he said.

The tracking wasn't limited to in-game performance. Players were given bracelets to wear at home, so that the team could monitor their sleep. They were told during practices to wear devices from an Australian-based company named Catapult, so the team could monitor biometric data such as heart rate and cutting speed. They were outfitted with individual water bottles so that the team could monitor each player's hydration.

"I never had any of that type of stuff before," Richardson said.

Initially, there was some pushback, especially from the veterans. "Things like tracking sleep feel like too much," Allen said. Richardson often felt like the Sixers were "babysitting" the players. But as time went on, he and his teammates grew to appreciate how much effort the team was putting into maximizing their performances. The charting also provided the players with a form of competition where they could actually succeed. Players took pride in seeing their name at the top of the deflections list the day after a game. Some compared heart rate levels after practices. They'd lobby assistant coaches for more merits. The younger players, most of whom were fringe talents fighting for their NBA futures, viewed these metrics as an avenue toward proving their worth.

"Every day was like a tryout and lots of those numbers were visible in practice," Davies said. "I'd kill myself on the court."

Recognizing the reality of his job, Brown devoted as much energy to preparing for practices as he did for games. He'd map out the sessions to the minute, and apply lessons learned as the son of two professional teachers. "He was so energetic," Richardson said. He'd keep film sessions short and to the point. He used visuals. He showed players data so that they could understand why their mistakes were problems. "He wouldn't pull a player for taking a bad shot," Pearson said. "But he would tell them why it was bad." He also did his best to make the players feel valued and comfortable.

"He was always telling us that we could come speak to him if we had any sort of issues with anything," Allen said. "I think that was the greatest thing about him."

Brown first passed this message along to Allen in October, a few weeks before the start of the regular season. It was a meeting with Brown the day after Allen had missed a practice, one made open to fans. He'd partied the night before, overslept, and, upon calling the Sixers that morning to let them know he'd be late, was told to stay home.

The next day he was summoned to Brown's office. He was told that he was fined. "But instead of scolding me he asked me if there was anything going on in my life, he just wanted to make sure I was all good," Allen said. "It was great to see our coach actually cared about his players."

The interaction earned him Allen's admiration. It also laid the foundation for a problem that would plague the Sixers for years to come.

———————

Jason Richardson had seen a lot over his twelve seasons in the NBA. This, though, was something new.

"I know we ain't waiting for no goddamned rookie who's not even playing," he shouted over and over.

It was a winter afternoon, and Richardson, one of the last remaining veterans on the roster, was settled into his seat on the Sixers' chartered plane. Everyone—the players, the coaches, the support staff, some executives—had already boarded. By this point the travel day schedule was routine: Practice in the morning, media availability afterward, 3 p.m. flight. Most players arrived at the airport between 2:15 and 2:45. Occasionally, one would hit traffic on the drive over and notify the team's head of security, Lance Williams, via text.

Nerlens Noel was different. Describing him as someone who'd be late to his own funeral would be a cliché. It would also be accurate.

"I definitely had to grab him by the collar a few times," Foster said.

A year earlier, scouting services had ranked Noel the top high school prospect in the country. A 6-foot-11 pogo stick with a 7-foot-4 wingspan, he could run and jump unlike any other player in his class. He enrolled in Kentucky and would have likely been picked first in the 2013 draft if not for tearing the ACL in his left knee during a late-season game.

That night, on the bus home, Kentucky coach John Calipari found Noel, head lowered, shoulders slumped. He sat down next to him and wrapped his arm around Noel's neck.

"This is going to kill our team, that's how good you are," Calipari told him. "But this isn't close to the end for you. This is not going to hurt you at all."

Calipari explained how a torn ACL wasn't the injury it once was. Science, he said, had advanced to the point where players now almost always returned to the court.

"NBA teams won't be concerned," Calipari told Noel.

Noel spent the next four months rehabbing in Birmingham, Alabama, and in June was picked up by the Sixers in a draft-day trade. To Hinkie, Noel was the prototypical modern NBA center. He was big and mobile. He was athletic. He'd already proven that he possessed the proper instincts to protect the rim. If the Sixers weren't going to compete, what did it matter if Noel spent the year watching from the bench?

Hinkie permitted Noel to remain in Birmingham through September, an allowance some on his staff, who had scouted Noel at Kentucky and been briefed on his immaturity, viewed as a mistake.

Noel hadn't grown up with much structure. His parents separated when he was young. He and his three siblings lived with his mother in Everett, Massachusetts, a city just outside of Boston. She supported them by working double shifts as caregiver in assisted living facilities.

Noel learned at a young age just how much power his athletic gifts afforded him. His parents rarely attended school functions or games, and their absence created a power vacuum. Noel watched in high school as various adults—his high school coach, a former college assistant coach a former star recruit, a club coach, a low-level agent—all flocked to him, hoping to secure a piece of that soon-to-be-delivered NBA bounty. It wasn't a surprise that basic professional skills like punctuality seemed confounding. Noel had grown up watching the world revolve around him.

"I tell everyone who drafts one of my kids, 'You're getting a nineteen-year-old, not a twenty-four-year-old, you need to understand that,'" Calipari said. "Here, we're on top of them. They have no choice but to do the things we want."

"We knew Nerlens had some issues," one former Sixers front office staffer said. "Drafting him only made sense if we were going to surround him with vets."

Sixers staffers who had traveled down to Birmingham to check in on Noel's progress received troubling reports. In September, right around the start of training camp, he joined the team in Philadelphia. It didn't take long for the problems to present themselves.

Noel was almost always late, be it for a team flight, practice, or rehab session. Guessing his arrival time became a part of his teammates' pregame routine. He'd often show up to practices smelling of weed. Sixers security would sometimes receive calls from the team hotel about the stench of marijuana emanating from his room. He accrued tens of thousands of dollars in team fines during his rookie year, each one issued via a pink slip. Sometimes teammates would walk by his locker and see a stack of them on top of his chair.

"You understand that things happen, but when they become a constant issue, like you're late for everything, then you're not being a professional," Richardson said. "You're not taking your job seriously."

One problem was that Brown didn't seem to know how to address this sort of behavior other than by issuing fines. "He wanted to be more of Nerlens's friend," Walberg said. But Hinkie didn't push him either. He'd drawn a clear line between the work he was doing in the front office and what was happening out on the court. He rarely attended practices, almost unheard of for NBA GMs, who view those sessions as a prime opportunity to evaluate their players, build relationships with them, and show their support. "I don't see the value," he once offered a staffer as his reason. He told Pearson that much of this was by design; after all, the coaching staff and front office had different incentives and goals. Brown wanted to win games. Hinkie did not. He was better off devoting his time to other endeavors.

Noel did finally arrive at the airport that winter day. It was around 3:30 when he pulled up in his white Range Rover. His lateness had delayed takeoff by about a half hour. He parked his car, met Lance Williams by the TSA checkpoint, and climbed the stairs toward the plane's cabin. He walked by the coaches and straight to his seat. No one said a word.

The Wells Fargo Center was nearly full for the first time in months. Attendance during the season had dipped to an average of 13,869 fans per game—the second-lowest number in the NBA. Sometimes tickets would be available on StubHub for a nickel. Some fans would show up with brown bags covering their heads. Yet on this March Saturday night, 17,438 fans had filled the arena to watch the 15–57 Sixers take on the 26–46 Detroit Pistons. Dozens of reporters and prominent talking heads, vultures eager to pick at the wreck, had descended too. "We knew it was going to be a circus when ESPN flew in Stephen A. Smith," Carter-Williams recalled. In their locker room before the games, Sixers players could barely dress without tripping over cameramen searching for B-roll.

Two nights earlier the Sixers had fallen to the Rockets, their 26th straight loss, tied for the most in NBA history. One more would solidify their spot in the NBA record books. Their last win had come on January 29, in Boston, on a Turner buzzer-beater. "Tell you the truth, I don't even remember it," Thad Young told reporters before the game against the Pistons. Fifty-nine days had passed since then, all of February and now almost all of March. TV ratings had plummeted. Callers flooded Philly talk radio calling for Hinkie's head. Hosts labeled him a disgrace. Local sportswriters blasted him in their columns. The streak had also brought national attention to him and his plan, changing the narrative around both. "Embarrassing," is how Stan Van Gundy, a former Miami Heat and Orlando Magic head coach, described the Sixers during an early March panel on tanking at the MIT Sloan Conference. "If you're putting that roster on the floor, you're doing everything you can possibly do to try to lose."

For many Sixers fans, Sam Hinkie was more than just the man in charge of their favorite basketball team. *(Mitchell Leff via Getty Images)*

Some fans embraced The Process and all the losing that came with it. Others, not so much. *(Mitchell Leff via Getty Images)*

Joel Embiid, during his third year (but rookie season) in the NBA, celebrates a rare Sixers win. The victory came courtesy of a T. J. McConnell buzzer-beater over New York Knicks star Carmelo Anthony. *(Mitchell Leff via Getty Images)*

Friends of Brett Brown describe him as relentlessly optimistic. The ability to encourage players even in down times—Sixers lottery pick Jahlil Okafor *(right)* endured many during his two and a half seasons in Philadelphia—was one of the reasons Hinkie chose Brown to be the team's head coach. *(Mitchell Leff via Getty Images)*

No two players better represent the problems with The Process—from Sam Hinkie's draft misses to the dangers that come with treating people like assets—than Jahlil Okafor (left) and Nerlens Noel. (Mitchell Leff via Getty Images)

Hinkie was always more concerned with work than making friends. (Mitchell Leff via Getty Images)

Sam Hinkie looks on as Sixers managing partner Josh Harris *(center)* introduces Jerry Colangelo, the man chosen by Harris and the NBA to replace Hinkie at the top of the Sixers organization. *(Mitchell Leff via Getty Images)*

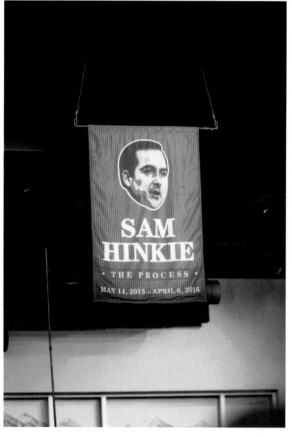

In May 2017, in front of a few thousand fans at their annual draft lottery party, *The Right to Ricky Sanchez* podcast honored Sam Hinkie—who had resigned a year earlier—by raising this banner to the rafters of Xfinity Live complex. *(Courtesy of Spike Eskin)*

At its heart, Sam Hinkie's plan was a simple one: Lose lots of games, take a lot of swings at the top of the draft, and hope that a few connect. The Sixers whiffed a few times. But they did hit twice, and the results—Joel Embiid and Ben Simmons—transformed the team into a championship contender. *(Mitchell Leff via Getty Images)*

Bryan Colangelo in January 2018, wearing a shirt with his trademark high collar, watches a Sixers win over the Chicago Bulls from the tunnel of Philadelphia's Wells Fargo Center. The Sixers would win 53 games that season, Colangelo's second full season as team president, and make the playoffs for the first time since 2012. *(Mitchell Leff via Getty Images)*

Markelle Fultz was supposed to be the team's third young star. Instead, a bizarre saga—featuring a series of mysterious injuries and him losing the ability to shoot—derailed both his own future and the team's plans. *(Mitchell Leff via Getty Images)*

Brett Brown and Joel Embiid, the last men standing from the original Process teams, embrace during a March 2018 win. *(Mitchell Leff via Getty Images)*

An orbital fracture sidelined Embiid for the Sixers' first Process-era playoff game. That didn't keep him from partaking in the pregame festivities, however. Donning a mask and acting as—to use his words—the "Phantom of the Process," he rings the team's makeshift Liberty Bell prior to the Sixers' 130–103 blowout win over the Miami Heat. *(Mitchell Leff via Getty Images)*

One of the upsides of coaching a team built to lose is that there's little pressure to win. By 2018, that had changed. As a result, so had Brown's demeanor. *(Gregory Shamus via Getty Images)*

Spike Eskin *(left)* and Mike Levin *(right)*, hosts of *The Rights to Ricky Sanchez* podcast, became the voices of Philadelphia's most ardent Process-supporting fans. By 2019, the Sixers had embraced the podcast. This photo is from a live show recorded that September, one in which Brett Brown *(center)* bought beers for the entire audience. Behind him hangs photographic proof, gathered by Eskin and Levin, that during his time with the Sixers Brown had aged like a U.S. president. *(Courtesy of Spike Eskin)*

The results of The Process, as seen in the Sixers' star-studded starting lineup for Opening Day 2019 *(from left to right)*: Josh Richardson, Ben Simmons, Joel Embiid, Tobias Harris, and Al Horford. *(Mitchell Leff via Getty Images)*

NBA commissioner Adam Silver, also in attendance at the conference, was asked to share his thoughts on the Sixers.

"You don't like to see any team have to go through a losing streak like they currently are and flirt with the longest losing streak in the history of the NBA," he said. "That's bad for everyone. It's potentially damaging to the players involved and the culture they're trying to create."

Brown tried his best to keep his players insulated from the attention bubbling around the streak. "Play Hard, Smart, Together and Have Fun!!" he'd write on the whiteboards before games. But by this point the team's failures had become one of the top stories in all of sports.

"All the players watch *SportsCenter* and see all the coverage," Pearson said. "You could tell it was weighing on all of them. If anyone in the world thought they, or the coaches, were trying to lose every game—if they just looked around they would have seen it wasn't true."

Against the Pistons the Sixers rolled out a starting lineup of Carter-Williams, Young, two undrafted players (Henry Sims and Hollis Thompson), and one who'd spent a chunk the previous season in the D League (James Anderson). The game remained close for the first few minutes, but midway through the opening quarter the Sixers began pulling away. They led by 19 at halftime and 30 by the end of the third. About a half hour later, with the scoreboard reading 123–98, the final buzzer sounded. The streak was over; the Sixers' seldom-used victory music blasted out of the Wells Fargo Center speakers. There were hugs in the stands and smiles on the court.

That night, players, coaches, and even members of the front office went out for drinks. Some coaches made the ninety-minute drive to Atlantic City. "Everyone felt the need to celebrate," Pearson said. The Sixers' season would end eighteen days later, with consecutive wins, bumping their record up to 19–63. They'd beaten Las Vegas' prediction, and even avoided finishing with the league's worst record. The Milwaukee Bucks, a team not built to lose, had won just 15 games—in the view of Hinkie and his supporters, delivering a point in his favor. Lots of teams were bad. The Sixers at least had a plan, and with it came a bright future.

They had cap space. Thanks to their terrible record and the Jrue

Holiday deal the previous year, they'd be receiving two high picks in the upcoming draft. Noel would be returning to the floor the following season. And Carter-Williams had just become the third player since 1951 to lead all rookies in points (16.7), rebounds (6.2), and assists (6.3); he'd later be named Rookie of the Year. Reinforcements seemed to be on the way. Harris and his partners were happy. The only direction left to travel was up.

Chapter 7

THE RIGHTS TO RICKY SANCHEZ

They'd come to Northeast Philadelphia because their leaders had summoned them. Now all their eyes were fixed on the TVs hanging from the bar's walls. A suited man standing inside a midtown Manhattan hotel event room a hundred miles north was reading off a list of numbers and teams.

"The 10th pick will go to...," began NBA deputy commissioner Mark Tatum. He paused to open a large, sealed white envelope with the number 10 etched in red letters on the front. About two hundred Sixers fans, mostly young, mostly raised on a diet of basketball analysis found outside the mainstream media, stood shoulder to shoulder in Miller's Ale House, fingers crossed, waiting for Tatum to reveal the answer.

It was May 20, 2014. The crowd, about half of whom wore T-shirts with either Sam Hinkie's name or face plastered across the front, had gathered to hear the NBA announce the results of its annual draft lottery. To discourage teams from tanking, the league had decided years earlier to shift to a system that, in theory, would randomize the draft order. Instead of the best pick simply being awarded to the worst team and so on down the line, all teams that failed to make the playoffs would receive a list of four-number combinations. The worse a team's record, the more combinations it received. On a designated night every May, each team would send a representative into a sequestered room, along with a select group of reporters, NBA executives, and security officials, where a machine would be filled with fourteen Ping-Pong balls numbered between 1 and 14. Four balls would be randomly chosen. Whichever team held the first combination would receive the draft's first pick. This would be repeated twice, with picks 4 through 14 then doled out in reverse order of win-loss record.

The Sixers, the league's second-worst team the previous season, entered the night with a 19.9 percent chance of receiving the top pick, about five percentage points lower than the league-worst Milwaukee Bucks. The upcoming draft class was considered a deep one, but most scouts and analysts had three players graded ahead of the rest: Kansas wing Andrew Wiggins, Duke forward Jabari Parker, and Kansas center Joel Embiid. Hinkie's plan of tanking a season in order to nab a franchise player depended on the lottery. The results would also determine whether or not the Sixers would receive the first-round pick they had acquired from the Pelicans in the previous year's swap of Jrue Holiday for Nerlens Noel, which the Pelicans had agreed to send only if it fell out of the draft's top five.

Tatum pulled a card out of the envelope. A Sixers logo appeared, signaling that the pick would indeed be going to Philadelphia. Cheers broke out throughout the bar. Here was a faction of fans enthralled by Hinkie and enamored with his plan. They applauded his adherence to his stance, and his promise to drag the Sixers out of NBA purgatory. Hinkie, they'd come to believe, was the savior they'd been waiting for.

"Everyone in the city is going to hate me," Hinkie had told Jason Richardson the previous year.

He was wrong about that. And there were two people—a comedy writer and a sports radio veteran—for him to thank.

Most kids grow up idolizing their sports heroes from afar. Spike Eskin's childhood was different. He wore Charles Barkley's clothes, slept over at Pete Rose's house, and was on a first-name basis with Mike Schmidt. Such was life growing up as Howard Eskin's kid.

For years, Howard Eskin was the most prominent and polarizing voice in Philadelphia's sports media. Dubbed "the King" by others (and himself), he was known for his mink coats, Rolex watches, and biting commentary. He was a workaholic who brought a Walkman into the delivery room so that he could follow the Phillies game as his wife delivered one of his sons—and shared the story with anyone who asked. He wrote columns, hosted popular radio shows, and served as an anchor on TV. One moment Eskin would break a big news story (such as the Eagles' owners trying to sell the team), the next he'd embark on a crass crusade against a coach. He asked tough questions at press conferences. He also turned them into performances. He loved the spotlight and, unlike traditional newsmen, had no qualms seeking it out. Some fans idolized him. Many more seemed to hate him. One even tried choking him at an off-site broadcast.

"It was weird having your dad be such a lightning rod," Spike, whose given name is Brett, said. There were the moments when the fathers of Spike's friends would tell him how much Howard annoyed them. There was the time when Howard arrived on a chopper to throw out the first pitch at one of Spike's Little League games. There were all the family outings where strangers would stop Howard to talk sports. Howard was aware of it all. "I felt bad," he said. "I mean I don't know what else I could've done. I was who I was." Like many fathers and sons, the two left the issues unaddressed, with Howard instead trying to make good the only way he knew how. "He tried to take me everywhere," Spike said. All-Star games. Training camps. Spring training. He'd introduce him to star athletes. It led to some cool photos. "But," Spike said, "there wasn't a lot of, like, Dad at home time."

Spike staged mini rebellions. He blanketed his arms in tattoos. He bleached his hair and gelled it upright. He dressed like the rock and roll fan he was. Yet something about his father's life drew him in. He studied broadcast journalism at Syracuse University from 1995 to 1998 and also worked at the student radio station. He was interested in music and sports, and a program director told him not to use the same name for both genres. A receptionist at his hair salon had begun calling him "Spike." He liked it. To everyone outside his immediate family, he's been Spike ever since.

After college, Spike worked a bit for a radio station in Philly before taking a job with an alt-rock station in Chicago, where he eventually became a program director. He stuck with music for more than a decade. "I mostly tuned sports out during that portion of my life," he said. Around 2008, at the age of thirty, he was named the midday host of Philly rock station WYSP, allowing him to return home, where his love of sports was rekindled. During the 2009–2010 NBA season, he requested a press pass for a Sixers game against LeBron James's Cleveland Cavaliers. He was granted a season credential and started attending nearly every home game. It was Eddie Jordan's lone season as head coach and the Sixers were awful. Spike fell in love with the team anyway. Sitting in the press seats just a few rows behind the basket, he felt he connected to the players, like he could read their emotions. He began blogging about the team and, the next season, frustrated by the press area's insistence on decorum, decided to purchase tickets instead.

In 2011, YSP flipped to sports talk, costing Spike his job. He had the option to pursue a music gig in another city, but there was another direction he was itching to pursue. Years earlier, he'd told an executive named Chris Oliviero that his preference was to spend his career behind the scenes. "I don't want people knowing who I am when I walk down the streets," he said at the time.

Now things had changed. The parts of his father's life that had spooked him as a child no longer seemed so bad. Believing there was a void in the Philly market, Spike had recently begun hosting his own sports podcasts. He enjoyed the back-and-forth with fans and having a voice to express his opinions. He created a website (SpikeEskin.com) to write about sports, changed his Twitter profile picture to one hiding his tattoos, and ceased running away from his last name. ("As a music radio guy I was just 'Spike,'" he said.) He live-tweeted games. He invited Sixers beat writers and national analysts onto his show. He hosted a few hundred fans for a party at the bar Chickie's & Pete's following the conclusion of the 2011 NBA lockout and, over Twitter, convinced Sixers forward Andre Iguodala to show up.

"People will think that you're an expert if you just talk like it," Spike said. "At the time there was no one talking about the Sixers. I became Sixers Guy."

The Sixers analysis boosted Spike's profile. In 2012, the local CBS radio station hired him to serve as its sports editor, run its social media, and host a 10 p.m.-to-2 a.m. show about once a week. One day, he came across a blog post on LibertyBallers.com, a Sixers fan site attached to the SB Nation network. The post began with a sarcastic note referring to Howard Eskin as an "always intelligent, unbiased, and level-headed reporter." The description and tone made Spike laugh. He reached out to the writer, a twenty-one-year-old Philly native named Michael Levin. "That kind of shit, guys hating my dad, put me through college," Spike said. "I have no shame about that." That lack of shame would change not only his and Levin's lives, but the lives of everyone in and around the Sixers.

Like Spike Eskin, Levin grew up in Philly. But that's about all the two had in common. Eskin lived in Chicago during the Allen Iverson era. His fanaticism was fostered later. Levin was born in 1989 and raised in the Philly suburb of Bucks County. He fell in love with the Sixers as a kid, sitting in the family living room alongside his dad, watching Iverson dribble circles around opponents.

Even at a young age, Levin found himself processing the game differently than his peers. He loved the majestic three-pointers and emphatic dunks, but he was also fascinated by the strategy of team building, and what it was about the NBA that prevented certain teams—even ones with a star like Iverson—from achieving sustained success.

"That it was so hard for them to find a second star to play with Iverson molded me," Levin said. "And that led to a frustration, which grew and grew."

Levin always enjoyed writing. He thought about becoming a sportswriter, but was wary of transforming his hobby into a profession. A TV production class in high school sparked a new passion. Levin enrolled in Ithaca College and turned his sights on Hollywood, but continued following the Sixers religiously. He spent his free time in the comments section of a Sixers fan website called Sixers Soul, which eventually got absorbed by SB Nation and renamed Liberty Ballers. In 2008, when Levin was nineteen, one of the site's editors asked if he'd like to write a draft preview. Soon after, he was part of the site's staff.

While at Ithaca, Levin landed a number of entertainment gigs, some prestigious (the Academy of Television Arts and Sciences Foundation's summer internship program), some not so much (penning obituaries for the Television Academy). Around that time he took over editing duties for Liberty Ballers. He graduated from Ithaca in 2011 and moved to Los Angeles, where he worked his way up from assistant on *How I Met Your Mother* to writer on the NBC comedy *Trial & Error*.

But the Sixers remained his passion, and Liberty Ballers was where that passion was applied. The Internet had changed the media landscape. You no longer needed a press pass to cover a team, and fans writing blogs weren't beholden to journalism's rules. From there an ecosystem was born, one full of nerdy, clever, less formal, proudly unobjective, and occasionally antagonistic sports coverage. Levin fit in perfectly.

"Most of the guys covering the Sixers didn't know what the fuck they were talking about," he said. "They were indebted to their sources on the team, which was just stuck in mediocrity. But everyone was tired of that way of thinking. Young people, our audience especially."

On March 7, 2012, in the midst of another Sixers slog toward a low playoff seed, Levin came across a Tweet from Howard Eskin stating that Sixers head coach Doug Collins would be starting Evan Turner for the rest of the season. Soon after, Levin received an email from Spike Eskin, inviting him to come on his WIP radio show.

"When you want to win a championship you have to start at zero," Levin said at one point during the guest spot. "They may as well lose every game, there's no sense in being mediocre. In the NBA you can't be any worse than mediocre."

The Sixers' owners seemed to agree. Collins was let go that spring and Hinkie was hired in May. Levin was attending a music festival in Napa at the time. He didn't know much about Hinkie, and his spotty cell service made Googling difficult. What he did know was that Hinkie was an analytics guy from the Houston Rockets, one of the NBA's most progressive teams.

"I was sleeping in a tent dreaming of what could be," Levin said. "I was ecstatic that they finally had a guy who I thought I'd mostly agree with."

That summer, Eskin and Levin started a Sixers podcast. "Mostly because there wasn't one," Eskin said. They did one show after Hinkie's first draft. In the previous weeks, both Eskin and Levin had taken part in an email chain where it was suggested, and agreed upon, that dealing Holiday would be the smartest move the Sixers could make. They then lamented how it would likely never happen. They were thrilled to learn that they were wrong.

"Last night was so exciting," Eskin announced during the opening segment of the first podcast.

The two recorded a second show the following week, and then a third the week after that. They were funny and energetic and, despite barely knowing one another, sounded like old friends. Conversations would veer from Sixers talk to the mocking grouchy writers. They spent the time in between shows batting potential podcast names back and forth. Some (*We Talkin' 'Bout Practice*) were homages to the Sixers' past. Others (*The Rebuild*) were tributes to the path they believed Hinkie was heading down. Others were just about poking fun at NBA and basketball lingo (*Good Length*).

One option stood out. It contained everything they were looking for: It was a nod to an arcane part of Sixers history that only the most fanatical die-hards would recognize. It involved a transaction. Also, it sounded ridiculous.

"This is *The Rights to Ricky Sanchez*," Spike Eskin announced during the third show. Intermittent laughs broke up his next few sentences. Ricky Sanchez was a Puerto Rican basketball player who had never actually played for an NBA team. He was drafted 35th overall in 2005. His rights (meaning the team he'd play for if he ever did decide to join the NBA) were traded to the Sixers two years later. The Sixers held on to those rights for five years before sending them to the Memphis Grizzlies in exchange for a reserve forward named Sam Young.

"I think there are seven people who get the name," Levin proudly stated.

Four months later, with the Sixers preparing to fly to Europe for a preseason exhibition, *The Rights to Ricky Sanchez* scored its first guest.

"No big deal, we just landed Sam Hinkie on our stupid little podcast," Eskin joked during the show's intro.

"Are you going to see Ricky Sanchez when you're in Spain?" Levin asked at one point.

"Can you imagine how long it would take to explain to Ricky Sanchez why a podcast is called *The Rights to Ricky Sanchez*?" Hinkie responded.

For about thirty minutes, Eskin and Levin giddily lobbed softballs at Hinkie. "You're a bit of a hero to a lot of Sixers fans that have been wanting the Sixers to sort of take a certain direction for a long time," Eskin told him, "having been stuck in sort of the middle ground since Iverson went away."

Hinkie was engaging and polite. He chuckled at Eskin's and Levin's jokes. He answered their questions in his usual simultaneously sincere and evasive way. He was also, per usual, self-effacing and deferential. He hammered home his talking points. At one point he referenced Jeff Bezos and how he "talks a lot about, like, you know, long-term deals being all that matters." At a different point, he added, "Nothing is known, exactly how things will turn out. I think a real key is just, like, Where does your self-worth come from personally? Like, does it come from the world telling you you're great, or the world reminding you, you know, every other day during an NBA season that you're smart or you're doing the right thing or that you're good at your job? Or can you stay focused on something that matters over the long term?"

It was an answer that hooked his interviewers. Already smitten with their new leader, Eskin and Levin were now ready to fight the rest of the NBA and its surrounding universe on Hinkie's behalf.

———

Not all fans were like Eskin and Levin. Not all fans had the stomach for losing.

Hinkie's first season, in which his Sixers won just 19 games and lost 63, was met with scorn. Attendance dropped even further. So did ratings. Some local media members viewed Hinkie's methods as a rebuke of everything they believed about professional sports.

One of the loudest critics was Howard Eskin.

"I'm not impressed," he tweeted when Hinkie was hired. He believed handing the reins over to a "numbers guy" was a mistake. He thought Hinkie was "clueless" about basketball. He didn't appreciate Hinkie's coy press conferences or reticence to speak on the record. He nicknamed him Waldo "because you could never find him." He called Hinkie's plan a Ponzi scheme and referred to his acolytes, a group that included his son, as the "Sons of Scam." Eskin might have been a polarizing personality, but when it came to Hinkie, his views represented the majority of the Sixers' elder fan base. Levin and Eskin wanted a title; some fans were just looking for a release and distraction after a long day of work. A tanking team couldn't play that role.

"A lot of the arguments about Hinkie's plan boiled down to: Why do you give a shit about other men in jerseys just playing a sport?" Levin said. "I think it is about hope and believing in something."

Spike and Howard spent hours debating the merits of Hinkie's plan. The two exchanged barbs on the air and trolled each other during family dinners. "Howard enjoyed poking a bit," Spike's wife, Valerie, said.

"I knew it was dumb," Spike said. "But I took the bait every time."

Levin was living in Santa Monica, but that didn't keep him from using his platform to fend off Hinkie's detractors. "Wins were treated as signs of progress. Losses were part of the plan," said Andrew Sharp, an NBA writer—and Hinkie critic[1]—who lived with Levin at the time. "It drove me crazy." Sharp would wake up once a week at 6:30 a.m. to the sounds of Levin yammering with Eskin. Listening from his bedroom, Sharp remembered thinking, "This is the saddest shit in the world. Here were two guys spending hours talking about a basketball

---

1   How did the *Rights to Ricky Sanchez* hosts react to this criticism? By turning #fuckAndrewSharp into one of the community's slogans. (Sharp participated in the bit.)

team that nobody cares about." But he also recognized that the two had stumbled onto something bigger.

"They don't take themselves too seriously and yet at same time they take all this stuff way too seriously," Sharp said. "It resonates with fans who care way too much but are also smart enough to understand that all this is ridiculous."

In the lead-up to the 2014 draft lottery, on the recommendation of one of Levin's writers, he and Eskin decided to throw a party celebrating Hinkie's first year. Eskin ordered up fifty black T-shirts with Hinkie's name on the front. Some WIP colleagues suggested a bar in Northeast Philly called Miller's Ale House. Eskin called them up. He tried explaining that a bunch of basketball fans would be coming, but no, not for a game. This was a lottery. He told the bar to expect somewhere between thirty and forty people.

The day of the party, two hours before the 4 p.m. start time, Eskin received a call from the bar. Some kids, worried about missing out on the free tees, had shown up early. Eskin arrived soon after. By 5:30, all the shirts were gone.

The crowd drank beers and booed former Sixers head coach Doug Collins, then an ESPN analyst, anytime he appeared on TV. Eskin acted as emcee, while Levin followed along from L.A. They cheered upon learning that the Sixers would be receiving the 10th pick from the Pelicans, and chanted "No! No! No!" every time Tatum prepared to announce a result. When he announced that the Orlando Magic had landed at No. 4, ensuring that the Sixers would be picking in the top three, the fans roared as if they'd just witnessed a championship-clinching jump shot.

"The third pick in this year's draft goes to," Tatum said next, "the Philadelphia 76ers."

It wasn't the ideal result, but in the view of those gathered, the Sixers closing the night with the draft's third and 10th picks was their biggest win in years.

Upon returning home that night, Eskin called Levin.

"Dude, there're people who care," he told him. "This is a real thing."

Chapter 8

THE SECOND COMING

I n the months leading up to the 2014 draft, no NBA franchise scouted the basketball team at the University of Kansas more vigorously than the Cleveland Cavaliers.

The Cavs were coming off a tumultuous season, their fourth straight missing the playoffs, and still reeling from LeBron James's decision four years earlier to bolt for Miami. Cavs owner Dan Gilbert responded by firing his general manager (Chris Grant) and his head coach (Mike Brown). He then handed the keys to an NBA lifer named David Griffin. Griffin had broken into the NBA twenty-one years earlier as an intern with the Phoenix Suns. By 2007 he was senior vice president of basketball operations in Phoenix. In 2010 he left for a similar job with the Cavaliers, and now he was running the show. With the Cavaliers miraculously winning the draft lottery, despite entering the evening with just a 1.7 percent chance of landing the No. 1 pick, he'd have his choice among three players grouped together at the top of most draft boards: Duke forward Jabari Parker and Kansas teammates Andrew Wiggins and Joel Embiid.

But first, Griffin needed a head coach. He tried pitching Bill Self, the head coach at Kansas, on the gig. Self declined the offer, but he shared his candid thoughts on his two star prospects. Self believed that Wiggins had All-Star potential. But the 7-foot-1 Embiid, Self said, was the sort of talent that comes around once in a generation, the kind of player who could change a franchise. After spending so much time around Kansas, Griffin and the Cavaliers had come to agree. The only question mark about Embiid was the stress fracture he had suffered in his lower back a few months earlier.

On a Monday night a little less than two weeks before the draft, Embiid arrived in Cleveland to work out for the Cavaliers. He met the team the next morning at their practice facility in Independence, Ohio. Griffin tasked Vitaly Potapenko, a 6-foot-10 assistant coach and former NBA player, to defend the nimble Embiid in the post. The Cavs figured Embiid would have no issue dancing around the older (thirty-nine) and slower Potapenko. But then he began throwing the 275-pound Potapenko "around like a rag doll," an onlooker said. He powered through him and easily moved him off the block. "The strength he had was mind-numbing," the onlooker said. Any worries about Embiid's back were dispelled.

The Cavs moved Embiid to the midrange. His jumper was fluid and smooth. He finished the workout by stepping out behind the three-point line. He splashed his first shot from behind the arc.

"How could you not draft me No. 1?" he shouted at Griffin.

He swished another.

"Look how good I am!"

Another ripped through the net.

"You need me, Griff!"

A fourth make.

"Come on, Griff, you gotta draft me!"

A fifth.

"I'm so good!"

A sixth.

"I gotta be No. 1!"

A seventh.

"How can you not take me?"

Smiles swept across the faces of Griffin and the rest of the Cavaliers brain trust. Griffin would later tell people that it was the best workout he'd ever seen. "He was like the second coming of Hakeem," he'd say.

His mind was made. "He told us there he was taking Joel No. 1," said Francois Nyam, one Embiid's agents at the time.

Embiid went to dinner that night with some Cavaliers decision makers. While devouring three orders of chocolate lava cake, he lobbed all sorts of questions at the executives sitting across from him, from X's and O's to asking why the Cavaliers had retired jerseys hanging above their practice court. He cracked jokes. He was polite. He made eye contact. "He was radically more engaged than most kids who come in for those things," said one attendee. The Cavs were smitten.

The next morning, Embiid awoke in his hotel room with his right foot screaming. "I can't walk," he told Nyam. About a week earlier, Bismack Biyombo, a Hornets forward from the Congo who was repped by the same agency, had landed on the foot during a workout in Santa Monica. Embiid told his agents he "felt something." They had all assumed it was just a sprain or bruise, but now they feared that it was more serious. Embiid pulled himself out of bed, laced up his sneakers, and limped into the Cleveland Clinic for his physical. He jogged on a treadmill for a few minutes, but the pain was too much. He underwent an X-ray. A thin stress fracture was discovered in the middle of his right foot.

The news began trickling out the next day. Sixers staffers, watching a draft workout from the sidelines that morning at PCOM, were giddy as they passed it along to one another. The team hadn't met with Embiid. But a few weeks earlier Hinkie had attended a workout put on by Embiid's agents in Santa Monica. He and his staff had also scouted enough of Embiid's games to recognize what it was that Griffin and the Cavaliers saw.

Later that day, Hinkie visited Brown's office. "Embiid got injured in Cleveland today," he said. "He might be available to us (at No. 3)."

On June 20, six days before the draft, a surgeon at the Southern California Orthopedic Institute inserted two screws into Embiid's fractured navicular bone to meld the crack. Embiid's agent, Arn Tellem, released a statement from the operating doctor, Richard Ferkel: "The surgery went very well and I'm confident that after appropriate healing he will be able to return to NBA Basketball."

That wasn't good enough for the Cavaliers. Griffin had a mandate from ownership to win and needed a player who could immediately help the team. Even if he wanted to take Embiid, the Cavaliers' doctors wouldn't give him the green light. The Bucks, meanwhile, had locked in on Parker, another Tellem client, at No. 2, and anyway, Embiid had no interest in playing there. "That place is corny," he hold Nyam. What he really wanted was to fall to the Lakers at No. 7. He'd been living in Los Angeles and grown comfortable in the city. "Work your magic," he told Tellem. Tellem knew there was no chance of Embiid plunging that far, so instead he and Nyam sold Embiid on Philadelphia. Tellem had grown up there. Nyam had moved there to play high school basketball. It took a bit, but Embiid bought in.

If the Sixers wanted him, he was theirs.

———

Joel Embiid is fond of comparing his life to a movie. The story, in his account, begins with a scout discovering him on the streets of Yaoundé, the capital of Cameroon, where Embiid grew up. It's a good opening scene, but not exactly true.

The story actually begins with an email.

"Best wishes brother!!!" Didier Yanga wrote to Joe Touomou in January 2011. "I'm sending you pictures of my nephew...Thomas' son, who is 2m06 tall and 17 years old. He's in 11th grade."

Eighteen months earlier, Yanga's nephew Joel Embiid had watched his first NBA game, a Finals matchup between Kobe Bryant's Los Angeles Lakers and Dwight Howard's Orlando Magic. Joel had grown up around sports. He excelled in volleyball, was an avid soccer fan, and also the son of a professional handball player. Yet something about the NBA spectacle was different.

"I had never seen anything like that," Embiid recalled. "The way they moved, and the athleticism, I thought it was the coolest thing in the world. I had that moment like, *I just wanna do that.*" He found a run-down hoop nearby and started playing regularly. "Kobe!" he'd shout after each shot. He'd extend his right wrist and freeze it in the air, just like he'd seen on TV.

He begged his parents to let him play. "But my brother wanted Joel to have excellent grades and not be distracted by anything else," Yanga said. Thomas served as a colonel in the Cameroon military. His three kids knew his edicts were not to be violated, and his wife, Christine, was just as strict, forcing Joel to memorize his school notes before playing outside and forbidding him from staying up late to watch NBA games. "I didn't even have any friends because all I ever did was sleep and do homework," Embiid recalled.

As Joel grew older he became more rebellious. After school he'd arrange a bunch of highlighted textbooks on his family's kitchen table and slip out to a nearby soccer field. He'd play until spotting his mom's Mercedes driving down the street, then dash back, hide his sneakers, and greet her from behind a stack of study materials.

Thomas and Christine planned for Joel to leave for France after high school, where he'd enroll at the National Institute of Sport and Physical Education. He'd continue his volleyball training—a sport they understood—and maybe earn a spot on Cameroon's national team. Thomas had followed this path and look at the life he now lived: Three beautiful children. A spacious home. A wife driving a Mercedes. The family even employed a maid.

But Joel didn't care about any of that. What he cared about, what he wanted, was to play basketball, to be like Kobe. Slowly, Thomas began reconsidering his stance. He reached out to his brother, who had played some high-level amateur basketball in the Ivory Coast and coached a bit too. Yanga wasn't an expert, but he knew enough to recognize the potential in his 6-foot-7 volleyball-playing nephew. He thought of an old friend of his, a man named Joe Touomou, one of the few bridges between Cameroon's cracked courts and America's lavish gyms. Touomou had grown up with Thomas and Yanga before leaving to attend Georgetown on a basketball scholarship. He was the first Cameroonian ever to play Division I and had worked as an international scout for the Indiana Pacers. He was the perfect person to illustrate all the opportunities basketball could provide.

Yanga explained the situation to Touomou, then sent him pictures of Joel posing in front of a doorway, to accentuate his height. Touomou received the photos on a Saturday afternoon. He saw how tall Joel was. He knew how athletic Joel's father was. He booked a flight to Cameroon and a few weeks later was in the Embiid home handing Joel a gym bag stuffed with leftovers from a previous camp—basketball jerseys, shorts, and a size 16 pair of white sneakers.

Thomas and Christine told Joel to wait upstairs. They sat with Touomou in the living room. Touomou began by explaining the potential he believed Joel possessed. He said he knew a local coach who could help him harness all that potential.

"Joel is stubborn," an unmoved Thomas said.

"All he wants to do is play sports," said Christine. "He needs to focus on school."

"Basketball can get him into the best schools," Touomou responded.

He was armed with examples. Look at Ruben Boumtje-Boumtje, he said, the first Cameroonian to ever play in the NBA. And look at Luc Mbah a Moute, an NBA forward whose father, in a similar conversation eight years earlier, Touomou had swayed. Both, thanks to basketball, had earned college scholarships.

The three spoke for more than an hour. Touomou could tell that the education pitch had softened Thomas and Christine. He told them to think it over, that he'd be back soon. Two days later, he returned to the Embiid home. Joel sat with them this time, and Christine served food. She and Thomas told Touomou that Joel could play, as long as he promised to remain focused on his academics. Joel looked on quietly, hiding his excitement.

In February, Thomas signed paperwork allowing Joel to join a local team led by a coach named Guy Moudio. Moudio gave Joel a tape of Hall of Fame center Hakeem Olajuwon to study. He used a medicine ball to build up Joel's strength. Moudio had to teach Joel some of the game's more basic skills, but he was impressed with what he saw and how Joel, despite being a novice, seemed to have an innate feel for the game. He mentioned his new pupil to Francois Nyam, a former French professional basketball player whose father was from Cameroon. Nyam was a cousin of Mbah a Moute's and had since become a fixture in the country's basketball community. He and Mbah a Moute were opening a basketball camp in Cameroon; that summer five attendees would earn an invite to Basketball Without Borders, a program organized by the NBA with the intention of spreading the sport across the world. An invite there was an opportunity to audition in front of a group of people with the power to fulfill the loftiest of dreams.

Joel was invited to participate, but while getting dressed on the morning of the camp's first day, he began thinking about all the players he'd be competing against. They were so advanced and he was still so raw. Anxiety overcame him. He spent the day at home playing video games with his younger brother instead.

The next morning, Moudio showed up at the Embiids' house. This was Joel's chance, and Moudio wasn't going to let nerves ensnare his prize pupil. He ushered Joel to the Yaoundé Sports Palace, and for most of the camp Joel was overmatched. "He couldn't catch a basketball, dribble, or anything," Nyam said. But like Moudio before, Nyam and Mbah a Moute were both impressed with the way Joel absorbed the game. "You could show him something completely new and he'd pick it up after, like, three tries," Nyam said. That was all the group needed to see. About a month later, Joel was standing on a court in Johannesburg surrounded by a group of NBA coaches and some of Africa's top prospects. He was skinny and raw, but also tall and agile. "His feet," said Monty Williams, a former NBA player who worked as a coach for that camp, "were unreal."

Impressed, Mbah a Moute and Nyam arranged for Joel to enroll as a junior at Montverde Academy in Florida, Mbah a Moute's alma mater and home to one of the country's top high school basketball programs. In September, Thomas and Christine drove Joel to Yaoundé Nsimalen International Airport. Joel was scared, but excited too. He barely spoke English, but he recognized the opportunity in front of him. He hugged his family, not knowing when he'd see them next, and boarded the plane.

———

Joel showed up to his first Montverde practice unsure what to expect. He watched his teammates, some of the best high school players in the country, kids who had spent years honing their skills, drill jumpers and glide across the court while he fumbled passes and dribbled the ball off his feet. On defense he didn't know where to stand. On offense he didn't know how to cut.

"He was new to everything," said Luc Mbah a Moute's younger brother, Roger Moute a Bidias, one of his Montverde teammates.

Joel's teammates taunted and teased him. He was an easy target. He was tall, but "really, really skinny," Moute a Bidias said. His English was limited to "good morning," and whatever lyrics he'd picked up from Bow Wow and Kanye West. His spoke with a heavy accent. He didn't have friends.

Montverde head coach Kevin Boyle blew his whistle, bringing practice to a halt. He was able to look past the mistakes, to see something his players couldn't. He told Embiid to get some water. Embiid stepped out of the gym. Boyle turned to his team.

"You laugh now, but in five years you are all going to go to Joel to borrow money because he's going to be rich," he yelled.

In his dorm room afterward, Joel collapsed onto his bed. His eyes welled with tears.

What am I even doing here? he wondered. He thought about calling his parents, about asking to come home. Maybe his mom and dad were right.

But then he thought about his soccer games back in Cameroon and how he'd always relished those moments when his team was down. He believed that's when he played his best. He was always competitive. This—exacting some sort of revenge on his teammates, beating them in practice—would just be his latest challenge.

He began studying Moudio's tape of Olajuwon every night and then practicing the moves the next day. During lunch breaks he'd seek out Boyle and ask for extra coaching. During free moments he typed "White People Shooting 3 Pointers" into the search box on YouTube so he could learn proper shooting mechanics from a group of people that he had discerned to be the best.

"I know it's a stereotype, but have you ever seen a normal, thirty-year-old white guy shoot a three-pointer?" Embiid recalled. "That elbow is tucked, man. The knees are bent. The follow-through is perfect. Always."

Slowly, his game improved. He suited up for a few JV games and played well. He realized he wasn't so far behind. His confidence grew. He remained shy around his teammates, but they no longer intimidated him. When hanging out with Moute a Bidias or the small group of fellow African teammates he mostly interacted with, his personality began breaking through. He'd beat friends in *FIFA* and then spend the rest of the day reminding them of his victory, and that mentality carried over into practices. If Dakari Johnson, a stud center ranked seventh in his class by ESPN, threw an elbow, Joel would reciprocate the next trip down, often forcing Boyle to jump in to prevent punches from being thrown.

Joel finished the season strongly, then linked up with a high-profile Amateur Athletic Union (AAU) team called the Florida Rams. "He'd do 360 dunks during warm-ups," said Chris Walker, a Rams teammate. Once, during a game in Atlanta, Joel dunked on an opponent, looked at the bench, and started dancing.

"We were like, 'Did that guy who never talks just do a shimmy?'" Walker said.

Joel's name began popping on college recruitment lists. He cracked ESPN's top-100 list. The Division I scholarship offers would soon be flying in. The problem was that as long as Johnson was enrolled at Montverde, Joel would be relegated to a reserve role.

Nyam poked around Florida's basketball community. Friends suggested he reach out to Justin Harden, the basketball coach at The Rock School, up in Gainesville. In April, Harden was told he might be hearing from Mbah a Moute about a talented kid who was looking for a new home. Harden did some research and called some friends. One was Norm Roberts, a Kansas assistant whose son had played for Harden. Roberts had seen Montverde play earlier that year.

"I'd take that kid in a heartbeat," he told Harden.

Three months later, Harden was parked outside a Walmart with his two young sons sleeping in his Sonata's backseat when Mbah a Moute finally called. The two chatted for about twenty minutes. Harden told him about his program and coaching style. Mbah a Moute explained Joel's situation.

"He didn't want Joel to have a free ride," Harden said. "He just wanted him to have the opportunity to play through mistakes."

Both men liked what they heard. Joel was spending the summer with the Mbah a Moute family in Milwaukee, where Luc was playing and living. In October, a few days before the start of school, Harden and his wife picked Joel up at Gainesville Regional Airport. They drove to a local Moe's Southwest Grill to share a bite. Joel, who was consuming thousands of calories a day—he tasted Nutella that summer for the first time and spent afternoons gorging on spoonfuls straight from the jar—ordered "the biggest burrito they had," Harden said.

Harden talked to Joel about the team and the school and told him about the couple, a local State Farm agent and retired preschool teacher, who'd be hosting him. A few weeks later, Joel took the court for his first practice.

"He was mesmerizing," Harden said. "I had never seen anyone able to move that gracefully."

He was still learning the game. He was often whistled for setting illegal screens (he'd spread his legs out past his shoulders and use his knees) and jumping over opponents' backs for rebounds. But those watching closely started seeing the signs of something special. Joel had immersed himself in basketball over the summer, sometimes even dribbling up and down Milwaukee's streets on afternoons when he couldn't get to a court. But there was more to it. "You could see a brilliance there," Harden said. Joel picked up new plays easily. He effortlessly adapted them to counter defenses in ways Harden hadn't previously conceived. He often did so during practices, just moments after seeing Harden demonstrate the play for the first time.

By this point, Joel's English had improved. But outside of a few African teammates who he felt comfortable joking with—"We relied on each other," said teammate Alain Chigha—he mostly kept to himself. "In Cameroon, if you're 6-foot-10, people make fun of you," Nyam said. "It made him an introvert." The questions lobbed at him from classmates about Cameroon bothered him. "They thought I grew up poor, in the jungle, killing lions," Embiid said. He missed his family and hated living under another family's roof. His new school's stricter academic standards bothered him. He spent most of his free time alone in his bedroom, playing *FIFA* and *Call of Duty*.

Occasionally that attitude infected his play. Harden pulled him during the team's semifinal matchup "because he looked like he didn't care." In other moments, a new character revealed himself. Joel challenged teammates to one-on-one games. He bombarded them with trash talk. Once, in a scrimmage toward the end of the season, he got tangled with Glenn Feidanga, a 6-foot-8, 230-pound senior. Feidanga whiffed on a punch. Joel, while being pulled backwards by Harden and teammates, unleashed a kick that grazed Feidanga's face.

"Sometimes he looked pissed off at the world," Harden said. "He did not have a great experience with us."

It didn't matter. Joel had enrolled at The Rock School so that he could land on the radars of college basketball's biggest programs, so that he could earn a shot at the NBA. He had done just that.

In September, Roberts dragged Kansas head coach Bill Self to Gainesville for an open scrimmage.

"Wow, he's tall," Self said as Joel walked onto The Rock School's practice court.

He and Roberts watched Joel shoot around and run up and down the floor. The footwork stood out, but other than that, Roberts was worried Joel hadn't done enough to sell his boss. He missed some jumpers. He was pushed out by his meatier teammates. He failed to assert himself.

After the practice, Roberts turned to Self.

"What do you think?"

Self looked around to make sure none of the other college coaches present were listening. He paused a moment.

"In two years that kid's going to be the No. 1 pick in the draft," he said. "From now on, don't recruit anyone harder than him."

It didn't take long for other schools to catch on. Louisville head coach Rick Pitino visited The Rock School early in the season. So did Florida's Billy Donovan. Texas's Rick Barnes, Virginia's Tony Bennett, and Marquette's Buzz Williams joined the chase.

That October, Kansas invited Joel to its Lawrence campus for an official visit. He watched the team scrimmage, shot around with some players, and threw down a windmill dunk. He ate dinner—which included a dessert request of two orders of chocolate cake—with Self and the team. The group was taken aback by how quiet Joel was. Justin Wesley, a junior guard who served as Joel's host for the weekend, told Embiid there was a frat party they could attend.

"What's a frat?" Joel asked.

At the party that night, Wesley asked Joel what he wanted to drink.

"Can I get a Shirley Temple?" Joel asked.

"A what?" Wesley asked.

"A Shirley Temple."

Wesley had no idea how to make one. He hunted down a pledge to look it up and find the proper ingredients. In the meantime, Joel had all sorts of questions: What was the campus like? What were the girls on campus like? What was Self like? How hard did you have to work? How good could he get?

"He was kind of naïve," Wesley said. "He was clearly still getting used to the American culture, and he really didn't know much about the college basketball scene."

Kansas had purposely invited Joel on the weekend of Midnight Madness, the official start of the NCAA basketball season. Many schools turn the date into a pep rally. Kansas billed the event Late Night in the Phog.

Joel showed up at Allen Fieldhouse around 6 p.m. Rabid fans dressed in blue and white filled all 16,300 seats. Music blared over the speakers and cheers filled the room. Some of Kansas's players put on oversized tuxedo jackets and, standing at center court, danced to "Gangnam Style." The team scrimmaged. Joel watched in awe.

"It was crazy," he said. "We walked in there and everyone started clapping and yelling. I didn't know what was going on. I was scared. I was like, 'Are they clapping for us?' I just looked down at the ground. I couldn't believe it."

Joel enrolled at Kansas the following summer, his fourth home in four years, and once again found himself feeling overwhelmed. He was now part of the billion-dollar business that is Division I college basketball. There were expectations, and stakes, and he wasn't sure he could deliver. During a summer scrimmage with some teammates, Tarik Black, a thick 6-foot-9 senior, dunked over the top of him. That night Joel recalled looking up plane tickets home. A few weeks later, during the final day of the team's ten-day conditioning boot camp, Joel, complaining of back pain, quit before completing the required number of suicides.

"You big baby," Self barked. "Now you're going to have to come back tomorrow and do it by yourself." At the encouragement of his teammates, Joel repeated the drill, this time finishing. "But it all reminded him of when he had first come to Montverde," Moute a Bidias said. In October, Kansas gathered for its first official practice. Once again Joel was shocked by the size of the players and speed of the game. After practice, he approached Self in his office.

"Coach, you're going to have to redshirt me, aren't you?" he asked.

"Are you kidding, Jo?" Self responded. "You're going to end up being the best player we ever had."

Self spent the first few months of the 2013–2014 season bragging about his freshman center to friends. He was sure he'd successfully wooed a kid who in two years would be the first player to hear his name called in the draft. Scouts, flooding Kansas's gym to check out Andrew Wiggins and Wayne Selden, another projected first-rounder, were the first to inform Self that he was wrong.

"He's already a lottery pick, and might even be No. 1 *this* year," one told Self in the fall after watching a Kansas practice. "There's no way he's staying."

To the public, Joel remained mostly unknown. It was Wiggins who was pegged as the draft's most prized prospect, and it remained that way for the season's early months. But Joel worked hard—he continued studying Olajuwon clips; sometimes he'd walk into the office of an assistant coach, pantomime a Dream Shake, and then walk out—and was inserted into the starting lineup in December. One game later, against New Mexico, he scored 18 points, two of them off a smooth drop step, set up by a shimmy.

"Olajuwon!" shouted ESPN analyst Fran Fraschilla, calling the game courtside. Kansas won, 80–63.

After the game, Self pulled Roberts aside.

"We're holding this kid back," he told him. "He needs to start."

Joel was a sponge, and growing faster than any player Self had ever coached. He saw things—angles, openings, reads—that others players didn't even know to look for. Once, during a scrimmage, Joel, a teammate, and an opponent all chased a loose ball into the backcourt. Joel's point guard came up with it and dribbled back up the floor. Joel sprinted to set a screen. Self, in awe, blew his whistle.

"Jo, why'd you go set that screen?" he asked, wondering if Joel would respond the way Self thought, and hoped, he would.

"Because the man is in the backcourt," Joel said. "There's no one here to help."

Self smiled.

By January, Joel's internal doubts had evaporated. His teammates noticed a difference in his demeanor. Earlier in the year, Self's scrimmages, where fouls weren't called and out-of-bounds violations didn't exist, had disoriented him. Now "he was throwing elbows and taking advantage of those rules," said former Kansas forward Andrew White. Joel punctuated baskets with shouts of "And one!" He screamed "Can't guard me!" at seniors. He taunted teammates who failed to score on him.

"Everything changed for him at Kansas," Nyam said. "You go from the tall kid everyone is making fun of to getting all the attention and being on ESPN and the cover of *SLAM*, it made him a different person."

That confidence created a comfort, and that comfort pulled out a personality Joel had mostly kept hidden since arriving in the United States. He was still quiet and private. "He rarely talked about his family," Justin Wesley said. But he was also funny and smart. He'd heighten his accent during interviews. If he got in trouble around campus, he'd respond by pretending his English was poor. He told coaches, teammates, and reporters that, as a child in Cameroon, as part of a tribal initiation, he'd pierced a lion with a spear (sometimes the story was tweaked so that he killed the lion with his hands). Never mind that he grew up in an upper-middle-class home, nowhere near a jungle. Joel liked how the tale mocked the stereotypes he believed others held about his home continent. He enjoyed how others never seemed quite sure if he was joking. "Americans have crazy ideas about Africa," he recalled.

The fib made teammates laugh, but it also fit a trend of Embiid embellishing his backstory, one that would only grow more rampant in upcoming years, be it in magazine profiles or first-person essays. "My life is a movie," he'd say often. Joel's version didn't mention his uncle or the role he played in connecting him to the NBA world. It often had him playing basketball for three months prior to receiving an invite to Mbah a Moute's camp, when it was actually closer to six. It often claimed that the coaching at Basketball Without Borders was the first he'd ever received, erasing much of the sweat Moudio had put in. It featured the Olajuwon tape Moudio gave him, but almost never mentioned Moudio by name. Around this time, Joel also ceased speaking with Moudio, Touomou, and Yanga.

"At first it made me sad," Yanga would say years later. "But not anymore. I did what I had to do. I have no regrets. In our traditions, Joel is my son, and I am happy that he succeeds, especially by the basketball that I practiced and that I continue to teach."

In the meantime, Joel was cruising toward the draft's top slot (averages of 11.2 points, 8.1 rebounds, and 2.6 blocks in 23 minutes a game) until suffering a stress fracture in his back in March. He was sidelined for the NCAA tournament, and watched Kansas fall in the round of 32. The injury was a blow, to Kansas but also to Joel. He'd rocketed up the draft board of every analyst and scout. He was a seven-footer with a 7-foot-5 wingspan who could shoot, and post up, and block shots, and move his feet. His package of skills was rare. But it was possible the injury would scare some teams away.

A couple weeks later Kansas called a press conference. Seated alongside Self behind a table draped in a blue cloth, Joel, speaking deliberately, announced his plan for the following season.

"After thinking a lot," he said, "I decided to declare for the NBA draft."

The Sixers spent the week leading up to the draft studying their options. Going with Embiid was risky. His talent was obvious, but no one could say for certain when he'd return to the court, or, once he did, how long he'd last. Hinkie was never one to shy away from risk, but this was uncharted territory. It'd be dangerous for any team to bet its future on a big man with a bad back and flimsy feet—even more so for one full of borderline NBA players and coming off an ugly 19-win season. Hinkie would have other chances during the draft to improve the roster. Thanks to the previous year's trade of Jrue Holiday for Nerlens Noel, as well as some incessant dealing, the Sixers also owned the draft's 10th pick as well as a league-high five second-rounders. But the No. 3 pick was the crown jewel.

"One of the lights at the end of the tunnel all during the season—which was very hard, particularly down the stretch—was that we had two lottery picks coming," Hinkie said. "Everybody's all excited about that, and there was a bit of hype around that. It was all reasonable stuff about the cavalry's coming."

Drafting Embiid would neuter that cavalry. Without an immediate injection of talent from that No. 3 slot, the Sixers would likely spend another season in the league's cellar, a result that would likely anger some fans, serve as ammo to Hinkie's critics, and, despite their previous assurances otherwise, test the patience of ownership.

On the other hand, every one of Hinkie's actions over the previous twelve months—the dumping of good players, the losing of games, the dumping of even more players, the losing of even more games—had been about creating an opportunity to nab a star, and that opportunity had now arrived. Hinkie spent the week leading up to the draft speaking to all sorts of specialists and looking up studies on navicular bone injuries. He was told that Embiid would need approximately five to eight months to recover. In other words, he'd miss the season. After that, the belief was that he'd be good to go.

A couple hours before the draft's start, Hinkie called Self. "If you're drafting in the top three, you need a guy who can lead a franchise," he told Self, who was on his way to the draft. "Joel may be hurt, but he's going to be the only guy left with a chance at becoming a franchise player."

Later that evening, seated in his third-floor office, Hinkie watched NBA commissioner Adam Silver announce the draft's first two picks.

They went as expected—Wiggins No. 1 to Cleveland, Parker No. 2 to Milwaukee.

Five minutes later, Silver walked to the podium in Brooklyn's Barclays Center. "With the third pick of the 2014 NBA draft, the Philadelphia 76ers select Joel Embiid," he announced.

Joel, unable to travel due to the surgery, heard the news from a couch in Tellem's home. His parents were seated beside him. He pumped both his fists. A smile filled his face.

Chapter 9

TRUST THE PROCESS?

For all the hand-wringing, Sam Hinkie's plan was fairly simple. He believed an NBA team needed two stars to transform into a perennial contender. Fifteen minutes into the 2014 NBA draft, it appeared he was halfway there. But there was no time to celebrate. There was more work to be done.

The Sixers also owned the 10th pick, acquired in the previous year's draft night, and would be back on the clock in about thirty-five minutes. There were also the league-high five second-round picks that Hinkie had spent the previous year accumulating, and there'd be a host of other opportunities that would present themselves over the next few hours. For a team like the Sixers indifferent to on-court results and focused purely on asset accumulation, this would be the most important few hours of the year.

Hinkie was aware—more so than most—that the draft was an inexact science. He was open about this belief, too. He never tried selling himself as some sort of wizard; it's why he had been so adamant about amassing as many picks as possible. He viewed the draft like a lottery—the more numbers he owned, the better his chances were at hitting a jackpot. But he also recognized that there were actions he could take to boost his odds. "We put more resources into the draft than anything else," said a former colleague.

Like most GMs, Hinkie spent the year dispatching scouts all over the world. He wanted in-depth reports on every aspect of every prospect's game. Not just the basics, like whether they could shoot or defend, but also the minutiae, like whether or not they could finish at the rim with both hands and, if not, what was holding them back. He was someone who paid attention to details like where a player positioned his thumb while shooting, and how that might affect the rotation of his jumper. He wanted his scouts to do the same. "We did a lot more work, a lot more detailed work than other teams or other GMs require," former Sixers scout Frank DiLeo said. "But you could tell Sam was reading everything we were sending." Hinkie believed all information was valuable—like, say, if one of his scouts knew a friend on a different team was visiting a certain school half a dozen times over a few months—and could be weaponized.

After the season, Hinkie gathered his front office and coaches at the team's basketball offices at the Philadelphia College of Osteopathic Medicine, where the group spent more than a month evaluating, discussing, and debating players. His scouts often woke up with film assignments in their inboxes. These were assigned based on an algorithm developed, at the request of Hinkie, by Aaron Barzilai and Lance Pearson. "It was about coming up with a systematic way to determine how much info we have on guys and how much we should have on guys," Pearson said. This meant weighing the importance of games (for example, the more NBA prospects in a game, the better), but also cataloging who among the staff had watched which player how many times. It was about trying to approximate the point of diminishing returns.

"We didn't just use the so-called analytics stuff to spit out rankings," a former member of the Sixers' front office said. "We wanted to help make even basic things like watching film more efficient, too."

During the lead-up to the draft, Hinkie would call the entire basketball staff into one of PCOM's bigger meeting rooms. Together, the group of about twenty-five staffers would discuss every prospect. Hinkie encouraged everyone to participate. "Hearing a bunch of different views was something he deemed hugely valuable," Barzilai said. But, wary of even accidental leaks, Hinkie kept his views to himself.

Prospects were assigned a ranking of one through five in about a dozen different categories, from shooting off the dribble to pick-and-roll decision making. If a discrepancy existed between evaluations, Hinkie would have the attendees break for a few hours, watch film of the skill in question—maybe a point guard's ability to drive to his left—and then return to share what they learned.

"If you are going to invest in the draft in a big way, you better be investing in scouting in a big way," Hinkie said. "You better be trying to have an edge one way or another. You better be putting systems in place, a staff, and a way in which you make decisions that actually gives you an edge. Otherwise, you are just going to do something I call indexing. Where you take whoever is next on the board in the eyes of the public, and that's a dicey situation."

Draft night was the time for all that extra work to pay off. The Charlotte Hornets had selected a big man out of Indiana named Noah Vonleh ninth overall. The Sixers once again were on the clock. Holed up in his third-floor PCOM office alongside some team executives, head coach Brett Brown, majority owners Josh Harris and David Blitzer, and minority owner David Heller, Hinkie worked the phones and contemplated his options. Two whiteboards full of notes lined one wall. Binders featuring player rankings were splayed out on a table.

Hinkie and his scouts wanted Dario Šarić, a playmaking 6-foot-10 Croatian forward. Šarić, the twenty-year-old son of two former professional basketball players, had turned pro at the age of fifteen and had since established himself as one of Europe's premier talents. He was coming off a season in which he'd been named Adriatic League MVP and had led his team to a league title. Most scouts believed him to be one of the ten best prospects in the draft. "Our guys had him around six or seven," Pearson said. Hinkie had seen him play in Spain and the Sixers' primary international scout, Marin Sedlaček, knew Šarić's father and was a proponent of Dario's. But Šarić had recently signed a new contract with Turkey's Anadolu Efes, one that would keep him overseas for at least two more years. "It's a better option for me, to stay two years more in Europe, to get more experience, to bring my basketball to a higher level," he said at the time. This spooked most GMs. Few executive jobs offer less security and turn over more frequently.

Wasting a lottery pick on a player unable to contribute for a couple of years was a risky proposition.

Hinkie wasn't trying to add a few wins over the next few years. He had loftier goals, and assurances from Sixers ownership that they coveted the same things. Everyone was aware and in agreement that progress wouldn't necessarily be linear.

"Sam would say that this is a unique ownership group with very lofty ambitions," said a former colleague. "They were really focused on bringing a championship to the city of Philadelphia and were on board with what we were doing." Some, like Heller, a minority owner who began regularly showing up at the Sixers offices about a month before the draft so that he could participate in meetings, were even helping to push that plan forward. "It was really the first ownership group to apply the private equity model to running an NBA team," said a minority owner of a competing team. That model meant Hinkie had a runway that his peers did not, and with that came opportunity.

With the 10th pick, the Sixers drafted Elfrid Payton, a point guard from the University of Louisiana at Lafayette. The decision confused onlookers and observers around the league. Payton was one of the top point guards in the draft, but he played the same position as Michael Carter-Williams, the reigning Rookie of the Year. Sitting in attendance at Brooklyn's Barclays Center, Carter-Williams appeared just as befuddled.

"I'm not really sure if I'm going to be moved or not," he said minutes later during a live interview with ESPN reporter Jeff Goodman.

Hinkie wasn't worried about position overlap—he figured that stuff often sorted itself out in the long run. There was also no rule stating that he was required to keep Payton. He knew, for example, that the Orlando Magic, picking at No. 12, had scouted him extensively throughout the college season. He also knew that Payton had wowed Magic executives during his private workout.

Hinkie and Magic general manager Rob Hennigan quickly agreed on a trade. The Magic would draft Šarić and deal him to Philly in exchange for Payton. They'd also send the Sixers a 2015 second-round pick, *and* a 2017 first-round pick (which had been sent by the Sixers to the Magic two years earlier as part of the Andrew Bynum megadeal).

In the end, Hinkie had figured out a way to simultaneously grab the player he wanted *and* beef up his war chest.

Early in the second round, Hinkie picked up two long and athletic wings—K. J. McDaniels at 32 and Jerami Grant at 39. He also swung a couple minor deals, picked up another future second-round pick, and took a flyer on a twenty-year-old Serbian point guard named Vasilije Micić, who'd likely remain overseas longer for a few years, if not more. But the story of the night was what Hinkie had done in the first round. "You thought incrementally you're going to continue to grow," Sixers head coach Brett Brown said. After watching Hinkie select an injured player at No. 3 and then turn the No. 10 selection into a player under contract in another country with no buyout option, it was clear that there'd be no reinforcements on the way.

"Well, where are we now?" Brown asked Pearson in his office that night. He already knew the answer.

———

In August, Hinkie completed his purge. Thaddeus Young, a veteran forward and the team's leading scorer the previous season, was sent to the Minnesota Timberwolves as part of a three-team deal. In return, the Sixers received yet another first-round pick and Luc Mbah a Moute, the career reserve from Cameroon who was a longtime mentor of Joel Embiid's.

Now the Sixers were ready for the season. If Hinkie was Leonardo da Vinci, then the team's opening-day roster was his *Mona Lisa*. Five of the fifteen players were rookies. Only two had more than two years of legitimate NBA experience.[1] Seven had gone undrafted out of college—three more and the Sixers would already eclipse the record for the most undrafted players to suit up for one team in an entire season. Combined, the fifteen players were making about $25 million, nearly equal to what the Knicks were paying an over-the-hill Amar'e Stoudemire.

---

1   Technically, Malcolm Thomas, a 6-foot-9 forward, was entering his third season in the NBA, but his "experience" consisted of a grand total of 135 minutes played for four different teams.

This was a team built to lose.

"The Thad deal really hit us hard," Pearson said. "Before that there was still some uncertainty about how deep the rebuild would go. That was one of those moments where it became very clear."

The season tipped off on October 29 in Indiana. The Sixers lost. They lost again two nights later in Milwaukee, and again the following night at home, and again two nights after that, and again two nights after that, and then they traveled to Toronto and they lost there and they traveled to Dallas and lost there and they traveled to Houston and lost there and they flew to San Antonio and lost there too.

Hinkie never instructed Brown to intentionally lose games. But he didn't mind watching his lottery odds improve every night. A player would be signed to a ten-day contract one day, inserted into the starting lineup the next—"Tim Frazier would come in and you'd shake his hand and say, 'Nice to meet you, you're the starting point guard,'" Brown said—and then waived nine days later. One time Brown began barking for a player to sub into the game—only to be informed by his assistants that he was addressing the player by the wrong name.

"We'd have to pull up video of guys we vaguely knew and quickly get Brett a summary of their strengths and weaknesses," Pearson said.

The Sixers played six more games in November. They dropped all of those. They opened December at home against the Spurs and lost that game too, dropping them to 0–17, one defeat shy of tying the mark for worst start in NBA history. A win in Minnesota on December 3 kept the Sixers out of the record books, but the season was already lost.

Amidst it all, Brown did his best to promote a positive environment in the locker room. Recognizing that employing a roster full of individuals clawing for jobs could undermine team unity, he did his best to insulate his players from Hinkie's plan. "Because of Brett, it never felt like we were playing for a team that wanted us to lose," McDaniels said. Brown rarely berated players, and when he did, it was for lack of effort, not mistakes. He often huddled with them on the side and inquired about their lives away from basketball. He invited guest speakers. He organized field trips, including one to the University of Pennsylvania to meet psychologist Angela Lee

Duckworth, whose work on "grit" earned her a "genius" grant from the MacArthur Foundation. He continued holding his current-event "State of the Unions."

"He'd come in and talk about, like, the stars, like, what new star they found," said Isaiah Canaan, whom the Sixers acquired in February. "He opened my mind to lots of things off the court." Brown also made a point of being open with the media and effusive when detailing the improvements of his players. Buddying up to the press often softened the coverage of him and his player, and also helped create a connection with the few die-hard fans following along.

The geniality was appreciated, but with a young team devoid of veterans it was not always the proper approach. The night before media day, Carter-Williams and Tony Wroten were busted by a New Jersey State Police officer for smoking marijuana in a parked car on the highway. A couple months later, Carter-Williams, who'd convinced the Sixers to allow his stepfather to attend practices and felt untouchable, failed to get back on defense during a blowout and, when confronted by Brown, pointed to the scoreboard. Nerlens Noel, who after being drafted sixth overall missed his entire first season due to an ACL injury, returned to the floor, but continued showing up late and smelling of weed. He and Carter-Williams also "hated each other," said the agent of one of their teammates. The feud dated back to their days as AAU teammates in Boston.

The biggest headaches, though, came from the team's biggest player.

Late on the morning of October 16, Joel Embiid was alone in his apartment in downtown Philadelphia's Ritz-Carlton when his cell phone began to buzz. It was his agent. There had been an accident back in Cameroon. A truck, its brakes had broken. It had charged into a schoolyard. A lot of kids were playing. Embiid's ten-year-old brother, Arthur, was one of them. He was dead.

Grief and guilt overtook Embiid. More than three years had passed since he'd last seen Arthur's round face and sweet eyes. He was angry with himself, angry that he hadn't carved out the time to make it back to Cameroon, angry that he hadn't brought his brother with him to the United States.

He spent the night in his apartment, mourning alongside Hinkie, Mbah a Moute, and Brown, who skipped the Sixers' preseason game that evening. "That, for me, was one of the darkest nights of my life," Brown said. "To see Joel in the state that he was in, and to feel very helpless on anything you could do to help other than to be with him. It was a long night." Hinkie, who as a kid lost his older brother to suicide, could relate to Embiid's sorrow better than most. "To learn that you have lost a sibling or a child is unfathomable," he said in a statement released at the time by the team. "We are poorly designed for that kind of loss."

Embiid flew back to Cameroon for the funeral. He spent about three weeks there before returning to Philadelphia toward the end of the month. He was already despondent over the foot injury that was sidelining him for the season. Now he was emotionally shattered, out of shape, and with nothing but *FIFA* and *Madden* to serve as distractions.

"When you're going through so much, loss of your brother, that you haven't seen in like three–four years, and you just had surgery and all that stuff, you've got thoughts coming in your mind," Embiid said.

On the surface, Embiid seemed fine. Better than fine. His ability to master American humor was uncanny. He was jolly in front of cameras and clever on social media. He tried recruiting LeBron and Kim Kardashian (for different purposes) over Twitter. He live-tweeted a fake date with Rihanna, writing, "RENDEZ VOUS tonight (that's actually French words) I bet she will love it when I speak French. They all do actually." It all went viral, making him a sensation.

In reality, Embiid was depressed. He'd show up late to team flights and practices. He'd stay up all night and sleep in the afternoon. "I was a vampire," he said. He amassed all sorts of team fines, none of which altered his behavior. He repeatedly defied the team's insistence that he keep his surgically repaired foot in a walking boot. He preferred walking around in flip-flops, even when getting off a team bus during a snowstorm in Boston. He drank Shirley Temples instead of water and devoured fried chicken fingers instead of baked chicken breast.

In the past, when he was healthy and playing, he could get away with consuming an entire plate of brownies. But now he was blowing off cardio sessions, which, due to the injury, were limited to begin with. As a result, his weight ballooned up to nearly 300 pounds (he weighed in at 240 pounds at the NBA Draft Combine in May). The team tried filling the fridge in his apartment with healthy food. The staffer tasked with restocking the supply would usually discover the previous week's delivery unopened.

"It was a really hard year for him," said Francois Nyam, Embiid's agent at the time.

There was no question Embiid was acting unprofessionally. But there were understandable reasons. "I think if he could have played immediately there would have been no problems," Pearson said. Here was a twenty-year-old kid (he turned twenty-one in March) who in the span of four years had seen his entire life uprooted. He'd gone from playing volleyball in Cameroon to basketball in the NBA. He'd changed homes four times in four years, and now had to cope with the death of his younger brother.

In late December, Embiid was in the visitors' locker room in Portland's Moda Center watching the Sixers–Blazers game on a TV when James Davis, a Sixers strength coach, approached him. Davis had been told to record Embiid's weight. Embiid refused. He didn't see the purpose. He wasn't playing—why did his weight matter? Davis continued insisting. He had a job to do, and he couldn't leave without getting a number. Embiid tried ignoring him. Davis refused to let up. Finally, Embiid lost his patience, unleashing a verbal tirade.

"He was reacting emotionally to someone with a job that was frustrating to him," said Pearson, who witnessed the incident. "But I've been in other situations in locker rooms where there have been fistfights with coaches and players. This was not that. This was a four on a scale of one to ten."

After the game, Brown was told about the altercation. The team flew to Utah that night. Embiid was sent home.

"Joel has all the resources that he needs back in Philadelphia," Brown coyly told reporters before the Sixers' game the following day against the Jazz. "It's more of a structured, stable environment where he has the machines that he can lift on, the people that he can see, team-doctor-wise. He's at an interesting stage of his recovery. Imagine when you are a big man like Joel Embiid, and you are trying to make sure his diet and his weight are where they need to be so we can help him. We feel like we can achieve that better in Philadelphia."

The Sixers spent the next week playing in Golden State, Phoenix, and Los Angeles before returning to Philadelphia. One afternoon that week, a few hours before a game at the Wells Fargo Center, Brown was ushered into a large room. Nearly every member of the Sixers' basketball staff was awaiting him.

"Why are we here?" Brown asked. He knew the meeting was about Embiid, but didn't understand why dozens of his colleagues felt compelled to meet with him in this sort of setting.

One of the assistant coaches stood up. "Coach, we're here because there's a problem with Joel," he said. "He's disrespected just about everyone in this room and has become a major distraction."

Brown was livid. "Jesus Christ!" he screamed. "You mean to tell me my entire staff is here and this is going on and no one told me?" He turned to Billy Lange, an assistant coach whom he'd designated as his chief of staff. "Billy, why the fuck didn't I know about this? Why wasn't this brought to my attention? I got the whole fucking staff here for one guy!"

Lange believed he had tried passing along the staff's concerns. He tried reminding Brown.

"You did not tell me," Brown shouted. "I'm sitting here and I've got my whole staff here—I've let everybody down."

Brown promised to address the issues. But disciplinarian was never a role he was comfortable playing.

"Even after that meeting nothing changed," said a person who was present. "It was a fucking circus."

———

Hinkie was aware of it all. But he felt it best to devote his energy elsewhere, to asset hunting and preparing for the following summer's draft and laying a new foundation for the future. The day-to-day stuff was left to Brown. This, Hinkie believed, was the way it had to be. "The coaching staff and front office are operating under different incentive systems," he once told Pearson. One group was trying to win games; the other was constructing a team that it hoped would lose. These two values could coexist, but only to a point.

Part of this was continuing to modernize his front office. Courtney Witte, a former college basketball player and the team's longtime chief scout, was let go. Sachin Gupta took on even more responsibility. Hinkie also recruited Ben Falk away from the Portland Trail Blazers, naming him vice president of basketball strategy.

Falk was twenty-five, wore glasses, and had hair like Shaggy from *Scooby-Doo*. He wasn't tall and his basketball career had ended before high school. But what he was was brilliant. He'd scored 1600 on his SATs. He'd landed an unpaid job with an NBA analytics guru during his freshman year in Maryland. After he graduated, the Blazers hired him to be their "basketball analytics manager." Players and staff nicknamed him "Wiz." He was great at crunching numbers, but "he was also very helpful in the basketball part beyond analytics," said Blazers head coach Terry Stotts. Stotts credited Falk with convincing him during one off-season to change the way his teams guarded opposing pick-and-rolls (big men were told to stay back at the rim and concede pull-up jumpers), a tweak that bolstered the Blazers' defense. More than that, Falk approached his job like Hinkie: He was relentlessly curious, had no interest in regurgitating NBA tropes, and understood the difference between process and results.

Gupta and Falk became Hinkie's chief lieutenants, making the Sixers the rare team to be led by a group of executives who had never even played college ball, let alone in the NBA. The three spent countless hours huddled together, searching for potential edges. A favorite was hunting for second-round picks. The group recognized that most GMs considered them to be like scratch-off tickets, investments generally not worth the time or trouble. Hinkie disagreed. For one, players drafted in the second round weren't granted guaranteed contracts. This gave Hinkie leverage to sign them to a team-friendly, risk-free, high-upside deal. After the 2014 draft, Hinkie offered his top second-round picks, Jerami Grant and K. J. McDaniels, similar four-year contracts, the longest offer permitted. The first two years would be guaranteed with a salary around $850,000, about $300,000 more than the minimum teams were required to pay second-rounders and a major boon for kids about to earn their first paychecks. But there was a catch: The last two years of the deal were not guaranteed. If the player stumbled, he'd be cut; if he played well, he'd be drastically underpaid for four years. These deals came to be known around the league as Hinkie Specials.

As was the case often with Hinkie, this strategy set off alarm bells throughout the league. The players' union advised agents to reject these offers. "You can understand a team wanting to have some financial control early on, but to attempt to impose this on players in that position was very cold," one union executive said. "It's playing within the rules, but we didn't think the right way to do business." Some agents were able to protect their clients. Grant took the deal, but McDaniels, on the advice of his agent, Mark Bartelstein, rejected Hinkie's offer. "That's just not something we would sign," Bartelstein said. "We negotiated a lot but Sam had a structure he really wanted and he didn't want to come off of that." Bartelstein explained to McDaniels that he was better off accepting the one-year, unguaranteed $507,336 offer granted to all second-rounders and taking his chances on the free agency market, either the following summer or, if he got cut, over the upcoming season. McDaniels did and, after being traded in February, signed a three-year, $10 million contract with the Rockets in July.

Hinkie began scooping up second-rounders wherever he could.[2] A favorite tactic was using all the cap space he had to absorb other teams' flotsam, and then charging a pick as a broker's fee. An added bonus was that it happened to be a way to save his owners millions of dollars.

NBA rules stipulated that all teams spend a certain minimum on player salaries (90 percent of the cap). In the 2014–2015 season,

---

2   Between the 2014 and 2015 drafts, Hinkie picked up seven second-round picks, including one for the year 2020, a draft so far into the future that it would feature a crop of players who at the time of the deal were still in middle school.

that number came out to $56.8 million, meaning the Sixers entered the season about $30 million short. There was no punishment for failing to reach this mark, just a rule forcing a team to divvy up among its players the difference between its total payroll and the "floor." There were loopholes, though, ones Hinkie was more than happy to exploit on behalf of his owners.[3] One was that a team had all season to reach the floor. Another was that if a team traded for a player, his salary for the year would count against the cap, even if he were waived, and even though he'd be paid at a pro-rated amount. Twenty-five players suited up for the Sixers over the 2014–2015 season, mostly on minimum salaries. But Hinkie made sure to acquire a few with bloated contracts as well, pushing the Sixers above the floor and doing so while also keeping that money out of the pockets of their players (and their commission-seeking agents).

The union was furious. So were agents, who were already exasperated by Hinkie's ways and agitated by one of the league's thirty teams essentially removing itself from the marketplace. Hinkie frustrated many of them. He was difficult to deal with. He ignored texts. He tried crushing them in every negotiation. He wasn't interested in strengthening relationships over two-hour lunches, or placing phone calls to check in or pass along player updates. "It was heavy lifting dealing with him," said one prominent agent. For many of them, this represented a swift change from how business was typically conducted. For all the money it brings in, the NBA is a small world. There are a few fringe shops here and there, but the same dozen or so agents represent the majority of the league's players, a status that often granted them the upper hand in negotiations.

"This is a world where you have to deal with the same people for a long time in many different settings," said an assistant general manager of a different team. "The my-way-or-the-highway thing, it doesn't work. If I completely annihilated you this time, then why would you help me at all in the future?"

---

3 And which, thanks to the Sixers, would be closed in future collective bargaining sessions.

There was more to the resentment, though. It wasn't just that many agents felt slighted. Fair or not, many of them believed Hinkie to be dishonest.

In December, the Sixers acquired thirty-three-year-old forward Andrei Kirilenko from the Brooklyn Nets. The Nets were desperate to wipe Kirilenko's $3.3 million off their books, and, for the price of a second-round pick, the Sixers were more than happy to help.

But Kirilenko had no desire to play for a tanking team. More important, he was a father of two whose wife was pregnant and on bed rest in their Brooklyn home. Kirilenko had stopped accompanying the Nets on road trips and his agent had informed all suitors that he would likely be in and out until his wife gave birth. Nets general manager Billy King had told Kirilenko's agent that Hinkie had agreed to waive Kirilenko after the deal so that Kirilenko could sign wherever he wanted on his own timeline. The problem was that the message was never passed along to Hinkie.

After the deal, Hinkie asked Kirilenko to report to the team. He figured Philadelphia being so close to Kirilenko's New York City home made this feasible. The goal was to showcase Kirilenko to the rest of the league and then flip him to another team for a future asset before the February trade deadline.

Kirilenko refused. In early January, the Sixers decided to try bullying him into reporting. They began fining him around $50,000 for every day he refused to show up, which continued until the union mediated. Only after the passing of the February 19 trade deadline did Hinkie finally agree to a buyout.

That same week, Hinkie dealt Carter-Williams to the Milwaukee Bucks. Carter-Williams hadn't grown the way the Sixers had hoped, with his shooting regressing even further. But his raw tools intrigued the Bucks. "We liked Michael's ability at the time to run a team, we liked his size and his fit with our roster," John Hammond, then the Bucks' general manager, said. Hinkie agreed to trade him in exchange for the rights to a future Lakers first-round pick that the Suns owned. It was a savvy deal. The Lakers and their star, Kobe Bryant, were both on the decline. Hinkie recognized there was a strong chance this pick would end up in the lottery, and even in the top five, and that Carter-Williams's numbers were mostly hollow, and so he pounced.

Old-school fans and media panned the move—*How can you trade the reigning Rookie of the Year?* Fans and reporters more steeped in the sport's advanced metrics and in favor of Hinkie's plan praised it. The trade was in line with Hinkie's general approach—he'd taken an 11th pick and a year later turned it into a likely top-five selection—but in his haste to complete the deal he'd failed to notify both Carter-Williams and his agent of the impending trade.

"I was pretty up-to-speed and pretty involved. As far as I heard I was involved in the long-term plan, especially with me, Joel [Embiid] and Nerlens [Noel]," Carter-Williams told reporters a few days later. "It was really us three that was the core group and were told that we were going to be [there] for a pretty long time and we really want to build around [you guys]. I understand that things change and plans change. I guess that Sam and the rest of those guys thought that to move me was the best move. That's on them and it is what it is."

Later that week, Carter-Williams's agent, Jeff Schwartz, issued a directive inside the office of his agency, Excel Sports Management. "He told all his colleagues and employees that there'd be no more dealing with Hinkie or the Sixers," a longtime basketball executive said. Schwartz, one of the league's most prominent and powerful agents, typically represents around thirty players at a time and his firm usually represents around 25 percent of the league.

Hinkie's view was that all this would be mended when the Sixers eventually took that next step. Maybe Schwartz could enforce his Sixers ban with his lower-level clients, but if the day ever came where Hinkie was offering one of his players a max contract, would Schwartz or any other agent really be able to block a deal—and be willing to reject a possible commission—because of an old grudge?

"It wasn't that Sam didn't know how to act," said a former Sixers colleague. "It was that he was making business calculations and had different priorities."

Hinkie didn't feel the need to kowtow to agents, and he certainly wasn't going to put those relationships before his chase for high-level assets, like a potential top-10 pick. Unlike many of his peers, he had no line. It didn't matter if he was chasing an All-Star, a lottery choice, or the chance at a future second-rounder. In his view the job was black and white, and he had trouble seeing the ways in which carrying this mentality was laying the foundation for his process to be cut short.

It wasn't just the players and their representatives whom Hinkie was alienating. Executives with other teams grew frustrated with his lowball proposals. "He was always throwing out the worst fucking offers," one opposing general manager said. His propensity for taking hours to respond to calls and texts in the middle of negotiations frustrated everyone. Opposing owners noticed all the open seats in their arenas whenever the Sixers came to town and worried that Hinkie's strategy was hurting business. "It's not complicated," said Milwaukee Bucks co-owner Marc Lasry. "No one likes coming to see a horrible team." Over the summer, at the behest of the rest of the league's GMs and in response to Hinkie's plan, the NBA nearly flattened the draft lottery odds so as to not reward teams for losing (the potential change was surprisingly and narrowly shot down in an October vote among NBA GMs).

Worse, in the wake of their draft night decision to send the Sixers Šarić and a first-round pick for the rights to Elfrid Payton, the Orlando Magic began telling colleagues that Hinkie had only managed to fleece them because he had a friend inside Orlando's offices passing along inside info. The allegation was never substantiated, nor, for that matter, did it explain why Magic general manager Rob Hennigan felt the need to part with *two* extra draft picks to get Payton. Even if there was a man on the inside, he had no power to force Hennigan into agreeing to a trade.

Around the same time, the Pelicans issued an accusation of their own: The Sixers, they said, had not fully disclosed Jrue Holiday's injury history prior to the two teams' 2013 draft night deal.[4] Holiday had suffered a stress fracture in February 2014, about seven months after being traded. That he had undergone a physical with Pelicans doctors

---

4 The accusation would make it into the press in June 2015. Contrary to reports of a $3 million fine from the NBA, the two sides settled for an amount closer to $1 million.

before the trade, or that the injury the Sixers were accused of not disclosing had never prevented him from playing and had nothing to do with the stress fracture, was beside the point. None of it prevented Pelicans general manager Dell Demps from lamenting to colleagues how Hinkie had lied to him. All that mattered was how the accusations fit with the image so many around the NBA had of Hinkie.

Everyone—agents, opposing owners, opposing executives—began excoriating Hinkie and the Sixers to reporters. A narrative began to form, one that Hinkie declined to push back on. Contrary to popular belief, he was more than happy to chat with reporters on background, but rarely offered on-the-record opinions.[5] He didn't see the value and was worried about doing the very thing he was often accused of—celebrating himself and his methods while running a last-place team.

"[Hinkie] is the biggest fraud I have ever encountered during my 40 years in sports media," wrote Angelo Cataldi, one of Philadelphia's most prominent sports broadcasters, in a column on the website PhillyVoice. "He is a charlatan, a snake-oil salesman. He is the Pied Piper of the young and the naïve, people who are not savvy enough to spot the con."

This, in turn, triggered aggressive responses among his supporters, both inside and outside the league, and it all coincided with a point where sports were suddenly being consumed from the perspective of management, with fans and media members pretending to be GMs and viewing players as "assets" that are bought and sold. Hinkie was now the face of this. Suddenly, he represented something greater than the Sixers, whether he wanted to or not. To detractors he represented everything that was wrong with the data-over-people modern GM. To his supporters, he was a revolutionary leading the army of progress onto the beaches of an anachronistic NBA. Hinkie never claimed such a role. But that didn't stop the rest of his detractors—both inside the

---

5 The one anecdote he would share with reporters on the record? That his favorite author is Robert Caro, the Pulitzer Prize–winning journalist who spent decades working on biographies of Robert Moses and Lyndon B. Johnson. (No one ever accused Sam Hinkie of being subtle.)

league and out—from projecting it onto him so that they could pick it apart.

"Tanking wasn't unique, but he went further than anyone else and the people tried to make it sound like he was reinventing the wheel," one GM said. "That was one of the reasons he was met with so much resistance. All that stuff poisoned the public well."

The losses piled up as the season inched along. Ownership, previously in Hinkie's corner but now hearing the noise from friends and the media, began pushing him for a timeline. "But Sam didn't believe in setting dates like that," a colleague said. "There was a plan on where we were going and how we were going to get there, but Sam knew it needed to be flexible so that you can properly react when things don't go your way."

The pressure was starting to build. Hinkie, Gupta, and Falk thought about ways to explain their vision, and Hinkie presented all the progress he believed the Sixers had made. Nerlens Noel had returned to the floor and made the NBA's All-Rookie team after nearly averaging a double double and flashing some advanced defensive skills. Joel Embiid's fractured foot was healing well. Dario Šarić was a year closer to coming over. They'd added three first-round picks and six second-rounders to their war chest and, after finishing the season on a 10-game losing streak to fall to 18–64, the league's third-worst record, would once again be drafting in the lottery.

"They tell us every game, every day, 'Trust The Process,'" guard Tony Wroten told *ESPN The Magazine*'s Pablo Torre in January 2015. Hinkie never publicly deployed the phrase, but it would become a rallying cry around the Sixers and their faithful. No phrase better represented Hinkie's vision or the war he was now fighting.

Chapter 10

LOST UNICORNS

A crowd of around 150 NBA scouts, executives, and coaches piled into the Impact Basketball training facility in Las Vegas, about five miles south of the Strip. The 2015 draft was just two weeks away and ASM Sports, one of the world's most prominent basketball agencies, had chosen the gym to host a "pro day" for its prospects. Ostensibly, the NBA people were there to watch a handful of NBA hopefuls, but that wasn't exactly true. There was only one player whom everyone in the league was yearning to see: Kristaps Porzingis.

Porzingis, a 7-foot-3, nineteen-year-old Latvian, had spent the previous two seasons playing in Spain's Liga ACB, widely considered the second-best league in the world. He'd held his own against the older and more seasoned competition and his talent tantalized evaluators everywhere. He was huge and could dribble and run the floor and shoot. A series of rule changes (the prohibiting of hand-checking ball handlers and, as a counter to the increased reliance on one-on-one play, the permitting of zone defenses) instituted by the NBA to loosen up the game was slowly relegating traditional centers to the sidelines. The days of plodding seven-footers running the show from the paint were no more. The game had evolved. It was quicker. Space on the court was a priority. Three-pointers were all the rage.

From here, a new type of style was emerging, that of "positionless" basketball. What if, instead of having one guy who could dribble and another who could shoot and a third who could block shots, you ignored traditional positions and just put your five best players on the court? GMs were slowly recognizing that this was the most effective way to go about building a team, and in this ecosystem there was nothing more rare, and therefore more valuable, than a big man who could both protect the rim on one end and spread the floor on the other.

Porzingis, some evaluators believed, could be exactly that, and this would be the lone chance for most teams to scout him on American soil prior to the draft. Typically, prospects spend the weeks leading up to that night crisscrossing the country, auditioning for teams on their turf. Andy Miller, the president of ASM Sports, had a different idea, a way to seize control of the draft process and attempt to dictate where Porzingis landed. Only a handful of teams were shown Porzingis's medical report and buyout terms (he was still under contract with Baloncesto Sevilla). Only one team (the Portland Trail Blazers) had been granted an interview. Only one (the Los Angeles Lakers, who owned the No. 2 pick) had been granted a private workout. The rest were forced to come watch him that June day in Vegas, in a setting that Miller and Porzingis's trainers could control.

The workout lasted fifty minutes. Porzingis dazzled. His movement was fluid. His dunks were explosive. His jumper was smooth. Magic general manager Rob Hennigan, who had tried convincing Porzingis to enter the draft the previous season and was desperate for him fall to Orlando at No. 5, left the workout dismayed.

"He won't get past No. 4," he told friends.

One of the teams selecting before the Magic was the Philadelphia 76ers. Sam Hinkie was present for the performance and, like almost everyone sitting in the gym, was enamored with Porzingis's skills. But he also wanted to know more. He'd hoped for a meeting with Porzingis while in Vegas. Miller demurred. Hinkie, though, could be relentless, and few areas energized him as much as attempting to dig for every morsel of information during the lead-up to the draft. He waited for nearly every team employee to clear the gym, then approached Miller in the lobby.

"You said that I would get a meeting with him here," Hinkie said.

"I said, 'I'd try,' and it's not going to work out, Sam," Miller responded.

Miller didn't think the Sixers would be a good home for Porzingis. As the agent for Nerlens Noel, he'd seen firsthand how the Sixers handled their young players. "He thought the place was a mess and didn't like how Sam did business," said a former colleague. He also remained bitter about Hinkie's attempt two years earlier to sign Khalif Wyatt, an undrafted player represented by one of Miller's youngest agents, to one of his nonguaranteed, four-year deals (a Hinkie Special). He felt Hinkie was taking advantage of a novice. But there were practical reasons for Miller to keep Porzingis out of Philadelphia, too. The Sixers already had two young big men on the roster. Adding one more would have meant a crowd and likely left one of his clients riding the bench. Miller's hope was that the Knicks would nab Porzingis at No. 4. If the Knicks passed, Miller figured the Magic would pounce.

Hinkie was the wild card, the person capable of derailing the plan. Miller wanted to keep the Sixers from drafting Porzingis *and* from trading the pick to a team looking to leapfrog the Knicks. Had he and Hinkie shared a strong relationship, he might have considered having an honest conversation. Instead, he devised a different plan.

Hinkie returned to Philadelphia that weekend. He asked Miller if Porzingis could come by the team's facility. Miller agreed, then canceled the night before. Like all prospects, Porzingis arrived in New York a few days before the draft. Hinkie asked for an interview. Miller said yes, then canceled at the last minute. Hinkie, aware he was being given the runaround, offered to send a van up to New York on Wednesday, the day before the draft, to drive Porzingis to and from Philadelphia. "Sure," Miller responded. He couldn't say no without tipping his hand. That morning, he called Hinkie and told him that Porzingis had food poisoning. Hinkie asked if he could send some representatives up to New York. Miller said okay, but that he couldn't make any promises. That day, some Sixers staffers took a Cadillac SUV and met Porzingis at a photo shoot for the website Athletes Quarterly. Inside the studio, while standing outside the bathroom door, they heard what sounded like a person throwing up. They returned to Philly empty-handed. Hinkie told Miller he could rent out a gym near the hotel the following morning. "Let me see how he feels in the morning," Miller responded, before rejecting the idea the next day.

On draft night, Hinkie huddled in his office alongside his top advisers, members of ownership, and Brett Brown. As expected, the Minnesota Timberwolves selected Kentucky big man Karl-Anthony Towns first overall. Next up was the Los Angeles Lakers, who had spent the week debating two players: Ohio State point guard D'Angelo Russell and Duke center Jahlil Okafor.

Five years earlier, Okafor would have been the easy call. He'd been named National Player of the Year as a high school senior and led Duke to a national championship while becoming the first freshman to be named Atlantic Coast Conference Player of the Year. He was massive—nearly 6-foot-11 and about 275 pounds—with huge hands, deft feet, a soft touch, and a full arsenal of low-post moves.

But he was also slow, and uninterested in defense, and he rarely passed the ball. He'd entered Duke in 2015 as the projected 2015 No. 1 pick; by late March he'd been passed on most draft boards by the more nimble and well-rounded Towns.

Hinkie, like many others, recognized all of Okafor's flaws. He knew that the new rules allowing zone defenses would make him easy to defend and that when opponents had the ball he'd be too slow to keep up. Some of the intelligence compiled on Okafor—such as his problems picking up new plays—was concerning, too. Russell, on the other hand, was a player he believed to be a perfect fit for his young roster—a savvy, sweet-shooting floor general who could grow along-side his two young big men and aid their development.

Earlier that month, the Lakers were leaning in that direction. That changed as the draft approached. They went with Russell at No. 2. The Sixers were up. Porzingis was interesting, but they were wary of his pencil legs, poor rebounding numbers, and propensity for fouling out of games. Hinkie didn't mind that he'd never interviewed him. (Okafor, on the advice of his agent, Bill Duffy, had also refused to meet with the Sixers. "Bill thought the whole thing was a disaster and didn't want his guys anywhere near it," said an associate.) But Hinkie's draft strategy was all about finding value. Reaching for a player like Porzingis, or Emmanuel Mudiay, the next best point guard on the board, would be antithetical to this approach.

Hinkie, as always, worked the phones, but found no compelling offers for the pick. If anything, he believed, Okafor would have more trade value after spending a year putting up numbers, just like Michael Carter-Williams had. From here, the decision was easy. The goal was to accumulate as many assets as possible. It didn't matter that Okafor played the same position as two of the Sixers' previous lottery picks. Hinkie believed drafting was more like blackjack than anything else, and he was playing the odds, and chances were slim that all three of his picks would hit. "And if they turn into modern versions of Tim Duncan, Ben Wallace, and Hakeem Olajuwon," he'd joke to colleagues, "then that's a good problem for us to have to figure out."[1]

Hinkie talked through the possibilities and risks with his staff, then notified the league that Okafor was the pick. There was no eruption of applause in his office, no celebratory high-fives. The Knicks took Porzingis at No. 4. Fans in attendance at the Barclays Center booed. ESPN's cameras caught one kid wearing a Knicks jersey crying. The pick was widely criticized, but within months Porzingis would establish himself as one of the game's premier young talents.[2] "He can shoot, he can make the right plays, he can defend, he's a seven-footer that can shoot all the way out to the three-point line. That's rare," future Hall of Famer Kevin Durant would say of Porzingis in January. "That's like a unicorn in this league." The label would stick. And while Miller's runaround hadn't discouraged Hinkie from taking Porzingis, it did restrict his ability to fully scout him. Hinkie had made a point of entering every decision with as much data from as many different sources as possible, and for good reason. To him, every workout,

---

1   The counter to this would be to wonder whether Duncan, Olajuwon, and Wallace would have all become All-Stars if they'd been forced to split practice and game minutes with one another.

2   Not the first time Knicks fans have looked foolish, and certainly won't be the last.

every conversation represented a data point. Accumulating more than anyone else was one of his goals. Perhaps one more entry would have nudged him toward Porzingis, preventing the chain of events that would keep him from seeing his process through.

The 2015–2016 season started in a familiar way for the Sixers: with lots and lots of losing. They dropped their first 18 games,[3] tying the mark for most losses to begin an NBA season (it was also the third consecutive year they had lost at least 17 in a row). The next game was a Tuesday at home against the 2–14 Los Angeles Lakers, a gift from the schedule gods. The players were all aware what one more loss would mean. "It was on Twitter, *SportsCenter*, everywhere," said Nik Stauskas, a guard the Sixers traded for in July. "That's when it all really hit us. It was like, 'Are we really that bad?' None of us wanted to be in the record books."

A sea of Lakers purple and gold greeted Stauskas and his teammates that night. Two days before, the thirty-seven-year-old Kobe Bryant had announced that he'd be retiring at the end of the season. This would be his last game in Philadelphia, one of the cities he grew up in, and it was sold out. Bryant buried three of his first four shots, all three-pointers, each bucket met with raucous cheers. The Sixers battled, though, and pulled out a 103–91 win. The players were buoyant in the locker room afterward. "Guys were smiling and having fun for the first time all year," Stauskas said.

The good vibes wouldn't last long.

The Sixers lost their next 12 games, falling to 1–30, the worst 30-game start to a season in NBA history. "The effort was there, we just had a lot of guys who were fringe NBA players," Stauskas said. "I think having so many guys on the brink, it wasn't the best thing for us. It's just basic human nature that guys are going to look to score and showcase themselves instead of playing the right way."

---

3   This, after losing their final 10 games the previous season.

By this point, all the losing, and all the noise surrounding the losing, had become routine. Shunned agents and irked opposing owners, irritated by how the Sixers were draining the league's bottom line, continued lobbying Sixers managing partner Josh Harris to move on from Hinkie. Some fans and members of the media shook their fists. Others—represented by the hosts of the *Rights to Ricky Sanchez* podcast and its boisterous following—vociferously defended Hinkie. They threw parties and made T-shirts in his honor. They adopted *Trust The Process* as a rallying cry.

Due to stress, Hinkie lost twenty pounds between November and January.

"This is serious for our fans, for our staff, for our players," he told ESPN's Zach Lowe during a rare and extensive interview that April. "You want to perform. You want to meet expectations. You want to play well. You want to tamp down all the noise that comes with a record or a streak or those kinds of things because those are not productive to some larger mission."

Most detrimental were the hits delivered off the floor. They started in June, twelve days before the draft, in the Los Angeles office of Dr. Richard Ferkel, Embiid's orthopedist. Embiid had recently started scrimmaging after missing his entire rookie season due to a stress fracture in his right foot. There were three-on-three games with teammates in Philadelphia where he "literally almost ran all our bigs out of the gym," Sixers forward Robert Covington recalled. "It was the first time I'd seen him, and for him to dominate like that, it was like, 'Well, damn.'" There were pickup games with a group of NBA veterans in Santa Monica. "You could see that he was going to be a superstar," Jamal Crawford, one of those vets, said. It had been a grueling year for the Sixers. Embiid's impending return represented a much-needed sign of hope.

The checkup was supposed to be routine. All five previous MRIs had shown Embiid's foot healing nicely. Then Ferkel looked at the results of the CAT scan. There was a problem. The fracture in Embiid's navicular bone had widened. A new screw would need to be put in, meaning Embiid would once again be forced under the knife, only this time the surgery would be more complex.

Ferkel called the Sixers. He shared the update with Embiid. The news devastated him. It was determined that weak bones were mostly to blame, but some within the Sixers organization believed Embiid's refusal to wear a walking boot during his rehab had caused the setback. The Sixers, who preferred to keep their injury updates vague, issued a statement: "A standard CT scan on Joel's right foot revealed less healing than anticipated." Embiid flew to New York for a series of follow-up tests at the Hospital for Special Surgery. In August, two screws in his foot were replaced and a bone graft, using bone from his hip, was performed. Embiid was ruled out for another season.

———

Embiid's injury meant Okafor would open the season as the team's starting center. He was impressive early on, racking up 26 points and seven rebounds in his NBA debut and scoring 20 or more points in five of his first eight games.

But there were problems bubbling beneath the surface.

"I was in a dark place," he would say years later.

It all traced back to his childhood. One day, when he was just nine years old, Okafor was sitting in the living room of his Oklahoma home watching music videos on BET when his mother started coughing. He laughed. Dacresha Benton—"Dee" to family and friends—was always joking around. Benton gasped for air. Okafor laughed again. Two weeks earlier Benton, twenty-nine, had been diagnosed with bronchitis. Okafor thought it was funny how she was mocking herself. He figured he'd tease her back.

"I'm going to take your Oreos," he said, knowing Benton hated when he raided the family's snacks. He left for the kitchen, waiting for Benton to break character and tell him no. She kept wheezing, each breath more shallow and labored and painful than the one before. Okafor realized something was wrong. The family's phone was broken. He and his half sister sprinted to a neighbor's house to dial 911.

The ambulance arrived. Paramedics ripped open Benton's shirt and applied CPR. She was whisked to the closest hospital. Sad and scared, Okafor sat in the waiting room alongside his sister, aunt, and grandmother, waiting for news. A doctor emerged. One of Benton's lungs had collapsed. She was dead.

"It happened right in front of me," Okafor would tell a reporter from *Chicago* magazine eight years later. "I've put myself in her shoes, thinking about what she must have been thinking: I'm suffering and he's just looking at me, laughing."

Okafor was asked in that interview if he had stopped blaming himself.

"Yeah," Okafor initially replied. "But even now I still have to think, What if I could have known right off the bat that she wasn't playing? She would still be here."

Okafor's parents were separated at the time, with his dad, Chukwudi "Chucky" Okafor, having moved back to his native Chicago. After Benton's death, Jahlil went with him. Chucky had also grown up without a mother; his died of breast cancer when he was just eighteen months old, leaving his father, a Nigerian immigrant, alone on Chicago's South Side with six kids. He often worked three jobs at once, and Chucky took advantage. He brawled. He helped steal cars. He attended five high schools in three years. He also grew to be 6-foot-5, and could have perhaps fulfilled his dream of playing basketball professionally had he not been kicked off numerous teams—high school and college—for various transgressions. He wound up playing for a junior college on the Arkansas-Oklahoma border, where he fell in love with a 6-foot-2 former high school basketball star. He and Dee raised Jahlil, along with Dee's daughter from a previous relationship, in the tiny town of Moffett (population in 2005: 222), where Dee's mother lived.

Basketball had always been part of Jahlil's life. As a toddler he'd dunk on a rim made from a coat hanger that Chucky attached to a door. As a kid he received a new bedroom basketball hoop every year on his birthday. He loved the game, and, following Benton's death, Jahlil and Chucky devoted all they had to fulfilling their NBA dreams. Chucky had Jahlil run in weighted shoes. He taught Jahlil how to shoot with both hands. The two of them spent countless hours playing one-on-one. As an eighth grader, Jahlil, by then 6-foot-8, caught the eye of DePaul's basketball coach, Tracy Webster, who offered him a scholarship. The spotlight was now shining on him. He was accepted into Whitney Young, a prestigious, highly selective magnet high school, and within a couple of years had shot up to 6-foot-11 and climbed to the top of nearly every high school ranking of players. The more prominent colleges came calling. Okafor chose Duke.

Everything was going according to plan. But every now and then Okafor would hint at his internal demons.

"My deepest fear is losing someone else close to me," Okafor told *Chicago* magazine during his senior year of high school. "That's something I think about way more than I should. I'll be in my room thinking, What if my dad's not here? Or, if I'm driving: What if I lose my aunt? What if I lose my sister?" Everything he was doing, he told friends, was about trying to make his mom proud, but he worried about basketball defining him. He softened his deep voice so as to not intimidate people and lamented to Jay Rehak, his teacher in a senior-year TV production class, how all his classmates' scripts cast him as an athlete. "I'm more than just a basketball player," he told him. The fame that came along with being the top basketball prospect in the country overwhelmed him. He once failed to turn in an assignment Rehak had sent via email. "I didn't see it," he told Rehak afterward. Rehak asked how that was possible. "I can't check my school email account," Okafor replied. His rising fame had caused his inbox to be flooded with messages.

He managed to keep most of these fears and feelings bottled up in high school and during his lone season at Duke. Doing so while in the NBA would be a new and more difficult challenge.

On a Saturday night in early October, a few hours after completing training camp and with the Sixers' preseason opener three nights away, Okafor went out drinking in the Old City neighborhood of Philadelphia. This was a new habit for him. "Alcohol was never something we ever had an issue with," said Dr. Joyce Kenner, the principal at Whitney Young. He was just nineteen, but his size and fame granted him entry into most clubs and bars.

At around 2 a.m., Okafor and a friend were walking near the corner of 2nd Street and Walnut when they passed two men sitting in a parked Chevrolet Camaro. The window on the driver's side was open. The man and Okafor yelled at each other. Okafor tried punching the driver through the open window. The driver and passenger leapt out of the car. The passenger knocked Okafor to the ground and pulled out a gun. He pointed it at Okafor's head. "Look at me," he said.

U.S. Park Rangers, who patrol nearby Independence Hall, spotted the commotion. The gunman tossed his weapon—a 9mm was recovered by authorities the next day—and ducked into a garage at the nearby Sheraton Philadelphia Society Hill Hotel. The driver climbed back into his car and fled. Both men got away.

Officers returned to the scene to collect statements from Okafor and his friend. They were gone. "It appears to me that [Okafor] was intoxicated," a ranger wrote later in his report. "I observed two other males keep him stable several times."

A few days later, a ranger, unaware that the team didn't practice at Wells Fargo Center, showed up at the arena in uniform looking for Okafor. Authorities were still searching for the gunman and the ranger wanted to know if Okafor had any details that could help. A message was passed along to Lara Price, the team's executive vice president of business operations. Price called Hinkie and then Lance Williams, a former government agent serving as the Sixers' director of security. "There's an officer here in uniform looking for Jahlil," she told him. Williams met them inside. The ranger shared the details: The intoxication. The fight. The gun. He also told Williams that this wasn't the first time he'd seen a seemingly drunk Okafor stumbling around the area. Concerned for Okafor and furious at Hinkie for ignoring previous warning signs, and for what he considered to be his gross and dangerous propensity for treating players as assets, Williams dialed up his boss.

"Sam," he said, "you need to speak to Jahlil. He could have been killed."

The incident was kept quiet for nearly two months. Okafor continued playing. Hinkie spoke with him a few times. Others did as well, but Okafor kept drinking, and often with his dad. The night before

Thanksgiving, the Sixers, 0–15 at the time, traveled to Boston. They led for most of the game, and pushed the lead to 11 with less than seven minutes remaining. The Celtics fought back, but with 2:51 left in the game Okafor converted a three-point play, giving the Sixers a five-point lead. That elusive first win was within their grasp. But the Celtics wouldn't go away. The Sixers turned the ball over. They tossed up contested shots. With 39 seconds left, the Celtics took a two-point lead on a Jae Crowder three-pointer. The Sixers put the ball in the hands of Phil Pressey, a 5-foot-11 guard who had gone undrafted two and a half years earlier and who, coming into the season, owned a career scoring average of 3.1 points per game. He missed an open look in the paint with three seconds left. The Celtics held on for the win.

"I remember just being upset because I thought we were about to get our first win," Okafor said. "And I just decided I'm going to go out that night."

Okafor and some friends walked out of a Boston nightclub around 2 a.m. The hood of his gray sweatshirt was pulled over his head. A small group of people congregated outside. "The Sixers suck!" one yelled. Okafor approached some women in the group and tried getting their phone numbers.[4] His advances were rebuffed. Arguing escalated into shouting. Okafor began slurring insults. "We got money, you broke-ass niggas," he yelled, and repeated, the words melding together. One man tried stepping in front of Okafor and guiding him to the side. Okafor knocked his hand away, then shoved a third man to the ground. A couple of men tried holding him back. Okafor began swinging his fists. Another man punched him in the back.

For a moment, tensions mellowed. Friends led Okafor down the street. Then more insults were lobbed at him. He turned around and fired back. "You broke-ass bitches!" he shouted repeatedly. The crowd around him swelled. "Monn-eeeey! Monn-eeeey!" he yelled while rubbing his fingers together. Onlookers taunted him even more. He darted out toward the street. "Wassup then!" he yelled while lunging

---

4   According to a statement provided to police the next day by an alleged victim.

after a man. "Wassup then!" He swung his right fist. There was more running. A person fell through a glass storefront. A woman screamed. Okafor jogged away.

"I don't remember a lot of it, because I was really intoxicated. And me being drunk, I wasn't in my right state of mind," Okafor would recall a few years later. "I remember being taunted—just random stuff I would hear all the time on the court. I just reacted differently."

That afternoon, while awaiting takeoff on the team plane, Okafor handed his cell phone to Lance Williams. "Duff wants to speak with you," he said, referring to his agent, Bill Duffy. Duffy told Williams that TMZ had contacted him—they had a video of Okafor fighting people on a Boston street. About four hours later, the Sixers landed in Houston. By then the video had gone viral and was plastered to the home screen of every sports and gossip website and playing on a loop on ESPN. "I messed up," Okafor texted Tyus Jones, a former Duke teammate and longtime friend. He went straight to his hotel room that night. Williams joined him soon after. He found Okafor crying. "It's going to be okay," Williams said. He asked him if he wanted to join the team downstairs for dinner. Okafor said no. They spent Thanksgiving night alone, eating room-service hamburgers, waiting for Chucky's flight to land.

The next day, Williams received a call from Jerome Pickett, an executive vice president and chief security officer for the NBA.

"He said the commissioner had called to ask how come one of our players is on TV fighting and nobody from the Sixers has called me," Williams said. Silver was furious. He knew the Sixers had been aware of how Okafor was spending his nights, and now it was clear nothing had been done. Episodes like these damaged the league's image. Of more concern was how they put Okafor in danger.

The TMZ video opened the floodgates. On November 27, CSN Philadelphia broke the news of the gun incident. Three days later, the *Philadelphia Inquirer* reported that Okafor had also been issued a ticket in October for driving his Maybach 108 miles per hour—63 miles per hour over the speed limit—while crossing the Ben Franklin Bridge. Hinkie's detractors, now armed with even more ammo, were able to claim the moral high ground. The team was a circus! All that losing had poisoned the environment! A veteran mentor could have protected Okafor! Hinkie viewed players as assets, not people! The last one in particular stung Hinkie, but, true to form, he kept his views to himself. Some supporters spoke up on his behalf. "Saying that people wouldn't get in trouble if there were some veterans around, that's just crazy," Spike Eskin said during an episode of *The Rights to Ricky Sanchez* that week. "You just can't make up an excuse and use it for everything." But even Hinkie's staunchest backers could sense that the narrative had taken on a life of its own. It had permeated every corner of the NBA universe, and even reached some corners some outside the sporting world, but most important, it had reached Harris's ears.

A few days later, Harris enlisted the law firm Mintz Levin, which he'd worked with in the past, to depose Hinkie; Brown; Brandon Williams, a team executive; Lance Williams; and Allen Lumpkin, the team's longtime director of basketball operations. The deposition questions were straightforward: The men were asked about the Okafor incident, and about Embiid's blowups the previous season, and everything else swirling around the organization. They were asked about protocols and systems. They were asked who knew what, and when, and what each person did with that information. The answers were passed on to Harris. Big changes were on the horizon.

Chapter 11

THE COUP

One evening in the fall of 2015, Scott O'Neil, the cocksure CEO of the 76ers, walked into an upscale San Francisco seafood restaurant overlooking the bay. His dark hair was slicked back, as always, and he carried with him pitch material: customized Sixers jerseys with the StubHub logo stitched to the top and pictures illustrating how the logo would pop on TV.

For years, O'Neil had pushed the NBA to relax its restriction on jersey sponsorships. He believed it to be an untapped revenue source. The NBA, like many major men's American professional sports leagues, had long rejected such proposals, out of fear of offending traditionalists, but O'Neil knew that would soon change and desperately wanted to be first. He called his friend Scott Cutler, the recently hired president of StubHub. Cutler was intrigued. Soon after, O'Neil, Chris Heck, his longtime friend and the Sixers' chief revenue officer, and Jake Reynolds, his brother-in-law and the Sixers' vice president of sales and service, were boarding a flight to San Francisco.

At dinner that night, O'Neil pitched Cutler on his vision. He illustrated how he had taken over the Sixers a few years earlier and "how the Sixers had to take things down to the studs to rebuild it back up," Cutler recalled. O'Neil explained how the Sixers were accumulating draft picks and building around promising young players. He described how they were selling this strategy to their fan base. Any concerns Cutler might have had about attaching his company to a team that had become synonymous with losing were quickly dispelled. Changes governing the rules on jersey sponsorships, O'Neil pointed out, wouldn't be instituted until the 2017–2018 season.

"By that time," he told Cutler, "we think we're going to have one of the most exciting teams in the league."

The pitch and its timeline was never run by Hinkie. He might not have known it, but his time with the Sixers was coming to an end.

The relationship between O'Neil and Hinkie was tenuous from the start. Hinkie preferred to keep his inner circle tight. O'Neil, meanwhile, held aspirations of being more than just a marketing guru. "He wanted to be the guy that could run both basketball and the business side," said a well-connected NBA insider. In his previous job, as president of Madison Square Garden Sports, he helped draw up the Knicks' 2010 free agency pitches to LeBron James, Dwyane Wade, and Chris Bosh (which were unsuccessful), and a year later pushed MSG chairman James Dolan to trade for Carmelo Anthony. He was comfortable enough around the basketball side that he could often be found on the practice court in shorts and a T-shirt, "kicking the shit, fouling and knocking the hell out of some of our players," said Donnie Walsh, the Knicks' president of basketball operations from 2008 to 2011.

O'Neil broke into the business the early 1990s, as a marketing assistant for the New Jersey Nets. He was around twenty-four at the time and a few months into the job when Jon Spoelstra, the Nets' president,[1] spotted him trying to repair a paper jam in a Xerox machine.

"Why are you fixing that?" Spoelstra asked.

"Because it's broken," O'Neil responded.

Spoelstra called O'Neil into his office. O'Neil thought he was getting fired.

---

1 And, yes, father of the future Miami Heat head coach.

"You ever sell sponsorships?" Spoelstra asked. The Nets were a dull team playing in an insipid arena planted on top of a Jersey swamp. "The sponsorship staff was beaten down from all that failure," Spoelstra recalled. He had noticed O'Neil, who'd recently graduated from Villanova University with a marketing degree, around the office.

"I needed someone who had some chutzpah," Spoelstra said.

He promoted O'Neil, giving him an office and additional responsibility, but O'Neil craved more. "I wanted to be the boss since I was three years old," he once told *The Villanovan*. He took a job with the NFL's Philadelphia Eagles in 1994, then received an MBA from Harvard Business School, then returned to the Eagles, then linked up with a nascent apparel company called AND1 before joining the NBA and climbing to senior vice president of marketing and business operations. He developed a reputation for being "intelligent, intense, and curious," said Peter Feigin, the president of the Milwaukee Bucks and former vice president of marketing and business development for MSG Sports. "He has the ability to be abrasive at times, but he's all about growth. When Scott has a project he puts his own time and demands results on it, which are above and beyond what a normal person would do, and his expectation is things will be done extremely well and focused. He keeps that intensity and expects it from everyone around him."

MSG hired O'Neil in 2008 to help the company rehabilitate in the wake of a $11.5 million sexual harassment and discrimination lawsuit brought against them and former GM and coach Isiah Thomas. O'Neil secured million-dollar deals with marquee brands like JPMorgan Chase, Delta Airlines, and Coca-Cola before clashing with the temperamental Dolan and leaving in 2012. A year later the Sixers hired him to replace co-owner Adam Aron as CEO.

"One of Scott's mantras back then was, 'Make sure you're ready for when you do have that 50-win team,'" said Fred Whitfield, a longtime friend of O'Neil's and the chief operating officer, team president, and a minority owner of the Charlotte Hornets. "When you're running business operations in the NBA, you don't really have control over what happens on the court, but your goal should be to get your stuff in a position so that when you do have a 50-win team, you're able to maximize every opportunity that comes with it."

O'Neil froze ticket prices. He bolstered the sales staff, making it one of the largest, and youngest, in the NBA. "He invested in a ton of human capital to get through the tough times," Feigin said. The group adored O'Neil, who emphasized culture, community service, and work-life balance. His staff was tireless, energetic, and creative. Sales of season ticket packages were celebrated in the office with a ringing of a bell and a quick dance party. The sales staff would vote on all sorts of awards, and then pass around totems like a Brett Brown–signed hard hat and championship belt.

Recognizing the difficulty of marketing a last-place team, the group got creative. Season ticket holders were invited to meet-and-greets, with both players and Brown. On-court experiences, like high-fiving players as they came out of the tunnel, were dangled. The tactics helped the Sixers increase their season ticket sales from around 4,600 during the 2013–2014 season to 7,100 in 2015–2016, with a 90 percent renewal rate. O'Neil put himself on the front lines of the battle. Whitfield recalled coming to Philadelphia for games and accompanying O'Neil on visits to some Wells Fargo Center suites. "The fans there weren't very pleasant," Whitfield said. "They were really saying nasty things about what was going on and how painful it was to continue spending well-earned dollars on a losing product." O'Neil would channel Hinkie. "Be patient with this," he'd say. "We do have a plan in place and we're going to turn the corner." But behind the scenes his patience was wearing thin.

Forbes had ranked the Sixers one of the least valuable teams in the NBA. They averaged a measly 13,940 fans per game in 2014–2015, the league's lowest mark, and just 14,881 the following season, the NBA's third-worst figure. And the TV ratings were even worse: an average of 23,000 viewers per game during 2014–2015, a number more suited for a late-night infomercial than an NBA game. O'Neil's job was getting more difficult and he was growing frustrated by Hinkie's insistence on keeping him at arm's length.

In February 2015, O'Neil was ready to launch a new marketing campaign. The tagline *This Starts Now* would replace the current slogan of *Together We Build.* The words would be splayed across a photograph of three of the team's lottery picks: Nerlens Noel, Joel Embiid, and Michael Carter-Williams. The campaign was introduced on the afternoon of February 17. Two days later, Hinkie traded Carter-Williams to the Milwaukee Bucks for a future first-round pick. O'Neil was embarrassed. Furious too. Whatever semblance of a relationship that had once existed between him and Hinkie was now broken. O'Neil began voicing his displeasure—to Harris, but also to the NBA. He'd known Adam Silver for years, both from his time in the league office and as part of a small group of team executives (called the Team Advisory Committee) who reported to the NBA's Board of Governors. He also left Hinkie out of his pitches to potential business partners, never even mentioning his name.

"Sam did it to himself," O'Neil said. "Someone had to take the hit."[2]

On December 7, 2015, the press was told to show up early for that night's game against the Spurs. No other information was shared. They congregated in an interview room at the Wells Fargo Center and noticed three microphones set up. One was assumed to be for Sam Hinkie, another for Josh Harris. The group began guessing who the third person could be. Some assumed it was Brett Brown. Others thought that perhaps Jahlil Okafor, who'd been at the center of a number of recent off-court incidents, would be speaking.

At around 5:30, Harris and Hinkie walked in. They were flanked by an older man. He was tall. He wore a big championship ring on his right hand and had a face that exuded old-school authority. Some in the room recognized him from the decades he'd spent in and around the NBA.

---

2   O'Neil never did agree to an interview for this book. I did, however, introduce myself to him in October 2018 outside the visitors' locker room in Detroit. I told him I was writing a book on The Process and that I found it funny he had sort of become the bogeyman to Hinkie loyalists. His response was the quote above. The words "off the record" were never muttered and I had clearly identified myself as a reporter.

"We are pleased to announce Jerry Colangelo as chairman of basket-ball operations and special adviser to the 76ers," Harris said, reading a prepared statement in his typical drawl. Hinkie and Colangelo sat on either side of him.

"This season, to date, has not been easy for us and even more diffi-cult than we anticipated," Harris added. "Our situation necessitated a review to make our organization better."

Harris had been drowning under the complaints for months, from O'Neil, who wanted a more linear path, and from others through-out the league as well, and he began pushing Hinkie for markers of progress. Hinkie and his staff, feeling the walls closing in, tried devising more effective ways to present the steps they believed they had taken. They had two young lottery centers on the court (Nerlens Noel and Jahlil Okafor) and tons of draft picks and Dario Šarić was a year closer to joining the team and Joel Embiid's health was improving and thanks to all the losses another lottery pick was on the way. It would soon all be visible and evident. They just needed to remain patient.

But the Okafor saga—the drunken videos, the reports of reckless and dangerous behavior, most of all the ensuing bad press—had moved Harris out of Hinkie's corner. It didn't matter that Hinkie was running a private-equity-like playbook—take over a distressed asset; tear every-thing down—or that he was doing exactly what he'd told Harris he would. Harris wasn't used to his business being in the papers every day. "We own this chemical company that was $50 billion, but nobody cares about the price of propylene," he once said. "But the Sixers starting lineup, everyone has an opinion." He didn't like the constant criticism, or the way the narrative had seemed to permanently turn. Less than three years earlier Sixers fans had showered him with cheers at the press conference introducing Andrew Bynum. He missed that feeling.

He'd asked Hinkie to address some of the public concerns. Hinkie never did. Harris knew that Silver, who had expressed his displeasure with tanking both privately and publicly, was eager for the Sixers to make a change. He asked for help.

Silver was delighted. He suggested a few names. One was Rod

Thorn, a septuagenarian NBA lifer who served as Sixers president under Harris from 2011 to 2013 before leaving to become the NBA's president of basketball operations. Another was Colangelo.

Colangelo, seventy-six at the time, was as revered and respected as anyone around the NBA. He'd climbed from the working-class Hungry Hill neighborhood of Chicago Heights—where he grew up in a house built by his Italian immigrant grandfather two doors down from a saloon—to Phoenix Suns general manager, a position he earned at the age of twenty-eight. He held that job until 1987 when, as part of a group of investors, he purchased the team for $44.5 million. He was the kind of executive who, in the 1990s, told assistant coaches that "my word" was as binding as an actual contract and would fly his players, coaches, and every member of their families to Hawaii for postseason vacations. He was a member of the Basketball Hall of Fame, a four-time NBA Executive of the Year, a Phoenix luminary with hands in nearly every one of the city's professional sports teams—"Jerry is the primary arbiter of what goes on downtown," former Phoenix mayor Terry Goddard once said—who had since taken over and revitalized the USA Basketball program. He had relationships in every corner of the league office and all across the NBA, from agents to team executives to the media, and enjoyed nurturing them. From this standpoint, he was the antithesis of Hinkie.

At home in Phoenix in late fall, Colangelo received a call from Silver. He wanted to know if Colangelo would be open to speaking with Harris. Colangelo didn't know him, but he loved team building, relished challenges, and, as others around the NBA have put it, was never one to turn down an opportunity to be labeled a savior. Colangelo told Silver to pass along his number. Around the beginning of December he and Harris spoke over the phone.

"Josh shared with me what the circumstances were," Colangelo said. "He asked if I would be willing to serve in an advisory capacity to help them through their difficult circumstances at the time."

Harris had always been susceptible to persuasion as an NBA owner. Former Sixers head coach Doug Collins, a sort of larger-than-life NBA legend and for someone new to the world of professional sports a cool dude to know, was the first to have Harris's ear. Then came

Hinkie, whose fluency in finance appealed to Harris's private equity background. Now it was Colangelo's turn.

"This is not a deviation from our plan," Harris said during that introductory press conference. Later he added, "To be completely clear, I continue to have the utmost confidence in Sam." Hinkie put on a good face. "This is a really good day for the Sixers," he said. He added that he was eager to lean on Colangelo as a resource.

That night, Spike Eskin and Mike Levin recorded a *Rights to Ricky Sanchez* show to react to the Colangelo news.

"Welcome to an emergency episode of *The Rights to Ricky Sanchez*," Eskin announced to start the show. "The Process has, uh..." He trailed off.

"I'm interested to see how you finish this sentence," Levin said.

"I don't know," Eskin responded.

Colangelo and Harris agreed to a three-year deal. The plan, Colangelo said, was to "get acquainted with all the people, all the basketball people, and come to some judgments myself." Most of his work would be conducted long-distance from his home in Phoenix, but he did pay a number of visits to the offices, especially early on.

One of Colangelo's first calls after taking the job was to Mike D'Antoni, the sixty-four-year-old former Coach of the Year who, while with Colangelo's Suns, had pioneered the frenetic and explosive "seven seconds or less" offense.[3] D'Antoni's two most recent stints—with the Los Angeles Lakers and New York Knicks—had ended poorly and he was looking to get back into the game. Many around the league believed Colangelo was bringing in Brown's eventual replacement.

D'Antoni was hired as an associate head coach. He tweaked some of Brown's actions and added some new sets. "It was a little awkward at first," Sixers guard Nik Stauskas said. "None of the players wanted

---

3   The strategy behind it was exactly as it sounds—that the best looks on offense typically came within the first seven seconds of a possession.

Brett to be fired, but we knew D'Antoni had been a head coach and we weren't really sure what it meant." D'Antoni's easygoing disposition and self-deprecating sense of humor helped break the tension. When he joined the Sixers, they were 1–27. Four games later they upset the Suns in Phoenix.

"Man, I'm good," D'Antoni told Sixers players in the locker room afterward. "I come in and you guys start winning right away."

Colangelo wasn't done tinkering. He met often with Hinkie. He told him he had no qualms with the decision to tear down the team, but he did push for changes along the margins. He believed Hinkie needed to do a better job of selling his plan in the media. "[We] talked about how it would help if I would be more open—if we did a better job of bringing fans along with us," Hinkie said. Colangelo was also adamant about bringing in a few veterans to help guide the younger players. "There seems to be a void of leadership, player-wise," Colangelo said during his introductory press conference.

The day before Christmas, a little over two weeks after Colangelo had come on board, the Sixers traded two future second-round picks for Ish Smith, a twenty-seven-year-old point guard. Smith was a slight but speedy journeyman who was averaging a solid but unspectacular 8.9 points and 5.7 assists per game. He'd played 25 games for the Sixers the previous season. The coaches loved him, and were ecstatic about his return.

"We just needed anyone who could consistently dribble, get the ball to an open man, so the coaches didn't have to generate every single basket," Lance Pearson, then the coordinator of coaching analytics and special video projects, said. "He also knew what it means to grind and stay on a roster. We felt there were a lot of lessons he could share."

Hinkie didn't disagree. Before the season he'd tried signing Kendall Marshall, a former lottery pick rehabbing from a torn ACL, for that very reason. "We had strong desires for a point guard who could help us play at a high tempo, and get our best players the ball in positions where they could be successful," Hinkie said. "Someone to throw a post entry pass. We thought Kendall was that guy." But Marshall's recovery took longer than the Sixers anticipated. He didn't return to the court until early December. By that time, the wheels on the Sixers' season had already come off.

Still, signing a player like Marshall wasn't the same as trading for one like Smith. Hinkie had spent his entire reign collecting second picks. To him, they were precious assets, not bait to be dangled as a means for acquiring a backup point guard.

Colangelo also called David Falk, a prominent agent and one of Hinkie's most ardent critics, about adding Elton Brand, a former No. 1 pick, to the player development staff. Brand, thirty-six, had played sixteen NBA seasons, including four with the Sixers (2008–2012). He was a former Rookie of the Year and a two-time All-Star. He was intelligent and well liked, so much so that the Hawks, his previous team, had offered him a front office gig. But he was still trying to figure out how to spend the next phase of his career. Falk notified Brand of the Sixers' interest. Brand spoke to Duke coach Mike Krzyzewski, who'd coached Okafor and worked with Colangelo on Team USA, and met Hinkie for breakfast.

Hinkie explained to Brand what he was looking for, and how the Sixers thought he could help. He told him he'd get a company credit card to take teammates out to meals. Brand wasn't sold. He didn't need the money. He'd earned nearly $170 million over his career. Also, the Sixers were bad. Really bad. "Players didn't want to come work out for the team, they couldn't get any veterans. It was a low point," he recalled. Was *this* really a situation he wanted to join? "I'm going on a vacation," he told Hinkie. He said he'd think it over and be back in around three weeks. "If you still want me, let me know." The Sixers did, but for a different role. "Sam came back and said that the Sixers actually wanted me to be on the team," Brand said. "He told me I wouldn't even have to play." After some introspection, Brand signed on.

Initially, Hinkie went along with it all. Then, not long after his hiring, Colangelo came to him with another proposal, only this one was more of a demand, and the type not typically made of NBA GMs. "We really thought the front office could be restructured," Colangelo said. "Sam would remain in power, but someone else would be brought in to sit alongside him and you would have a couple people rather than one running the show."

Colangelo and ownership whittled a list of candidates down to two names. One was Danny Ferry, a former Duke star and NBA champion who'd previously served as the general manager for the Atlanta Hawks and Cleveland Cavaliers. Harris had pursued Ferry in June 2012, for the role Hinkie now occupied, but Ferry had instead taken the job with the Hawks.

The other was Jerry's son, Bryan, leading many to believe that this had been Jerry's plan all along.

"They were the top two candidates in everyone's estimation," he said, pushing back against the charge of nepotism. "I did not even participate in those interviews, I thought it was inappropriate for me." Bryan had served as Suns general manager under Jerry and then later moved on to the Toronto Raptors. He was named Executive of the Year in 2007 but had also been replaced in 2013.

Ferry, whom Harris had tried to hire in 2012, was the first choice. The offer intrigued him. He'd left the Hawks a year earlier—it was reported that he'd read an "offensive and racist comment" from a scouting report about an African player out loud during a conference call—and was looking to get back in the game. He'd worked alongside Brett Brown in San Antonio and considered him a close friend. Brown, in fact, was one of the people selling Ferry to ownership. "Brett really wanted the Sam thing to work as well," said a friend. "He really liked Sam and respected him and knew he had great value, but also knew he was in trouble. He was trying to piece something together." Ferry told Brown he was interested but only if Hinkie was on board. Hinkie wasn't thrilled, but recognized the situation. He liked Ferry as a person, respected him as a basketball mind, and figured if he had to partner with someone, Ferry would be a good choice.

Harris called Ferry soon after.

"We're trying to bring in someone with a different perspective and different feel to work with Sam," he told him. He stressed that the two would work as partners. Ferry and Hinkie discussed what the partnership would look like. Who would communicate with ownership? Who'd be the lead voice with players? How would responsibilities be divided? Who'd get final say on trades and draft picks? If the two disagreed, how would that be presented to ownership? Sometimes Hinkie would pull out an org chart. The process dragged on. What was supposed to take a few weeks lasted a couple of months. "They were comfortable with each other, but Sam couldn't get comfortable with how it would all work," said a longtime NBA executive—understandably, given that no other team operated with two men sharing the controls.

Ownership was losing patience. Bryan had been contending for the Brooklyn Nets' GM vacancy before being passed over at the last minute. He was now available and interested in the job. Jerry started lobbying ownership on his behalf.

Around the end of March, Bryan and the Sixers entered negotiations. On April 5, Hinkie went on ESPN writer Zach Lowe's podcast. He talked about how helpful Jerry Colangelo had been. He shared his thoughts on Joel Embiid. He explained why he didn't expect tanking to spread across the NBA. He expressed optimism about the Sixers' chances in the upcoming draft lottery.

"We have the highest ever chance at the No. 1 pick because of some of our moves. I think we are like 53 percent for one of the top two picks and a coin flip from having two top-five picks," Hinkie told Lowe. "It is funny how some 76ers fans are turning it into March Madness."

The following afternoon, Hinkie sent a thirteen-page letter to Harris, Colangelo, and the rest of the Sixers' ownership group.

"To the equity partners of Philadelphia 76ers, L.P.," it began. "I hope this letter finds you well. I have been serving the Sixers at your pleasure for the past 34 months. Atul Gawande, a Surgeon at Brigham and Women's Hospital in Boston, remains (from afar) one of my favorite reads. He laughs that reading scientific studies has long been a guilty pleasure. Reading investor letters has long been one of mine." Five paragraphs later—which included a Warren Buffett anecdote, a quote misattributed to Abraham Lincoln ("Give me six hours to chop down a tree and I will spend the first four sharpening the axe"), a subtle jab at Scott O'Neil ("I can assure you that when your team is eventually able to compete deep into May, Scott will ably and efficiently separate the good people of the Delaware Valley from their wallets on your behalf. Worry not.")—Hinkie reached his point.

"Given all the changes to our organization, I no longer have the confidence that I can make good decisions on behalf of investors in the Sixers—you," he wrote. "So I should step down. And I have."

About two hours later, the letter—deemed a "manifesto" by the media—was leaked to ESPN. Rumors circulated that Jerry Colangelo was the one to do so. He denied the accusation.

"Ultimately, Sam made the decision, he didn't want to be part of our new structure, and so he resigned," Jerry said. "That's what transpired, he was not pushed out. Every intention was to keep him because he really was valuable in the sense of his expertise. There was a lot of misinformation, in my mind, that was out there. About who did what and who said what."

Sixers players began sharing the news with each other in a group chat. "It was sad how it happened," said Robert Covington, who was drafted by Hinkie. Some players scanned the letter. The *Philadelphia Daily News* ran a headline the next morning: "SCRAM HINKIE: Sixers GM abandons ship." Hinkie showed up at PCOM for that day's practice to say some goodbyes. Afterward the team set up rows of chairs across the gym floor. Harris and Brown addressed players and staff.

"I wanted Sam to be here to see this whole thing through," Brown told them.

A little over a month later, the Sixers announced a deal with StubHub, placing the company's logo on the team's jerseys. O'Neil celebrated the announcement on Twitter with the hashtag #process2progress.

Chapter 12

#HEDIEDFORYOURSINS

Spike Eskin was on his computer in his Philadelphia home when he saw the news flash across Twitter: Sam Hinkie was resigning. Furious, Eskin texted his podcast partner, Mike Levin:

"We have to do a show."

Levin, despondent, tried pushing back.

"I'm not in the mood."

"We have to," Eskin replied. "People need to hear from us." He went down to the mini studio in his basement and dialed Levin.

Neither man was shocked by the news. There had been signs: the hiring of Jerry Colangelo, the trading of second-round picks, the prevalence of Hinkie-disparaging columns in local papers. But seeing Hinkie's reign officially come to an end and seeing *how* it had ended left both men feeling betrayed. Teams fire GMs all the time, but this seemed different. Eskin and Levin felt connected to Hinkie, and not just because on an international scouting trip a few years earlier he'd emailed them a cell phone photo of a player under the subject line of "Ricky Sanchez."[1] They and the thousands of fans they represented

---

1   Levin had also sat down with Hinkie three times for off-the-record chats. "He would always come back extra buoyant after those," said Andrew Sharp, the

believed in Hinkie and what *he* represented. They were the infantry in the war Hinkie was waging, at least in their own eyes. These fans fought the battles that Hinkie declined to engage in, and they delighted in it, sometimes even more than they delighted in watching the Sixers play games.

Their leader, however, was now gone. Levin, Eskin, and thousands of others weren't sure what to do.

"If you're listening to the podcast looking to feel better...," Levin said on the show, his voice soft and sad, "you're not gonna."

He paused and took a deep breath. He sighed.

"It's always been about more than just the team and just, like, this idea," Levin continued. "It's..." He tried completing his thought. "I don't know." He took another breath. "It's unfortunate that you can bring in a guy with a vision and shove him out the door when he executes that vision."

"They didn't even have the balls to fire him," Eskin said. "If you thought what he was doing was bullshit, then fire him. At least have the guts to fire him. It's disgraceful."

A few weeks later, Levin came up with an idea. He and Eskin were looking for ways to promote the upcoming *Rights to Ricky Sanchez* lottery party. The Sixers, for the first time since Hinkie's arrival, had finished the previous season with the NBA's worst record (10–72, one loss shy of the worst mark in league history), and had a 26.9 percent chance of landing the draft's No. 1 pick, the best odds in the league.[2] This was always a big night for Sixers fans, and even bigger for the *Rights to Ricky Sanchez* crew, but with Hinkie gone the night would now take on even more meaning. It would be a celebration of the future but also a tribute to the past.

"Let's rent out a billboard," Levin told Eskin. They pooled money from family, friends, podcast sponsors, and the SB Nation Sixers site Liberty Ballers. Eskin drove out to the South Philadelphia stretch of

---

sportswriter who lived with Levin at the time. "It was like someone coming home from a good date."

2   Their own pick had a 25 percent chance of landing at No. 1. They also owned a Kings lottery pick that had a 1.9 percent chance of hitting the jackpot.

I-95 approaching the city's sports stadiums and arenas, parked his car, snapped a picture of a billboard that he wanted to rent. He sent it to Clear Channel Outdoor, who owned the space.

On April 25, drivers passing by the sports complex were greeted by the words HINKIE FOREVER, written in a bold white font. Beneath the letters was an advertisement for the lottery party. On the left was a giant picture of Hinkie's face, faded and colored like Barack Obama's in the "Hope" posters from his 2008 presidential campaign.

"It was about showing them that we're not blindly devoted," Levin said. "That we believe in The Process and if you guys keep fucking up we're going to be out."

The night of the draft lottery, around three thousand Sixers fans flooded South Philadelphia's Xfinity Live!, a large beer-and-restaurant hub tucked into the sports complex where fans without tickets congregate during games. Sixers jerseys and hats were everywhere. T-shirts with Hinkie's face, too. Chants of "Trust The Process!" filled the room, the words growing louder and louder. The phrase had appeared in an *ESPN The Magazine* feature about Hinkie. Eskin had printed the phrase onto T-shirts for the previous year's lottery party and the slogan took off, though in the wake of Hinkie's ousting it had come to serve less as an embrace and more as a jab.

When it was time for NBA deputy commissioner Mark Tatum to announce the lottery results, the fans inside Xfinity Live!, standing shoulder to shoulder, all looked up toward the large TVs hanging from the walls. Tatum started at No. 14 and worked his way down. The Sixers made it to the final five. The final three. The final two. It was just them and the Lakers now. Tatum paused to open a large envelope. A Lakers logo emerged. Fans, unable to bottle up their excitement, hopped up and down like pogo sticks. Others leapt onto tables and pumped their fists. Strangers high-fived. It looked like an EDM party. "Trust The Process!" they shouted over and over, thanking Hinkie for the gift left behind.

There was little debate who the No. 1 pick would be. The 6-foot-10 Ben Simmons, not yet twenty years old, was everything you could ask for in a prospect: big and strong and fast with arms and shoulders that could blend in on *American Ninja Warrior.*

He also possessed a preternatural feel for the game, promoted by his father, Dave Simmons, a South Bronx native who had played professionally in Australia for more than ten years. Ben spent most of his childhood in Newcastle, along the shores of the South Pacific. He enjoyed the outdoors—bodysurfing, playing tennis, running on the shore alongside the family's golden retriever—and competing with his dad, older sister, and four half siblings, but what he loved most was basketball. Dave started all his kids at a young age. Even as a boy Ben was preparing for life in the NBA. He hung an Allen Iverson poster in his room. He played with older kids so he could develop skills as opposed to relying solely on his size. As a teenager he'd regularly stand in front of his bathroom mirror and recite answers to imaginary interview questions—*What'd it feel like to hit that game-winning shot? What's it feel like to be an NBA champion?*—ones he assumed he'd be fielding within a few years.

When Ben was fifteen, his godfather, David Patrick, an assistant coach at LSU and a former teammate of Dave's, came to visit the family's Melbourne home. Impressed, he called in some connections and got Ben an invite to an All-American Camp in Long Beach, California. Simmons impressed and vaulted up all the recruiting rankings, making the NBA a reality. He decided the best way to pursue his dream was to try his hand against the better competition in the United States. He enrolled in Florida's Montverde Academy, one of the top high school basketball programs in the country.[3] He grew as a player and the team won in bunches, and by his junior year he was one of the nation's top recruits and receiving invites to work out alongside stars like LeBron James.

The top colleges pursued him. He chose to play for Patrick instead, giving LSU its most significant basketball recruit since

---

3   The same school Joel Embiid had enrolled in after coming over from Cameroon.

Shaquille O'Neal nearly thirty years earlier. He starred on the court, leading the team in points, rebounds, assists, steals, and blocks. But little else that season went as planned. LSU finished 19–14 and missed out on the NCAA tournament.[4] Questions sprung up about Simmons's "character." He was omitted from the list of finalists for the Wooden Award—given annually to the top player in the country—after failing to meet the minimum requirement of a 2.0 GPA. He once told Patrick that he only gave full effort on defense if he respected the players he was being tasked to guard. He also attempted just three 3-pointers during the season, leading some around the NBA to believe that he was shooting with the wrong hand (he shot with his left but did nearly everything else with his right). Worse, he scoffed at the idea that his crooked jump shot could limit his NBA ceiling.

"Your jump shot, what do you say to those who say, 'He's got to learn to shoot better'?" ESPN's Chris Broussard asked him during an interview in the lead-up to the 2016 draft.

"There's nothing to say, I averaged 20," Simmons responded.

A narrative began to form, one depicting him as a self-centered diva more interested in future dollars than present wins. That he was one of the first basketball phenoms to come of age in the social media era, thrusting his life under a microscope in a way few athletes had experienced before, didn't make his life easier. But there was more to it, a reason behind the attitude, namely that he didn't respect the institution he was playing for.

"The NCAA is really fucked up," Simmons said to a documentary crew that followed him that year. "Everybody's making money except the players.[5] We're the ones waking up early as hell to be the best teams and do everything they want us to do and then the players get

---

4   According to a FiveThirtyEight.com study, Simmons at the time was just the second No. 1 prospect (according to ESPN's rankings) in fifteen years to not lead his team to the NCAA Tournament.

5   Simmons is not the only one to hold such views. In a landmark piece for the *Atlantic*, Taylor Branch, a Pulitzer Prize–winning historian known for his work on the civil rights era, described the NCAA as having "the unmistakable whiff of the plantation."

nothing. They say education, but if I'm there for a year, I can't get much education."

He wasn't at LSU by choice. He didn't care about that world, about the classes or the grades, the NCAA's tournament or its awards. If it were up to him, he'd have spent the season in the NBA.

"[LSU head coach Johnny] Jones said, 'We need to make up a punishment if you miss another class,'" Simmons told the camera at a different point. "I missed my next class about preparing for better study habits. I'm going to the NBA next season. Why bullshit if it's not going to help me?"

Before the draft the Sixers were the only team Simmons worked out for. He loved the idea of playing for Brett Brown,[6] who had coached his father in Australia. He arrived at the Barclays Center on June 23 in a dark three-piece suit. A little after 7:30 p.m., NBA commissioner Adam Silver made the pick official. It was a special day for Simmons, but also the Sixers and their recently hired president of basketball operations, Bryan Colangelo. Yet for Colangelo there was no escaping the shadow of his predecessor. "He was always sensitive and read everything written about him," said a friend. And the jabs were now coming from everywhere. Earlier that week, Simmons had posted a picture on his Instagram account of him working out for the Sixers. He captioned it with "Trust the process." More telling, though, was the sign caught by ESPN's cameras during the draft. It was held up by a fan in the stands, wearing a Sixers T-shirt. It read, "Hinkie died for your sins."

————————

Sam Hinkie wasn't dead. He'd just moved with his wife and four kids to Palo Alto, grown out his stubble, and shaved off most of his hair.

"The more I thought about it, the more obvious it became that a sort of gap year here was right," he wrote on Twitter in September 2016, beginning a string of ten tweets, his first ever posted. He added, "I've

---

6   Whose job seemed secure after Mike D'Antoni left in May to become the head coach of the Houston Rockets.

always been focused on learning as fast as I can and figuring out how I can do things better. So a period like this felt super rare. And there may be no better place on the planet to learn right now than right here." He asked for reading recommendations. Joel Embiid sent him a link to a story on himself.[7]

After resigning, Hinkie had considered getting away. But "I didn't think it would be the most fatherly thing to do," he told *Sports Illustrated's* Chris Ballard. He wasn't interested in jumping at the next job offer, either. Instead, he took the advice of Paul DePodesta, a friend and Billy Beane disciple working as an executive for the NFL's Cleveland Browns: "Treat this as a rare opportunity to refocus the next twenty years of your life."

Hinkie's days mostly followed the same pattern. He'd wake up early, accompany his two oldest boys on a scooter ride to school, then spend the morning working on "creative tasks."[8] Sometimes this meant wondering things like, "Why do we watch basketball games front to back? Why not watch games back to front, or out of order?" He'd rarely take out his phone. Texts were ignored. "You can't let someone else's agenda hijack your day," he told Ballard. If his wife needed him, she knew to call twice.

Afternoons were spent meeting with all sorts of Silicon Valley types. Health care start-up founders. Hedge fund managers. Artificial intelligence developers. Stanford MBA students. "My people," Hinkie said. He met Ballard one morning at Facebook, where he had spoken with members of the company's virtual reality team. Sometimes, upon meeting new people, he'd tell them that he was "like a founder that got pushed out for professional management."

"Oh, first time?" was a common response.

"There's not the sense of shame for failure here that there is some other places," Hinkie told Ballard.

Nearly three thousand miles east, Hinkie's vision for the Sixers was coming to life. Tanking had finally yielded a No. 1 pick, but

---

7 It was by Kevin O'Connor of The Ringer and titled "An Ongoing Process."
8 Ballard's description.

there was more. Dario Šarić, the 2014 lottery pick who had spent the previous two seasons playing in Turkey, was finally coming over. In Robert Covington, a former undrafted wing with a smooth jumper and quick hands, the Sixers had finally struck gold with one of the dozens of players Hinkie had plucked from the scrapheap. The new 125,000-square-foot palace of a practice facility, across the Benjamin Franklin Bridge in Camden, New Jersey,[9] and which Hinkie had helped design, was finally opening.[10]

Most important: Joel Embiid was finally suiting up.

More than two years had passed since the Sixers had drafted Embiid third overall. The first year was a disaster, and so this time he and the Sixers, led by Dr. David Martin, whom the team had hired away from the Australian Institute of Sport, elected to take a different approach. Embiid met with former NBA center Zydrunas Ilgauskas, who'd suffered the same injury early in his career. He moved out of the Ritz-Carlton residence and into an apartment downtown. He got a chef. Martin drew him up a sleep schedule. He even spent some time rehabbing at a plush sports science facility in Qatar.

"We wanted to go outside the box and do something creative and shake Joel's world up a little bit and make it exciting," Brown said.

---

9   Why Camden and not Philadelphia? "We were looking for a site in Philadelphia and were pretty much decided on it when the state of New Jersey passed the Economic Opportunity Act, which had some frankly really amazing tax incentives," said Alan Razak, principal of the development firm AthenianRazak, which ran the project. Under the act, which was signed into law by then-governor Christie in 2013 as a way to entice business to come build in the Garden State, the Sixers were eligible to receive a tax credit equal to the amount of their full investment (in this case, about $80 million). The only requirement was that they create 250 jobs by the time the site opened, which they were able to do by transferring all their business and basketball operations to the facility.

10   It also featured dozens of pro-Process messages covertly written in black Sharpie by a Hinkie-loyal Sixers fan who happened to be one of the electricians hired for the job. He billed himself Son of Sam. These messages included, among other things, a "TTP"—"Trust The Process"—on a label fastened to the light trimmings hanging in the owners' lounge and a "Hinkie died for this..." on the inside of one of the fuse panels in Colangelo's new office. The story was reported by John Gonzalez of The Ringer.

By training camp Embiid was back on the court, dazzling Sixers players and coaches. He'd yet to play a single game and still was clearly the best player on the team. He had everything, from the Olajuwon-like footwork to the feathery touch. And then there were the vicious dunks, on teammates both old and young. There was a dunk during a scrimmage over the outstretched arms of a leaping Nerlens Noel. "One of the most violent dunks I've ever seen," said Gerald Henderson, a veteran signed by the Sixers that summer. There was a dunk on veteran big man Elton Brand. "He did a one-two, middle, then came the drop step, and just banged on me," Brand said. "I may or may not have fell into the wall. It was one of those bad ones."

The Sixers opened the season against the Thunder on the last Wednesday night in October in front of 20,487 fans, a rare Wells Fargo Center sellout. For months Sixers fans had obsessively tracked Embiid's return. Cell phone videos of his noncontact workouts from the previous spring became viral hits. Local reporters received Twitter messages inquiring which Sixers tickets offered the best view of Embiid's pregame routine. For three years Sixers fans had watched a team built to lose do exactly that, waiting for the things sports fans covet most of all: a sign of hope. Embiid was that.

At a little after 8 p.m. the starting lineups took the floor. Embiid, his hair grown into a tight afro, strolled to center court for the jump ball. He was eager and nervous and only knew one way to react. Twenty-seven seconds into the game he received the ball on offense for the first time. Standing at the top of the key and behind the three-point arc, he immediately rose up and flung the ball toward the hoop. It was on line, but rimmed out. The crowd, almost all of which had stood in anticipation, sighed.

Three minutes later, Embiid received another chance. He caught the ball at the top of the three-point line again, faked a shot, took two dribbles to the right, and then deployed the full arsenal of nifty footwork that had lifted him out of Cameroon and into the NBA. A spin toward his right shoulder, a pause, a spin back to his left, a plant. He rose up.

"Down it goes, for his first NBA hoop!" Sixers announcer Marc

Zumoff exclaimed on the broadcast. The crowd screamed. Embiid whirled his finger at the fans and, after turning to backpedal onto defense, vigorously bobbed his head. A few seconds later Thunder star Russell Westbrook drove to the basket and floated a shot up at the hoop. Embiid slid over and with his right hand violently swatted it away. The crowd roared again, this time louder.

In the second quarter Embiid buried his first three-pointer. There was another block and more Olajuwon-like Dream Shakes. "He can't guard me!" he shouted at Thunder defenders. He was showered with chants of "M-V-P." More smooth fadeaways. The words "Sam Hinkie" trended on Twitter. With nine minutes remaining and the Sixers up by three, Embiid walked to the foul line for two free throws. A quiet, three-word chant broke out, growing louder and louder as he prepared to shoot.

"And they're chanting, 'Trust The Process,' in a nod to Sam Hinkie,'" ESPN analyst and former NBA head coach Jeff Van Gundy said on the telecast, over the chuckles of broadcast partner Mike Breen. ESPN's cameras froze on a couple of fans behind the basket wearing Hinkie T-shirts.

Over the previous few months Embiid had adopted the slogan, changing his Instagram name to Joel "The Process" Embiid and asking the Sixers' public address announcer to include the nickname in his pregame introductions. In July, he posted an Instagram picture of himself and Hinkie laughing with the hashtags "#HeDiedForOurSins" and "#TrustTheProcess," the latter of which punctuated nearly all of his tweets. He'd post pictures of himself dunking on social media along with the caption "processing..."

Embiid and Hinkie had bonded in their two years together. Embiid, an NBA nerd who studied the salary cap and draft, was a fan of Hinkie's plan. The Process spoke to him in a way few things had. "I think a lot about what I went through and how it prepared me to be a better man. I really feel like I'm The Process," he told *Sports Illustrated*'s Lee Jenkins in a profile that was published earlier that day. "Like The Process is about me."

But the relationship went deeper. Hinkie had always been there for Embiid. When Embiid learned that his thirteen-year-old brother had been killed, Hinkie sat with him in his apartment, comforting a then-twenty-year-old kid whom he barely knew. When Embiid, in the midst of his rehab, could no longer take the torture of watching his teammates from the bench, Hinkie invited him to watch games in his suite.

The Sixers hung close with the Thunder. No one cared. Sixers fans had seen 199 losses in the previous three seasons—what was one more? Embiid's emergence and performance—20 points in 22 minutes, flashes of a franchise player—was more important than a single game.

"For him to come out here and the fans to see what we're all seeing," Brett Brown said that night, "for the city to be rewarded with a player that we all understand has unique gifts, special gifts, for him to go through all the things he's been through and play like he did on opening night, the city deserves it and he deserves it."

Embiid, seated at his locker large with a yellow ice bucket at his feet, summed up his thoughts on the evening a different way.

"Trust The Process," he said. Sam Hinkie may have been gone, but the Sixers were still his team.

———

Bryan Colangelo was just thirty years old the first time he became a general manager. His father, Jerry, the Phoenix Suns' owner and future Basketball Hall of Fame inductee, was looking for someone else to run the team's day-to-day operations. He wanted his lone son to be that man.

The cries of nepotism rained down. Bryan knew they would, too. It's why, after graduating from Cornell in 1987 with a BS in business management and applied economics, he'd turned down a job with the Suns and moved to New York City to work in real estate. "I wanted to establish my new identity in the business world and allow myself to grow outside of the organization," he said. He stayed there for four years before moving back to Phoenix and taking a job with the Suns. His first position was as a noncoaching assistant to head coach Cotton Fitzsimmons. He asked a lot of questions, watched a lot of film, and learned about every facet of the business. "We only had, like, eight people working in the office at the time," then–Suns assistant coach Lionel Hollins said. "There was a ticket manager, a marketing guy, a PR guy, and a receptionist. So we all did a little bit of everything."

Bryan's tenure as GM got off to a rocky start. He traded fan favorite Dan Majerle and legend Charles Barkley. Neither deal netted the team much in return, and his Suns lost in the first round in each of his first four seasons at the helm. Criticism mounted. Fans called for Jerry to take back the controls.

"I'm very sensitive to it, because I haven't been around long enough that my skin has thickened," Bryan told the *Arizona Republic* in January 1997. The writer, John Davis, asked him about nepotism charges. "I'm concerned about it," Bryan replied. The problem, according to then-Suns coach Danny Ainge, was he was fighting a battle he couldn't win. "The people that love Jerry want him to be just like Jerry, and that's a hard standard to uphold," Ainge told the *Republic*. "The people who don't like Jerry say that Bryan's only there because of his last name."

Bryan eventually turned things around. He made some smart trades and savvy draft choices. His best move was pairing head coach Mike D'Antoni with point guard Steve Nash, who propelled the Suns deep into the playoffs for four straight seasons and, by feasting on a steady diet of fast breaks and quick-trigger threes, revolutionized the way basketball was played. Thanks to that decision, and a few others along the margins, Bryan was named NBA Executive of the Year in 2005. Two years later, with Jerry having sold the Suns, Bryan left to run the Toronto Raptors on a five-year, $20 million deal. The Raptors made the playoffs in his first two years there, ending a four-year drought, and in 2007, Bryan was once again named Executive of the Year. But there were more misfires, ones from which he wasn't able to bounce back, like selecting Andrea Bargnani—a seven-foot Italian with a smooth jumper and an allergy to defense and sweat—and handing out a number of onerous contracts. By the 2010–2011 season, the Raptors had fallen back into the NBA's cellar. They won just 22 games that season, an especially dubious number considering their bloated payroll,[11] and just 23 the next. In May 2013 they informed Bryan that they'd be looking for a new GM. He was offered the opportunity to remain with the team and focus on the business end, but a month later, recognizing how diminished his role had become, he elected to resign.

Forty-eight and unemployed for the first time in more than twenty-five years, he figured he'd take some time off and wait for the right situation. "It was a little bit humbling that the phone call didn't come right away," he said. He stayed in Toronto, dialing up contacts around the NBA, meeting his wife and friends for lunches, and traveling to his son's AAU games. He did some scouting, at NCAA games and overseas.

The calls finally came around January 2016. By this point the Raptors had grown into a 50-win team, with some of Colangelo's moves helping pave the way. Kyle Lowry, whom he had traded for in 2012, had grown into an All-Star. So had DeMar DeRozan, whom he had drafted ninth overall in 2009. Dwane Casey, whom he had hired as head coach in 2011, had turned out to be the right leader for the group. Colangelo felt vindicated by Toronto's success, but seeing Masai Ujiri, the man who'd replaced him at the head of the Raptors organization, receive all the credit in the press angered him. "He'd always talk about how he felt he got ran out of town there despite being the smartest one," said a future Sixers colleague. "He had a lot of demons in terms of the Jerry stuff and felt the Raptors job was his chance."

One call came from the Sixers, who were now being run by Bryan's father and looking for an experienced executive to work alongside Sam Hinkie. The other was from the Brooklyn Nets, who had "reassigned" general manager Billy King. Bryan, wary of once again working for his father, pursued the Nets gig. He and the Nets' Russian-based owner-ship group, led by oligarch Mikhail Prokhorov, spent a little over a month talking. The Nets' liked what they heard.

Then came February's All-Star Weekend in Toronto. At a Saturday

---

11   They finished last that year in "payroll efficiency," a number measuring a team's wins per salary dollar spent.

night event, a number of the league's top executives, including San Antonio Spurs general manager R. C. Buford and Golden State Warriors president of basketball operations Bob Myers, approached Dmitry Razumov, the Nets' chairman, to lobby on behalf of Spurs assistant general manager Sean Marks, whom the Nets had recently interviewed. The campaign helped nudge the Nets in that direction. A few days later they officially handed Marks the job.

With the Nets' vacancy filled, Colangelo was left with two options. Neither was ideal. Taking the Sixers' offer would mean once again facing charges of nepotism. Passing would be betting that another team would come calling in the future, which was no sure thing. Eager to get back into the league, Colangelo chose the former. In April, three days after Hinkie's abrupt and surprising resignation, he was officially named the Sixers' president of basketball operations. Jerry stepped down as chairman but stayed on as an adviser.

Colangelo and Hinkie shared little in common. Hinkie preferred operating behind the scenes; Colangelo enjoyed being seen. Hinkie typically wore a subtle blue blazer; Colangelo wore suits custom tailored in Bologna, Italy, and shirts with crisp collars that crept up to his chin. Still, publicly, Colangelo was complimentary of Hinkie. He claimed he had accepted the offer believing that he'd be working alongside him.

"This is one of the most exciting jobs, I believe, that's out there in the league right now. It's a situation where my predecessor, Sam Hinkie, has done a nice job of establishing the assets and the resources to move forward in a positive way," Colangelo told reporters at his introductory press conference. "We're going to be measured in our continued building of this organization."

But he also made clear that the Sixers would be entering a new phase.

"We're really changing our focus toward winning," he said. "That's something that's a shift in culture."

It didn't take long for Colangelo to begin implementing these changes. He started by doing something Hinkie refused to do: establish a timeline. A plethora of A-list players were scheduled to become free agents in the summer of 2018. Colangelo knew the Sixers could have enough cap room to sign two of them, and that if they did, with Embiid, Simmons, and another lottery pick or two on the roster, they would instantly become championship contenders.

First, he believed, he needed to pull the Sixers' out of the league's basement. Otherwise no stars would want to come.

He began by signing two players Hinkie never would have considered to deals Hinkie never would have given out. (Gerald Henderson Jr., twenty-nine, for two years and $18 million; Jerryd Bayless, twenty-seven, for three years, $27 million). He told them he wanted veterans to teach the Sixers' young players how to act professionally. Both players struggled, either with injuries or production. (Bayless played just three games; Henderson had a balky hip and averaged just 9.2 points per game.) But they did help police the locker room in a way that Brown—because of his temperament and also more because criticism coming from fellow players always holds more weight—never could.

Early in the season, after a close home loss, Henderson overheard a couple of young Sixers laughing in the locker room. "What could possibly be so funny?" he shouted. The players tried defending themselves. Henderson stood up and raised his voice louder. "Some things were said that weren't too PC," he recalled.

The Sixers had once again started the season on a long losing streak; this time it took them eight games to record their first win. They responded by winning almost half their matchups over the next couple of months, but the small victories weren't enough for Colangelo, who wasn't prepared for the adulation Hinkie was continuing to receive. "We started hearing things off the record about how surprised he was by how much we all embraced Sam," Levin said. Colangelo responded by taking not-so-subtle digs at his predecessor—"There was a losing mindset," he said on a podcast with Yahoo! Sports' Adrian Wojnarowski in September 2016—and taking issue with all pro-Process commentary, whether it appeared on a mainstream platform like ESPN or a podcast hosted by a pair of fans.

"It seemed like they had their ears burning," Eskin said. "Like, when we would say something unsupportive or tweet something unsupportive of what they were doing we would hear about it. Not from Bryan—though it was made clear how he felt—but other basketball operations people."

————

On February 11 the Sixers won their 20th game—their highest mark in three seasons and twice their win total from the previous year. It should have been a time of celebration. Instead, they were ensnared in a cycle of chaos, much of it of Colangelo's doing.

A few weeks earlier, in the third quarter of a game against the Blazers, Embiid had landed awkwardly after a dunk. He hobbled around a bit, then jogged back to the locker room to have his left knee examined. "I just landed the wrong way," he told reporters afterward. "I'm great. The knee's fine. They did an MRI and stuff, everything looked good."

The injury was first deemed a "hyperextension." Then a few days later it was a "contusion." Embiid was held out of the Sixers' next three games. He returned to the floor on Friday, January 27, for a nationally televised contest against the Rockets, and put on his best performance of the season: 32 points, seven rebounds, four assists, three steals, and two blocks. "They didn't want me to push it," he said of the Sixers after the game. "They didn't want me to play at all, and I had to convince them." He'd always loved the spotlight, and the opportunity to play on ESPN wasn't one he was willing to pass up.

The Sixers traveled to Chicago but Embiid stayed back in Philadelphia. The following day the team announced that Embiid would miss the next three games. Three became five. Then it was seven. Sixers fans and reporters wondered whether the team was covering up a more serious injury. "It is taking so long because we are just erring, we will err on extreme caution," Brown told reporters. Two days later, with Embiid having missed eight straight games, Colangelo, who to that point had rarely made himself available to reporters, even off the record, went on local radio station WIP in an attempt to clarify the situation.

He started the interview by saying he'd like to be "forthright" about Embiid's injury but that he couldn't because of HIPAA laws. He dismissed the accusation of a cover-up. "I really don't understand the skepticism, because if there was something untoward happening, I'd be the first to call it out," he said. His explanation for Embiid's prolonged absence was that Embiid's knee had swelled up two days after that Rockets game. The hosts kept pushing. "If you want to get onto some other topics, I'm happy to stay on the phone," Colangelo responded. "But this is getting old." He'd felt under siege since arriving in Philadelphia. Now he was fighting back.

That night at Wells Fargo Center, a shirtless Embiid danced onstage during a Meek Mill concert. The moment was captured on the phones of attendees. The clips went viral. The sight—a young star hopping around despite having missed his team's previous eight games—became perfect fodder for the twenty-four-hour news cycle.

The Sixers practiced the following morning. Brown faced more questions. He answered a few before growing frustrated, telling reporters he had nothing else to add about "Joel dancing."

"Ask Bryan," he said.

Embiid was up next. "Meek invited me to the stage. I had fun. That's what I'm about, just enjoy life," he said. "But I don't think it was a good and I don't think it was a bad decision. I just thought about having fun." He added, "I saw people said I'm not playing and they expect me not to do that type of stuff. But, I mean, I'm twenty-two years old. I'm having fun. That's what I've been doing the whole year and I'm going to keep on doing that."

A few hours before the Sixers' home game that night against the Miami Heat, Derek Bodner, a local Sixers reporter, broke the news that in addition to the bone bruise Embiid had also torn the meniscus in his right knee. The Sixers, according to Bodner, had learned of the tear from the MRI Embiid had undergone on January 20, the night he'd originally suffered the injury. In other words, Colangelo and the team *had* been withholding information, and then lying when confronted. Even worse, they'd allowed Embiid to play against the Rockets despite knowing he'd torn his meniscus.

Colangelo addressed reporters that night. "On the MRI that was conducted shortly after the injury versus Portland, the MRI revealed obviously what we thought it to be—a bone bruise," he said. "There was also the recognition that there was a very minor meniscal tear. But it was not thought to be acute and it was not thought to be the source of the pain, inflammation, or symptoms." He said Embiid had been permitted to suit up for the Rockets game because his symptoms during the four days of practice leading up to the game were "nonreactive in any kind of way." The swelling, Colangelo claimed, had only begun after the game. "At this stage, once again, it's not thought to be a severe injury," he said. He wouldn't offer any sort of timetable for a return. Embiid sat out the next two games, then took time off during the NBA's All-Star Weekend.

The Sixers returned to practice the following week and announced that Embiid would miss the team's next four games, a proclamation he welcomed. "I wasn't too happy with the way it was kind of handled before," he told reporters. "I saw the day-to-day part—I was told that I was going to miss at least two or three weeks." It was another jab at Colangelo, and an acknowledgment that the Sixers had deceived their fans.

Four days later, Embiid was deemed "out indefinitely." He underwent another MRI. "It's quite simple," Colangelo said. "Joel developed a little bit of swelling and soreness. We're reacting in a way that's proactive." Two days after that, on March 1, the Sixers put an end to the charade. Embiid, they said, would be sidelined for the rest of the season.

While all this was going on, Colangelo was trying—and failing—to free up the logjam at center that Hinkie had left behind.

Hinkie had spent his Sixers tenure prioritizing talent, not fit, trading for or drafting centers in the lottery of each of his three drafts. It was a messy situation for Colangelo to inherit, and the clock was ticking. Noel was set to become a restricted free agent at the end of season. The Sixers would have the right to match any contract he was offered. Declining, though, would mean losing him for nothing. If the Sixers didn't view him as part of their future, they'd be better off trading him before February's deadline. Noel was aware that fighting for minutes with Okafor and Embiid could hurt his value on the open market. He had no intention of silently standing by while the front office weighed its options.

"I think it's just silly...this situation that we are in now with three starting centers," he told the *Philadelphia Inquirer*'s Keith Pompey before Media Day. "With the departure of [Hinkie], I would have figured that management would be able to get something done this summer." He doubled down on these comments at his press conference the next day. "I don't see a way of it working," he said. "You have three talented centers that can play 30-plus minutes a night. And it's just not going to work to anybody's advantage having that on the same team. That's how I'm looking at it. I'm not opposed to anything, but things need to be situated." Colangelo disagreed. "These are all young players not in a position to dictate circumstances," he told reporters.

The Sixers' biggest problem was that neither Noel nor Okafor were playing up to expectations. Noel flashed some promise but had delusions of grandeur, even resisting when Vance Walberg, an assistant coach from 2013 to 2015, proposed that he model his game after Tyson Chandler, an elite defensive player and dynamic rim-runner who rarely shot or dribbled. "His vision of himself was that he was going to become a scorer and jump shooter," Walberg said. "And Brett wanted to keep him positive so he kept shooting and working with him." Noel improved his foul shooting by seven percentage points (61 percent to 68) over his first three NBA seasons but never embraced the idea of serving as a role player.

Okafor, meanwhile, had failed to adapt to the NBA's frantic pace. He could score a bit, but was lost on defense, didn't pass, and couldn't rebound. He also remained haunted by the previous season's drama. "I had to go on the court in front of all these thousands of people, and I know they had all just witnessed what I did in that video and were judging me for it," he recalled. "So I remember not wanting to be on the court, being embarrassed to be out there. That was the first time basketball wasn't my escape."

Okafor, who was diagnosed with a small meniscus tear the previous March, began the 2016–17 season on a minutes restriction. Noel, who underwent minor knee surgery in October, began the season on the bench. The injuries bought Colangelo some more time, but not much. Noel returned to the lineup in mid-December. He played just 10 minutes off the bench despite Embiid sitting out. He sat the next game, then returned to the court for a matchup with the Lakers. Both Embiid and Okafor started and played more than 20 minutes. Noel played just eight.

"I need to be on the court playing basketball. I mean, I'm too good to be playing eight minutes," he told a group of reporters in the locker room. He grew angrier the more he talked. "That's crazy, that's crazy, that's crazy. Need to figure that shit out," he said. "Fuck it."

The Sixers tried trading Okafor. They came close in mid-February, but Colangelo didn't love the offers and on the day of the trade deadline dealt Noel to the Dallas Mavericks instead. The Sixers received backup forward Justin Anderson, veteran center Andrew Bogut (whom they waived), and two future second-round picks[12] in return. Noel was informed of the deal after a morning practice. A big smile stretched across his face as he hugged teammates. Brown, however, was stung. Noel was the last player remaining from his 2013–2014 team, his first on the job. He walked out of his office and pulled the hood of his sweatshirt tight over his face.

"This day sucks," he told point guard T. J. McConnell, who noticed tears welling in his eyes. Still, Brown understood why the move was made. "I'm happy for [Nerlens] in my heart of hearts," he told reporters that night before the Sixers' matchup with the Wizards. "[The Mavericks] have brought him in to grow him, to try to be a starting center. That does equal a commensurate paycheck. He will be rewarded if that's the way it plays out. That wasn't gonna happen here. It wasn't gonna happen here." And anyway, Brown now had more serious concerns. Colangelo had just announced yet another Sixers injury. Ben Simmons, Colangelo said, would miss the entire season due to a foot injury. Simmons had fractured a bone in his right foot on the last day of training camp, back in September. He underwent

---

12   Officially, it was a first-round pick, but it was heavily protected and eventually became two second-rounders.

surgery, and the team announced he'd miss about three months. The three months came and went. In January, the Sixers announced that Simmons had undergone a final scan; the results, they claimed, were "clean," but they declined to offer a timetable for his return. That changed in mid-February after Colangelo was informed by team doctors that Simmons's foot hadn't healed as expected. For the third time in four years, and despite Colangelo repeatedly assuring fans that Simmons was progressing as expected, a Sixers lottery pick would miss his entire rookie season.

"I miss Sam Hinkie," wrote Angelo Cataldi, one of Philadelphia's most prominent sports broadcasters, in a column on the website PhillyVoice. "That's right. One of the loudest critics of the ex-GM during his insufferable three years in Philadelphia has become, in a perverse way, a fan." Cataldi described Colangelo as a snake-oil salesman. "As the old joke goes, you can always tell when Colangelo is lying," he wrote. "His lips move."

With Embiid injured and Noel in Dallas, the Sixers lost their final eight games of the year, finishing the season with 28 wins. That mark was an 18-game jump from the previous season and a number equal to the total they had won the previous two. Things were looking up, too. Both Embiid and Simmons were scheduled to make full recoveries by the beginning of the upcoming season. And in the meantime Colangelo had a lottery pick—No. 3 in the draft, thanks to a previous deal made by Hinkie that allowed the Sixers to swap 2017 first-round picks with the Sacramento Kings—plus cap space and a war chest full of assets. If there ever was a time for Bryan Colangelo to step out from Hinkie's shadow and prove that he was more than just Jerry's kid, this summer would be it.

Chapter 13

"THIS IS NOT THE FUCKING KID WE DRAFTED"

Pre-draft workouts typically take place in front of small audiences and without cameras. This, on the Saturday night before the 2018 draft, was different. The Sixers had opened the doors of their Camden gym to their business executives and some of their players. Media members were invited, too. The workout was streamed live on the team's website, as was a post-workout interview with the Sixers' in-house reporter. This was a press junket, not an audition; a celebration of the team's soon-to-be-official acquisition of the player they believed would be their third star.

"Markelle Fultz is a franchise lead guard, future All-Star, and a player any organization can build around," ESPN draft expert Mike Schmitz wrote in a scouting report published that week. Fultz, nineteen, was coming off a magnificent freshman season (23.2 points, 5.9 assists, 5.7 rebounds, 1.6 steals, and 1.2 blocks per game) at the University of Washington. He was long and explosive and could score from anywhere. One possession he'd stop-and-pop from the top of the key, the next he'd use his 6-foot-4, wide-receiver-like body to bully his way to the hoop, the next he'd swiftly spin across the lane and dunk the ball with one hand.

By the end of the college season, nearly every evaluator in and around the league had Fultz ranked as the top prospect in the class. There were, however, a few exceptions. Danny Ainge, the president of basketball operations for the Boston Celtics, the team that happened to own the draft's No. 1 pick, was among them. "He thought Jayson Tatum"—a smooth 6-foot-8 forward out of Duke—"was the draft's best player," said a confidant. Ainge had given Fultz a chance in early June, bringing him in for a private workout, only to watch Fultz struggle. "There was no music, the gym was quiet, and there were just all these older white men staring at him," said Keith Williams, a longtime Fultz mentor who also worked as his chief representative for the majority of the pre-draft process. "He was nervous."

The Sixers owned the draft's No. 3 pick and weren't sure who to take. It was all but guaranteed that the Lakers would tab UCLA point guard Lonzo Ball at No. 2. That would leave the Sixers with all sorts of options. Brown loved Jonathan Isaac, a long and lithe forward out of Florida State. Colangelo liked him too, but he was also intrigued by Kansas wing Josh Jackson and Kentucky point guard De'Aaron Fox. He had all three ranked ahead of Tatum, but it was Fultz whom he and his front office, most vocally Marc Eversley, the team's vice president of player personnel, coveted most. Not only did they consider him the draft's top prospect, but they believed he boasted the perfect skillset to play alongside Ben Simmons, by then fully recovered from the foot injury that had sidelined him for all of the previous season, and Joel Embiid. Fultz could play both with and without the ball, and run, and create in the half-court, and also defend opposing point guards, an area where the taller Simmons struggled. Simmons and Embiid each had Hall of Fame potential, but they were not necessarily a natural duo. Fultz, Philadelphia thought, could be the bridge.

To get him, the Sixers believed they'd need to grab the No. 1 pick. That didn't faze Colangelo. He'd always been an aggressive GM, someone who, while running the Raptors back in 2012, had signed Knicks guard Landry Fields to a then-outrageous three-year, $18 million contract just to rob the Knicks of one of their top trade assets and thus their ability to trade for Steve Nash, a two-time

MVP and Canadian legend whom Colangelo desperately wanted to sign.[1]

Colangelo and Ainge, a former Suns colleague of his, agreed to terms about five days before the draft. They'd swap lottery picks and the Sixers would also send Boston a future first-rounder.[2] The Sixers would then officially sign off on the trade after meeting with Fultz in person.

Fultz learned of the deal while driving around his hometown with his mom and Kenneth Tappin, a longtime friend, on the Friday night before the draft. He groaned upon hearing the news. In the weeks leading up to the draft he'd told Tappin that Philadelphia was one of the two cities he was hoping to avoid (the other being New York). He was worried about living and playing in such major markets and also about being so close to his hometown of Upper Marlboro, Maryland.

A workout was scheduled for the following evening. Fultz and Williams drove up from Maryland, with Fultz spending the traffic-filled three-hour ride sleeping in the passenger seat. He strolled into the facility wearing a black Sixers hat over his high-top fade and was greeted by smiling executives. This was an exciting day for the Sixers,

---

1   It's worth going over the details here, mostly because they're kind of hilarious. The Raptors at the time were coming off a disappointing 23–43 season and Colangelo's job was in jeopardy. He believed Nash, then thirty-seven, whom he had signed eight years earlier in Phoenix, could once again transform his team. Colangelo offered Nash a three-year, $36 million contract, but he was worried that the Knicks, believed to be the other team Nash was considering, might steal him. The Knicks could only realistically get Nash by agreeing to a sign-and-trade with the Suns. This is where Landry Fields came in. The Knicks, being the Knicks, were lacking in assets, and Fields, a promising twenty-four-year-old restricted free agent, would have to be at the center of any trade package. So Colangelo decided to pry him away and neuter the Knicks' ability to participate in a sign-and-trade. It was a sort of brilliant move...until the then-recently divorced Nash took a pay cut to play for the Lakers so that he could be closer to his kids in Phoenix. Fields averaged 3.3 points per game in his three years with the Raptors and then retired.

2   It would be the Lakers' 2018 first-round pick that the Sixers would receive if it fell between No. 2 and 5. If the pick did not convey, the Sixers would send the Sacramento Kings' 2019 first-round pick, which Hinkie had secured in a previous trade. (It wound up being the Kings' pick, which was 14th in the 2019 draft.)

and for Colangelo, who was eager to put his imprint on the team he had inherited. Drafting Fultz would not only give the Sixers one of the league's best young cores, one that would no doubt spend the next half decade, if not more, filling the stands and competing for titles—it would also allow Colangelo to take credit for completing the Sixers' Process *and,* he believed, silence all those critics who twelve years later refused to see the botched Andrea Bargnani selection from his perspective.

"He was always bringing it up, trying to explain why it wasn't a bad pick," a Sixers colleague said.

A camera stationed along the sidelines was flicked on. Fultz put on a gray Sixers T-shirt, loosened up, and walked to the foul line. He missed his first shot and several more. He launched a series of three-pointers. Almost all of them clanked off the rim, his shoulders dipping after each miss. He looked nothing like the confident scorer who'd drilled 41 percent of his triples in college. The Sixers figured it was the combination of nerves and the long drive. And anyway, this was a show, not an actual workout—the on-court scouting had been conducted during the season. This night was about evaluating Fultz off the court. Fultz met with Colangelo and Brown, and also Simmons, Embiid, and Sixers wing Robert Covington. "Joel came up after I had finished and of course the first thing he said was, 'Trust The Process,'" Fultz recalled. The four players posed for a photo.[3] Fultz was affable and engaging. The trade was made official that Monday. Three days later, donning a new Sixers hat, Fultz shook the hand of NBA commissioner Adam Silver.

———

Most No. 1 picks grow up like Ben Simmons and arrive in the NBA having spent the majority of their teenage years in the spotlight. They land on scouting radars as high school freshmen or even in middle

---

3   "This should be legendary if it happens #TheProcess," Embiid wrote as a caption. Fultz responded by commenting, "Trust the process."

school. Their names pop up on rankings, their highlights on YouTube, and they are tossed into the machine that is the basketball-industrial complex. They learn fast the dangers of money and fame, and how the lure of both can corrupt family and friends.

Markelle Fultz's rise was different. He wasn't a child star. He didn't have years to prepare. As a 5-foot-9 freshman at Maryland's DeMatha Catholic High School, he wasn't even allowed to try out for the varsity team. He was relegated to the school's freshman squad instead.

"He was clumsy back then," Williams said. "He had big feet and was always tripping over them. He just wasn't smoothed out."

Fultz had met Williams when he was about seven years old. After Markelle attended a summer basketball camp, and begged his mom every morning to drop him off early so that he could get shots up before other campers arrived, Ebony Fultz, who raised him and an older sister as a single mom, began looking for ways to channel her son's passion for the game. A friend suggested that she reach out to Williams, a local trainer in his late thirties who had worked with a few NBA players and high-profile prospects like future All-Stars Kevin Durant and DeMarcus Cousins. Ebony knew Williams from high school. He told her to bring Markelle to his gym and that he charged $30 a session. Williams put his players, even the youngest ones, through grueling practices. He focused on cardio and strength building. Balls were often left on the side. Water breaks were limited.

Markelle, full of energy, loved every minute of it.

"Most little kids would leave my workouts like, 'Man, that old man is crazy,'" Williams said. "Markelle would be like, 'Oh, can I go again with the older kids?'"

Fultz's game improved. A college basketball scholarship seemed within reach. Markelle and Ebony wanted a high school that could help Markelle obtain one. It didn't matter if it was a private institution with bloated tuition. Ebony had spent years as a government worker, saving up enough money to move her family out of an apartment and into a house with a yard. "Sometimes things got tight—well, a lot of times things got tight," Ebony recalled. "I wanted to make sure [my kids] had what they need and a little of what they want." Markelle's future was an expense she was willing to incur.

Fultz enrolled in DeMatha, a prestigious local private school that had sent seventeen alumni to the NBA.[4] But what initially seemed like an attractive attribute wound up presenting a problem. There were too many good players attending the school, and no room on the varsity for Fultz. He was cut again as a sophomore, and the summer before his junior year, after shooting up to around 6-foot-3, considered transferring. Williams, who by then had stopped taking money from Ebony and become more father to Fultz than coach, believed Fultz had the talent and drive to become a McDonald's All-American, an honor bestowed yearly on the top high school players in the country. He encouraged Fultz to find another school, one where he could be the star. Ebony, however, wanted Markelle to remain at DeMatha. The school was strong academically and well connected to colleges and its alumni. The decision was left to Markelle. This wouldn't be the last time he'd be forced to choose between Williams and his mother.

He thought long and hard, then called Williams. "I'm staying at DeMatha," he told him. Williams was hurt, but he kept working for Fultz. He collected funding from Under Armour for his AAU team, the D.C. Blue Devils, so that Fultz could travel to tournaments and get noticed by scouts. DeMatha finally promoted him to varsity. Within a year Fultz was ranked by ESPN as the 12th best high school recruit in the country. The recruiting letters started arriving in bulk, eventually filling a seventy-quart storage bin in the Fultz home. Some schools got creative: Louisville sent a mock *Sports Illustrated* cover featuring Fultz; Penn State drew up a fake tweet of Fultz announcing his commitment to the school. But only one school had been there from the beginning. Raphael Chillious, a Maryland native and Washington assistant coach, had arrived early to a DeMatha game a couple years earlier and noticed a gangly kid on the JV who could do a bit of everything. At halftime, he called Washington head coach Lorenzo Romar.

"Coach, you are going to call me crazy, but I'm watching a 5-foot-9 kid, and if he grows into his body, he will not be an NBA player. He will be an NBA All-Star," Chillious told him.

---

4   As of August 2019, that number has climbed to twenty-three.

Romar was dubious.

"Coach, I'm serious," Chillious replied.

After Fultz's growth spurt, Chillious and Romar made Fultz their primary target. They attended all his AAU games. They talked with Williams about all the guards Romar had sent to the NBA. They called Ebony on Mother's Day. Fultz, with Ebony at his side, visited the school's campus in August. He committed a week later. The Huskies went just 9–22, and Fultz missed some late-season games with a knee injury, which was cleaned up with arthroscopic surgery, but none of that mattered. He'd already proven himself to be the best college freshman—and possibly player—in the country, and completed his journey. In the span of just over three years he'd gone from playing for his high school's JV to being selected No. 1 in the NBA draft.

———

The transition to being a pro was going smoothly. Fultz suited up for the Sixers' Summer League team in Utah a few weeks after being drafted and looked like the player who had starred for Washington, not the one rattled by the pomp that had welcomed him in Camden. He was fluid and bouncy, his long arms wreaked havoc, and his jumper was smooth. He scored 40 points in two games. Any lingering concerns the Sixers had from the poor pre-draft workout were put to rest.

Next up was the Las Vegas Summer League. During the third quarter of his first game Fultz stepped on an opponent's foot and sprained his left ankle. The injury wasn't serious, though it was significant enough for Philadelphia to shut him down. But Fultz didn't like staying off the court, and so during practice time he'd goof off on the side and figure out funky ways to shoot without putting pressure on his injured foot. Around a week later, while still in Las Vegas, he was cleared to begin shooting normally. He and Lloyd Pierce, a Sixers assistant coach, set up on one side of the team's temporary practice gym during an off day. Fultz launched dozens of jumpers. His form was disjointed. Only a few of the shots went in.

"I've never seen anything like that before," Pierce told colleagues afterward. "The kid can't shoot."

After Summer League, Fultz visited a basketball camp in Las Vegas and, at the request of the Sixers, Peak Performance Project (known as P3), a high-tech training center in Santa Barbara. He then returned to Maryland to pack up his stuff and continue training with Williams and Tappin, who had become his unofficial manager.

"My shot's trash now," he told Tappin. The two went to a gym one day after Fultz returned home from Summer League. Nearly all of his jumpers richocheted off the rim. He looked rusty and unsure, and he was releasing the ball closer to his chin as opposed to up near his eyes. Williams spent the next two months working with him on raising his release point to where it had been in college. "We mostly tightened it up," Williams said. "There were moments where he'd fall back a bit, but he was shooting fine."

While this was going on, Fultz watched as the circle around him, the one that had propelled him to this point, crumbled. It started a week before the draft, when he hired Raymond Brothers, a longtime NBA agent, to serve as his representative and attorney. Brothers had spent months wooing Williams. But after the draft, Williams, and others around Fultz, noticed a change. They first butted heads around Summer League, when Williams, against the advice of Brothers and the wishes of the Sixers, advised Fultz to sit until officially signing his contract, something NBA rookies often do.

"They called me and were like, 'What's wrong, Keith?' I was just, like, 'We don't have a contract, we don't have insurance, he shouldn't play,'" Williams recalled. "I think that rubbed them all the wrong way." A few weeks later, after Summer League, when Fultz made clear that he didn't want to visit P3, Brothers told the Sixers that Williams was to blame. "He used that as an opportunity to throw the dirt on me even though Markelle's telling him this is stupid, and then Philly gets mad at me," Williams said. "He was right. I didn't think he needed to be there. But I can speak for myself."[5] Ebony pushed Williams away too.

---

5 Brothers declined to comment, on or off the record.

She took more control of Fultz's schedule and finances. (He signed a four-year rookie deal, with the first two years and about $15 million guaranteed,[6] and also endorsement deals with Tissot, JBL, and Nike, all of which were negotiated with Williams's help and the latter of which was reported to be "multi-year" and worth about $1.5 annually.) She'd argue with Williams, and Tappin, but also with Markelle, whom she continued to view as her baby boy despite him now being a multimillion-dollar brand. They'd fight over cleaning out storage boxes in the family home. She'd call him dozens of times a day. One day, after a particularly trying fight with Ebony over his desire to purchase a new car, Fultz met Williams at the gym.

"He shot the ball worse than he had in weeks," said an onlooker.

Around September, Fultz moved into a house in Cherry Hill, New Jersey. "That's where everything went south," a friend said. Ebony got an apartment downtown but felt like she needed to exert even more control. Ebony's parents had left her as a child—she was raised by a grandmother—and when she became a mother she clung tightly to her own children. She'd bring Gatorade to Markelle's game for him and his teammates, but she'd also curse out AAU coaches who had the audacity to criticize her son. The pressure of life in and around the NBA only exacerbated these tendencies.

She'd become annoyed if Markelle had girls over at night. She installed security cameras around his home. She'd often eavesdrop and sometimes even call to scold Markelle about comments she'd heard. In response, Markelle began leaning more on Williams, especially when it came to checking in on nights out, which only angered Ebony more. "She would get upset that he were talking to him and not her, even though it was her that said make sure somebody knows where you're at," said the friend. "Once he moved up to Philly, her whole energy just started to change."

Williams stayed back in the Baltimore area, but drove up frequently to work with Markelle, early in the morning at the Sixers' training facility

---

6   The scale salary amounts for rookie contracts are outlined in the NBA's Collective Bargaining Agreement.

and in the evening at a local gym, and was confused by what he was seeing. Fultz's form was deteriorating. A small hitch had developed. He'd bring the ball up toward his face and pause before pushing it forward. "It's like somebody's holding my arms down when I'm lifting them to shoot," Fultz told Williams and Tappin. Williams, searching for answers, instructed Fultz to shoot while lying on the gym floor, or by dribbling the ball into his shot to create a rhythm—anything to help reset his muscle memory.

The Sixers were becoming aware that Fultz had a problem. One morning in early September, Brown approached Williams at the facility.

"What do you think is going on?" he asked Williams.

"It's mental, Brett," Williams replied. He told Brown he was working to fix Fultz's release point.

It didn't matter that he'd grown up with Markelle, spent years playing ball with him and accompanying him to buy G-Star clothes at the mall. It didn't matter that he'd always considered Ebony a second mom, or that he and Fultz had recently gotten matching tattoos—"F2G," for "faithful to the grind"—on the outside of their calves. Ebony didn't like how Tappin encouraged the nineteen-year-old Markelle to act independently, or how he told her that Markelle needed space, or how he tried explaining why there was nothing wrong with Markelle's new Cherry Hill neighbors excitedly wishing him luck on the street or leaving welcome-to-the-neighborhood gifts of Chick-fil-A, which Fultz had publicly expressed his affinity for, on his doorstep. "We need someone who's going to keep 'Kel in the gym, and you're not mature enough," she told him. A couple weeks after they moved in, Ebony printed dozens of flyers for Tappin to put in their neighbors' mailboxes, asking them to stop bothering her son. Tappin only distributed them to families that he thought had kids, which led to a fight, which led to her offering Markelle an ultimatum: Tappin or her. Tappin, knowing Fultz had no choice, moved out. That night, Ebony and Williams met Markelle at his home. Before long, Markelle and Ebony were yelling at each other. Crying, Markelle ran out of the house and into the street, barely avoiding a streaking car. Williams chased after him.

"The money did all this," Markelle, tears streaking down his face, sniveled to Williams. "I don't want this no more. You should have left me in college."

Fultz participated in a number of informal team scrimmages before training camp, never shooting the ball from outside the paint. Brown took it upon himself to "fix him." When that proved unsuccessful, he began consulting with team doctors, searching for a medical explanation.

"I remember getting a phone call and Marc Eversley is at my ass," Williams recalled. "He said, 'Keith, this is not the fucking kid we drafted. What the fuck is going on?'"

Two days into training camp, the rest of the basketball world began asking the same question. Mike Schmitz, the ESPN draft expert, tweeted a slow-motion clip of Fultz shooting free throws at Sixers practice, splicing it with film of him shooting foul shots at Washington. The juxtaposition was jarring, and the tweet went viral. It looked like two different players. Fultz had never been a great free throw shooter (he shot 65 percent from the line in college), but no one believed his form needed a complete makeover.

"My free throw's going to look the same as in college," Fultz told reporters after practice when asked about the changes. "I'm just trying to look at different ways to see how the ball can go in the hoop."

Brown, too, was asked about Fultz's new shooting mechanics. His response was more gruff. "Markelle has made some personal adjustments to his shot since we last saw him in Vegas, we've done stuff with him but really he's been with his personal trainer over the month of August and since Summer League ended," he told reporters. "He chose to look at some different things on his shot, heart's in the right place, trying to improve. Slowly, we're coming back into it and trying to recalibrate and get it back."

The quote made it back to Williams. To him, there was only one way to interpret Brown's words: "They were trying to establish a narrative to throw me under the bus." Brown and his staff tried working with Fultz, but his shot grew worse by the day and seemed to look different every time he entered the gym. At the free throw line during a preseason game, Fultz took a couple of dribbles, spun the ball up toward his shoulder, and tapped it back and forth between his left and right hands with his fingertips before shooting, as if someone had dared him to shoot without letting the ball touch his palms. He had told a friend that his shoulder was bothering him and the next day shared that explanation with Kevin O'Connor, a reporter from the website[7] The Ringer. "I'm just trying other things to make free throws," Fultz said. But he only seemed to experience shoulder pain while taking free throws. He'd dunk in warm-ups and toss full-court heaves in practices and make pull-up jumpers in preseason games—and all without showing any signs of discomfort.

The regular season tipped off in mid-October. Fultz played a total of 76 minutes while coming off the bench in the Sixers' first four games. He didn't take a single three-pointer. On October 24, the day after a Sixers win in which Fultz had scored just two points in 16 minutes of action, Brothers tried tossing his client some cover. "Markelle had a shoulder injury and fluid drained out of the back of his shoulder," he told ESPN's Adrian Wojnarowski. "He literally cannot raise up his arms to shoot the basketball. He decided to try and fight through the pain to help the team."

Brothers, however, had his facts wrong, and he was forced to correct himself later that day. "He had a cortisone shot on October 5, which means fluid was put into his shoulder, not taken out," was the quote he gave to ESPN.com later that day. "My intention earlier was to let people know that he's been experiencing discomfort. We will continue to work with Bryan Colangelo and the medical staff." The attempt left the public more confused but momentarily accomplished what Brothers intended. "If Markelle Fultz's bizarre shooting form is due to an injury, then why is he playing?" read a headline on CBSSports.com.

---

7 Or to use Sixers parlance, an "online media outlet." (About twelve people just laughed.)

Colangelo, eager to exonerate himself, was more than willing to answer the question. At the team's morning shootaround the next day, where it was announced that Fultz would sit out the Sixers' next three games due to "right shoulder soreness," Colangelo told reporters that Fultz had undergone a "couple" of scans and ultrasounds and that "the notion that there's anything structurally wrong or long-term in concern is clearly not the case. Nothing's wrong with Markelle Fultz." He added, "There was no medical reason not to play him. He was cleared to play and he wanted to play. That's why he was playing. His reluctance to shoot, obviously his shot mechanics have been affected by whatever's going on, or vice versa."

He pinned the injury on Fultz, and also Williams, who Colangelo said had worked with Fultz in August on altering his shooting mechanics, which, Colangelo implied, was likely the trigger for this mysterious shoulder injury (which, he was also implying, he wasn't sure existed). Brown read off the same script. "There is zero doubt Markelle tried to change his shot," he told reporters, who responded with a series of follow-ups, none of which Brown, back in the familiar role of team spokesman/meat shield, had good answers for.

How could you tell the injury affected Fultz?

"I don't want to comment on that."

When you did you become aware Fultz was injured?

"I don't know."

Did you know Fultz had a cortisone shot?

"I don't even remember."

The story gained another layer when Williams shot down Colangelo's accusations on a Philadelphia sports radio station that afternoon. "Oh my God. That's false. That's not true. That's not a changed shot at all. That's something that's been altered because of the injury."

He added, "You can look at his stats. He was one of the best shooting freshman point guards ever in terms of shooting off the dribble and catch-and-shoot, and that's what made him such a great pickup for Philly. That's what they were looking for, so why would someone who shot so well change his shot?"

Fultz visited a shoulder specialist in Kentucky. Four days later the Sixers made the inevitable official and announced that he would be out indefinitely with "soreness" and something called "scapular muscle imbalance"[8] in his right shoulder. But he remained with the team, and reporters coming in at the end of a November 6 practice watched him put the ball behind his back and casually toss it over his head in a manner that made it difficult to believe he was experiencing shoulder pain. "The crazier things got the goofier and sillier he got," said a Sixers staffer. These visuals were captured on reporters' cell phones and shared online, sparking even more questions. Soon after, the Sixers decided to make sure Fultz was off the floor before opening practices to the media.

He was kept out of sight for more than a month. On January 2, the Sixers announced that he'd been cleared for "gradual reintegration into team practices and training," and that the soreness was "dissipating and the muscle balance is improving." Two weeks later, Fultz was back shooting in front of reporters. His form looked different—but no better. His release point was still low, and he was still pushing the ball forward instead of smoothly guiding it up toward the rim, and it would start and stop, as if someone playing a video game was repeatedly pressing and releasing the shoot button. He'd dip his head after misses. "He can still impact an NBA game without having to shoot, he really can," Brown told reporters around that time. "He can impact an NBA game without having to shoot. But that doesn't make him whole." The line was meant as a compliment but came out backhanded.

Fultz spent the next three months rebuilding his shot with Sixers assistant coach Billy Lange. Many of the drills, like taking dozens of

---

8   Here is a description of the injury courtesy of the examining doctor, Ben Kibbler, and shared with PhillyVoice.com in February 2018: "The scapula is the base of stability so that your arm can do precise, powerful things to move a ball, shoot a ball in the overhead position. You've got to really have the shoulder blade in the right position of stability, it's the anchor to let everything else work. That's the problem. And when you have the shoulder blade not working well, the arm either is weaker or it's not positioned in exactly the right position, therefore the result is not very good, whether it's throwing a baseball or shooting a basketball." Kibbler, citing confidentiality concerns, declined to comment for this book.

shots from five feet away, were the type you'd see in a middle school gym. Every now and then Fultz would flash some progress—like a smooth midrange pull-up—but each step forward seemed to be followed by an airballed five-footer captured on a cell phone.

In late January, during a national broadcast of a Sixers game, play-by-play man Mark Jones told viewers that prior to the game Brown had informed him and the ESPN crew that Fultz was dealing with "some psychosomatic issues involved with getting over the hump and getting back on the court."

"I'm worried about the young man," analyst Doris Burke added.

The comments stung Fultz. "You really can't trust NO ONE!!" he tweeted that night. An angry Brown told reporters the next day that he'd been misquoted, that "there was no reference to any of that." But the damage had been done. Fultz was already leery of Brown, who he believed had promised him a starting spot before the season and then gone back on his word,[9] and of the front office, who he felt had tried forcing him to play a few weeks earlier during a trip to London. Living in a new city by himself with Tappin gone and Williams pushed to the side left him with few places to turn. He'd found some solace in Embiid's apartment, playing the card game Exploding Kittens and watching NBA games and highlights, but an argument between Ebony and some people in Embiid's circle had strained that relationship.

Frustrated, Brothers tried grabbing control of the narrative. The Sixers were scheduled to play on TNT in early February, and one of Brothers's former clients, Caron Butler, was slated to call the game. Brothers, without informing the Sixers, set up an in-game interview between Butler and Fultz.

Butler began the interview by reading a diagnosis off a paper, one that had not been mentioned before. "You have a case of scapular dyskinesis, which means you have to relearn things from a functional standpoint," he said. Then came the lob: "Tell me how you've been doing with that."

---

9   Even if Brown had made such a promise, Fultz's erratic shooting left him no choice but to go in a different direction.

"It's very frustrating," Fultz replied. He wore a solid black T-shirt and looked sad. "It's been tough, really, but at the end of the day I know it's going to make me better. It's been a long journey just trying to relearn it. I'm just going through it. I want to go back out there as quick as I can, but it's been a slow process." For the first time he was admitting that some part of him had forgotten how to shoot.

The gambit didn't remove any of the pressure swirling around Fultz. The end of every Sixers practice featured reporters standing as far out on the court as allowed, phones pointed in his direction. The clips would be viewed hundreds of thousands of times across the Internet and social media, and Fultz, active online like most teenagers, would see them all—and then retweet messages of encouragement.

"He just always thought the shot was going to come back and it never did," Williams said. "He had no answer for what was going on." Some of Fultz's teammates tried protecting him. "The kid's fucking nineteen, man. Holy shit. Y'all are sick," Sixers veteran J.J. Redick, signed by Colangelo in the off-season, shouted at reporters after a practice in early February. During an interview session later, Redick said, "I don't get the coming in here every day to, like, watch him shoot pull-up jumpers. It's a little obsessive." But in the absence of concrete answers there was little else for the public to do.

Some insight, or at least a view of the politics behind the saga, arrived in mid-February when PhillyVoice's Kyle Neubeck published an in-depth account of the ordeal. He revealed that Fultz had continued working with Williams through the season, often without the Sixers' knowledge, and that as recently as January Williams had led Fultz through a shooting session involving three different-sized basketballs. The story also contained an anonymous quote from a Sixers official throwing even more dirt on Fultz's mentor: "Markelle left [the Sixers] at the end of July, and the shot looked fine from our view until he showed up for training camp," the source told PhillyVoice. "He wasn't working by himself all that time." This narrative would be pushed heavily by the Sixers, Brothers, and others over the ensuing year, with reports coming out that Williams had worked with Fultz on tweaking his mechanics as early as the previous June, a charge Williams and others close to him and Fultz emphatically denied.

In response, Williams went on the offensive. He shared his side with reporters. He posted clips on social media of himself hitting jumpers, believing it would help his cause. "I wanted people to know that this is all easy to me, that I got perfect form, so why would I mess up his shot?" he said. But there was little he could do against the more powerful Sixers and Brothers. By then, Fultz had connected with Drew Hanlen, a renowned skills trainer who had worked with Embiid and whom both Ebony and the Sixers approved of. They'd agreed to work together over the summer. Williams had been cut out and the Sixers had been ostracized, and less than one year into it, Fultz's NBA career was already in jeopardy.

Chapter 14

CONFETTI

Despite the drama with Fultz, the Sixers were progressing just as Bryan Colangelo had hoped. In early October, a week before the season began, he signed Joel Embiid to a five-year contract extension. Doing so was dangerous. The deal was for the maximum amount permitted by the NBA's Collective Bargaining Agreement, a total of $146.5 million, and would climb to $176 million if Embiid hit certain markers (such as being named All-NBA)—despite Embiid to that point having played in only 31 games. Colangelo, aware of the risk, stuffed the deal with all sorts of injury protections, which were outlined across thirty-five detailed pages.[1] Two months into the 2017–2018 season no one cared. Embiid had become a bully in the post, adding some punch to his finesse, and the combination of his size and guile made the Sixers' defense impenetrable. Just twenty-three, he'd already established himself as one of the best players in the league. The combination of his contract and performance solidified his stats as the most important person in the franchise and the man who'd carry the Sixers into their next phase.

---

1   For example, if Embiid were to miss 25 or more games in a season due to an injury related to his previous foot and back issues, the Sixers could waive him and reclaim a portion of his salary.

Joining him there would be Ben Simmons, who, after missing his entire rookie season due to a foot injury, was, like Embiid, healthy and having no issues adjusting to the NBA. In a way, Simmons had benefited from the ability to spend a year learning about the league without having to step onto the court. Brown by this point had developed a playbook for keeping injured young stars engaged. "Unfortunately, I had a lot of practice," he said. He'd call Simmons into his office to study tapes of Magic Johnson. Sometimes during games he'd ask him for a play call. If Simmons wasn't with the team on a road trip, Brown would tell him to text his thoughts during the game.

Simmons enjoyed it all, but he struggled with the solitude that came with not being an active part of the team. "You're just doing the same thing every day," he said. "I had those days where I just wouldn't want to even go in." He tried combating the boredom by spending hours acting like a kid on vacation—watching *South Park*, playing *Call of Duty*, buying Nerf guns at Walmart—but the distractions carried him only so far. His whole life had revolved around basketball, and about making the NBA, and he'd finally made it—only to see it all taken away.

"I came to the States and no one knew who I was, then they kind of do, then I get injured and no one talks about you for a while," Simmons said at the time. "So it's kind of like now I've got to build myself back up."

He scored 18 points and pulled down 10 rebounds in his debut, and after the game, a five-point loss in Washington, he told reporters: "It felt like I was playing [NBA] 2K." Three games later he recorded a triple double—21 points, 12 rebounds, 10 assists—becoming one of the youngest and quickest to do so in NBA history. "We knew he was special the moment he stepped onto the floor," said Richaun Holmes, a center who played two seasons with Simmons in Philadelphia. Comparisons to LeBron James began popping up. Simmons, barely twenty-one years old, was already a physical force, but he also seemed to possess some of LeBron's other otherworldly qualities, both tangible (flinging pinpoint passes across the court) and not (manipulating a game's tempo), and he knew it too.

"It's easier to control things here than in college," Simmons told

David Patrick, his godfather and former college assistant coach, after an early-season win in Dallas.

Philadelphia entered the season pegged by Las Vegas oddsmakers as a 42.5-win team, and played at that pace for the season's first few months. The second half brought change, though. Embiid being released from his strict minutes restriction helped, and some savvy moves from Colangelo fortified the team along the edges. The first had come months earlier, when he lured veteran sharpshooter J.J. Redick with a one-year, $23 million offer. Redick, with his machinelike accuracy and ceaseless darting around the floor, immediately became a focal point of the Sixers' offense, opening up the court for Embiid and Simmons. Colangelo also scooped up Ersan Ilyasova and Marco Belinelli, two veterans marksmen who'd been recently waived by their respective teams and who fit snugly in the pass-happy scheme Brown had spent years rearing. The additional depth and shooting helped the Sixers end the season on a 16-game win streak, despite Embiid missing the final eight games with an orbital fracture suffered in a freak collision with a teammate.

At 52–30, the Sixers finished with nearly twice as many wins as the year before and third in the Eastern Conference. It was their best output since 2001, when Allen Iverson led them to the Finals. Five years after Sam Hinkie's decision to tear everything down, the Sixers were back in the postseason and the talk of the league. They were big and fast and explosive and, with Simmons leading the charge, beating teams by double digits. With the LeBron-led Cavaliers flailing and Boston Celtics star Kyrie Irving out with a knee injury, some experts even viewed them as the favorites to represent the conference in the Finals.

"The notion of the playoffs for me doesn't make me do somersaults," Brown told reporters toward the end of the regular season. "I want more."

———

Brown's playoff debut came on a Saturday night against the Miami Heat. Embiid, still recovering from the facial injury, welcomed the raucous home crowd by fulfilling the pregame tradition of ringing the team's 350-pound Liberty Bell replica. He wore a white Phantom of the Opera mask—he'd dubbed himself "Phantom of The Process" after being prescribed a mask following the injury—and the crowd exploded and the Sixers rode that energy and a dominant Simmons performance (17 points, 14 assists, and nine rebounds) to a resounding 130–103 win.

Game 2 followed a different script. The Sixers missed on 29 of their 36 three-point attempts and lost by 10. Afterward Embiid expressed his frustration on Instagram: "Fucking sick and tired of being babied," he wrote before deleting the post and clarifying his feelings to ESPN's Ramona Shelburne. "I promised the city the playoffs and I'm not on the court. I wish more than anything that I was out there. I just want the green light to play." Embiid had always fought the limitations imposed on him by the Sixers, going back to his refusal to wear a walking boot during his rookie season, and little had changed over the years. Now he had a new contract, which, combined with his skills and a budding friendship with minority owner Michael Rubin, only bestowed upon him more power, to both defy authority and command it.

Despite being listed as doubtful on the day of Game 3, Embiid returned to the floor in Miami. He wore a mask made from a mix of carbon fiber and a substance called polycarbonate, with protective eyewear built in. Embiid hated it, but he was told his type of fracture left him susceptible to reinjury. In any event, he adjusted quickly, dropping 23 points and dishing out four assists in a 128–108 win, and relishing every minute of his playoff debut. He hushed the Heat crowd after drilling three-pointers and stared down Heat players after swatting their shots. He took particular enjoyment in limiting Hassan Whiteside (five points in 13 minutes), an underperforming and over-paid Heat center he had squabbled with in the past.

"Whiteside is sooo bad!" Embiid exclaimed to his teammates in the locker room after the win.

Game 4 was close, but the Sixers squeaked out a 106–102 come-back win. The series moved back to Philadelphia for Game 5. Another victory would send the team into the second round.

Moments before tip-off, a rush of energy surged through the

charged-up Philly crowd. Hours earlier, the Philadelphia-raised rapper Meek Mill had been granted bail, ending a five-month prison term. Meek Mill, thirty, had been convicted in 2008 on charges related to the possession of drugs and guns (he denied the charges and in July 2019 was granted a new trial and judge by the Superior Court of Pennsylvania). He served eight months in prison and was placed on probation for five years—a period that was repeatedly extended—and in November 2017 a Philadelphia judge sentenced him to two to four years in prison for a pair of parole violations. He'd posted an Instagram video of himself popping wheelies on a dirt bike in upper Manhattan and was arrested that night, after performing on *The Tonight Show*, for reckless endangerment. His case, and life, had become a symbol for the United States' flawed criminal justice system, especially in regards to black men.

Michael Rubin had become one of his most public advocates. A stocky forty-six-year-old college dropout from Lafayette Hill, Pennsylvania, who preferred hooded sweatshirts to suits, he'd made billions of dollars in e-commerce. In 2011, he chipped in for a minority share of the Sixers. He was rarely present during Sam Hinkie's reign, but now the Sixers were rising. They had two young stars, both of whom had cracked the top 10 in jerseys sold. Only two NBA teams (the Golden State Warriors and Cleveland Cavaliers) sold more merchandise during the 2017–2018 season. Their attendance had soared—an average of 20,329 fans per game, the third-best mark in the league—and so had their local TV ratings (by 45 percent over the previous season). Their road games routinely sold out. The days of 10-win seasons and five-cent tickets were long gone. The Sixers were ascendant, and everyone wanted a piece. Rubin was no different.[2] As the Sixers became more prominent he started showing up to games and team events more frequently, befriending Embiid and loudly cheering him and his teammates on from a courtside seat.

Rubin first met Meek Mill at the NBA's All-Star Weekend in 2013.

---

2   "I don't think Josh [Harris] loves that Rubin gets all that PR for investing, like, $10 to $12 million," an owner of another NBA team said.

The rapper peppered him with business questions. The two stayed in touch, speaking on the phone a few times a week.

"I didn't really know anything about the criminal justice system when all this happened," Rubin recalled. "I didn't know anything about probation, and I didn't really care." Meek Mill's case shook him. "Meek used to always say to me, 'There's two Americas.' I'd be like, 'Dude, there's one America,'" Rubin said. "He was right. I was wrong. There's America, and then there's black America. I didn't agree with him, but he proved to be right."

Rubin visited Meek Mill in prison about a dozen times over the ensuing months and tried using his power and resources to fight on the rapper's behalf. The two got to work on creating an organization to advocate for criminal justice reform, but the case also presented Rubin with an opportunity to boost his profile. A publicist pitched media outlets on stories about Rubin and the battle he was waging. Reporters were asked to link to Rubin's newly created Instagram account.

Rubin had learned in the week leading into Game 5 that Meek Mill could be released any day. At around 3 p.m., a few hours before tip-off, he was told that bail had been granted.

"I want him at the game tonight," he told an associate over the phone. "Can I go pick him up or not? Will he be at the game or not?" He called Josh Harris, who owned Harrah's casino, which sat across the street from the state prison in Chester, Pennsylvania. Harris arranged for a helicopter to pick up Meek Mill and shuttle him and Rubin to a Philadelphia helipad. A black Chevrolet delivered them to the players' entrance at Wells Fargo Center. "He's gotta get a shower, and we gotta go win this game," Rubin told a group of reporters waiting in the parking lot.

"I need clothes," Meek Mill, wearing jeans and a solid burgundy shirt, said. He was asked how he was doing. "I feel great," he said.

Led by a phalanx of handlers and security, Meek Mill strolled through the arena's hallways and into the Sixers' locker room. His music had become the team's soundtrack, with Simmons and Embiid even visiting him in prison. He put on an Embiid jersey and was ushered to a courtside seat. A crowd of fans and media members, almost all carrying cameras and phones, congregated on the sideline, angling for a glimpse. The in-arena announcer welcomed him home. The lights went dark, and the team's Liberty Bell was rolled out toward midcourt. Carrying a small, makeshift hammer, Meek Mill strolled out to the spotlight. The crowd stood. The celebration had begun.

The game remained tight for the first half, but the Sixers caught fire in the third quarter and held off a late Heat really for a 104–91 series-clinching win. Confetti was fired into the air and the sold-out crowd belted out the lyrics to the team's victory song—*Clap your hands, everybody / For Philadelphia 76ers*—as it flowed out of the Wells Fargo Center speakers. In their plush locker room, Brown gathered his team. After every win, he would choose a "player of the game" to ring a miniature Liberty Bell. Redick, who had led the Sixers with 27 points, was called up. He placed a hand on Brown's shoulder. "Brett, congrats on your first career playoff series victory," he said, and handed the bell back. Embiid, standing behind Brown, and Robert Covington, a wing who'd been with the Sixers since 2014, leapt with glee while emptying bottles of water and a chocolate milk onto Brown. "Ring that fucking bell!" some players hollered. Brown, the lone survivor from the original Process team, soaked and shouting gibberish in his Bostralian accent, giddily complied.

"I was hired in 2013 and I sat with Josh Harris and David Blitzer and a few of the other owners and we talked about the vision, what we hoped to build, and through rough times and through adversity for sure, we didn't blink," Brown, white towel draped over his shoulder and gray hair soaked, said at the postgame podium. "We stayed strong in what we were trying to do."

Embiid, an All-Star on a max contract and fresh off his first series victory with a team that looked like it could go to the Finals, shared a similar thought. "Two years ago we won 10 games," he said. "To be in this position, I'm just excited."

———

Next up for the Sixers were the depleted Celtics. They'd won 55 games in the regular season, but Irving was now joining All-Star

Gordon Hayward, who had fractured his leg on the season's opening night, on the sideline while a balky hamstring had left young forward Jaylen Brown's status in doubt. The Sixers opened the series as heavy favorites—only to fall flat in Game 1. They misfired on 21 of their 26 three-point attempts and had no answer for Celtics rookie Jayson Tatum, the player the Celtics had chosen over Markelle Fultz, who racked up 28 points.

In Game 2, the Sixers came out swinging the ball, making their shots and suffocating the Celtics' offense, taking a 48–26 lead midway through the second quarter.

The Celtics responded with an electric 21–5 run to close the half, abetted by Brown's refusal to call a timeout and throw a life vest to his drowning players. The two teams battled in the second half, but a driving layup from Al Horford past the slower Embiid with just over eight seconds sealed a Game 2 victory.

The series moved to Philadelphia for Games 3 and 4. One more win would put the Celtics up 3–0, a deficit no NBA team had ever come back from.

The game remained close throughout, with Embiid dunking and drop-stepping and Simmons bouncing back from an ugly Game 2 performance (one point in nearly 31 minutes of action). But Tatum repeatedly punctured the Sixers defense with a series of smooth jumpers and slithery drives, and a series of careless mistakes—a season-long issue—cost them late in the fourth quarter. A miscue between Redick and Simmons with six seconds left led to an errant Redick pass, which the Celtics converted into a breakaway layup to take a two-point lead with 1.7 seconds left, stunning the Wells Fargo Center crowd. Brown called a timeout to draw up a play. Simmons took the ball on the right sideline, parallel to the top of the key. Belinelli, inserted into the game for his shooting, sprung open and curled toward the right corner. He caught the ball with his feet brushing across the three-point line and, while fading into the Sixers bench, flicked it up toward the hoop. The buzzer sounded as the ball went in. Belinelli's teammates mobbed him. Brown walked off the floor and to the locker room. A Sixers game operations worker launched pieces of red, white, and blue confetti into the air.

"We had drawn it to be a walk-off three," Brown said after the game. "And I thought it was."

But Belinelli's feet had been on the line when he released the ball. The shot, counting for two points, had only tied the game.

It took about seven minutes to clean up the papier-mâché and begin overtime. Belinelli drilled a jumper and Redick buried a three to give the Sixers a five-point lead. But once again the Celtics fought back. Their spread offense left Embiid on an island and opened lanes for Tatum to attack. He laid the ball in with 55 seconds remaining to cut the lead to two, his fifth and sixth points of the extra period. On the next possession Celtics point guard Terry Rozier picked off a lazy pass from Embiid, which led to an Al Horford free throw, trimming the Sixers' lead to one. Embiid on the next possession misfired on a fade-away jumper. Simmons grabbed the rebound with 19 seconds left and elected to shoot instead of kicking it out to kill the clock. His floater came up short. The Celtics called timeout. Boston head coach Brad Stevens had Marcus Morris take the ball out deep on the right sideline. Everyone except Horford, who Stevens knew would have the smaller Covington guarding him, was told to run back toward the opposite end of the court. Horford sealed Covington with his left arm and Morris tossed a lob pass over the top. With Covington's teammates all having evacuated the paint, there was no one to help him fend off Horford. He caught the ball at the rim and laid it in.

The Sixers had one more chance. Brown called another timeout. From half-court, Simmons tossed a soft, one-handed pass to Embiid at the foul line. Horford pounced in front of him and deflected it away. Seconds later the Celtics were celebrating a 101–98 win. The Sixers knew what this meant.

"Teams that are down 3–0 [in the series] have a record of 129–0. Just think about that number," Brown told reporters after the game. But he also said he wasn't willing to give up. "The number to me, zero, happens more out of spirit than talent. There's a breaking point we all have and I believe that, if we maintain our spirit, why couldn't we be the one?"

Motivating players had always been a strength of Brown's, but he decided to make a tactical adjustment for Game 4 too. T. J. McConnell, a former undrafted point guard who had impressed the Sixers during a 2015 Summer League audition and earned a contract that preseason, was inserted into the starting lineup. The son of a high school coach from Pittsburgh, McConnell didn't boast the skillset typically found in NBA players. He was barely six feet tall and not a good three-point shooter. But he was quick, tenacious—he'd pop 5-hour Energy shots before games—and a handful off the dribble. He reminded Brown of himself.

"My mindset was to make a lasting impression by how hard I worked on and off the court and try to do things the right way and be a professional," McConnell recalled. "I had to try and teach myself how to be a professional. We had a very young team and on the court [I was] just being like a Tasmanian devil and running all over the place."

He, Covington, and Embiid were three of the last holdovers from the Hinkie days,[3] and in the years since, McConnell had become a cult hero among Sixers fans. As the short white guy on the bench, he possessed the stereotypical traits often found in fan favorites,[4] but there was more to it. The love affair began with a game-winning buzzer-beater over Knicks All-Star Carmelo Anthony during the 2016–2017 season. McConnell had also appeared as a guest on the *Rights to Ricky Sanchez* podcast, recorded in October 2017 in front of a live audience, where his sense of humor and affinity for profanity further endeared him to the most ardent section of the team's fan base.[5]

"The facility we were at for practice my first season, that's part of The Process, too," McConnell said at one point, referring to the Philadelphia College of Osteopathic Medicine, where the Sixers previously rented space. "I walk into the facility and we got doctors playing, saying, 'Get the fuck off the court, we're tryin' to practice here.' And I mean, they're at one end and I'm at the other and I was like, 'No wonder we've only won 10 fucking games this year.'"

---

3   Along with Dario Šarić and Richaun Holmes.
4   Unfairly, it should be added, but that's a deeper conversation to be had in a different place.
5   In October 2019, *Rights to Ricky Sanchez* listeners inducted him into the show's Process Hall of Fame.

Most important, McConnell was in on it all. He knew when to take himself seriously and when to not and when to seem humble and when to boast, and he always seemed genuine. "I'm not supposed to be here," he'd often say of his NBA career. He'd never forgotten the email that his college coach had received from a fan after signing him: "I didn't know we were recruiting waterboys?"

Now he was starting a win-or-go-home playoff game, and his presence was immediately felt. He pushed the pace. He knifed into the paint. He pressured Rozier full-court. He scored a career-high 19 points, along with eight rebounds and five assists. Fans chanted his name. The Sixers extended their season with a 103–92 win.

The teams flew back to Boston for Game 5, which followed a familiar script. A close first quarter. The Celtics led by nine at halftime. The Sixers cut it to one entering the fourth quarter. Embiid was great. So was Tatum. Tied with 6:41 left. Two Simmons free throws. A Tatum dunk. Four straight points from Embiid. A three from Sixers forward Dario Šarić—one-point Sixers lead, 3:30 left. Tie game, one minute remaining. A Šarić turnover. With 22 seconds left, Tatum cut backdoor for a layup to give the Celtics a two-point lead. The Sixers called timeout. With his season on the line, Brown called for Embiid to get the ball in the post. Embiid walked onto the court, leaving his mask on the bench. "I felt like this could be the last possession of the season so I needed to be at my best," he would tell reporters later. He fielded the ball a foot below the right elbow. Celtics center Aron Baynes, 6-foot-10 and 260 pounds of muscle, bodied him up. Embiid took three dribbles to the left, his right shoulder and Baynes's chest crashing into one another like a battering ram against a metal door. No whistle was blown, and Embiid muscled the ball up off the backboard. It fell off the rim. Embiid tapped the ball up against the glass, corralled it off the bounce, and tried gathering himself. Rozier darted to the paint. He knocked the ball off Embiid's shin and out of bounds. Embiid, trying to lunge after it, collapsed to the floor.

Rozier extended the Celtics' lead to four with a couple of made free throws. Redick buried a quick three. The Sixers fouled Marcus Smart, who split two free throws. The score was 114–112, Celtics. Out of timeouts, Brown had Simmons try a full-court pass to Covington. Smart picked it off. The buzzer sounded.

As Boston celebrated, Simmons walked over to Embiid. "There's gonna be a lot of [championship] rings on this before we're done," he told him, holding up a hand.

He had good reasons to be optimistic. It had been a disappointing finish but a magical season. Entering the year, the Sixers' goal had been to make the playoffs. Now here they were, upset that they'd *only* advanced one round. They were young and talented and exciting and their future was bright. After the loss even Embiid couldn't help but think about how far he and the organization had come. And he knew exactly who to thank.

"Sam Hinkie did an amazing job," he said from the postgame podium. "Look at everything we've got. He's a big part of it. You got to give him a lot of credit.

"The Process is never going to end. Looking at where we are, it paid off."

Chapter 15

"UNKOWN" SOURCES

About four months earlier, with the calendar about to turn to February and the Sixers still searching for their footing, Ben Detrick, a freelance writer and vocal Sixers fan, received a message from an anonymous Twitter user.

"Ben, loving your Sixers content," wrote an account with the username Enough Sixers, which had no profile picture or bio information and followed Detrick and no one else. "Can you follow me back so I can send you a DM about an article?" Detrick obliged. The user, who declined to reveal their identity, had a tip for Detrick, one unlike any NBA reporter had ever received: that Bryan Colangelo was secretly operating five anonymous Twitter accounts. Not only that, but he was using those accounts to bash Sixers players, reveal confidential medical information, and send messages to reporters in an effort to influence coverage.

Detrick was skeptical. For one, the story sounded absurd. Also, he was a vociferous Hinkie supporter and someone who enjoyed taking public jabs at Colangelo. "Blaming Brett Brown instead of scrutinizing Bryan Colangelo's gruesome, mind-blowing incompetence is pretty weird," he tweeted in December 2017. He recognized that he was somewhat compromised. "As a strident critic of Colangelo's hiring in Philadelphia and his team-building performance over the past two years, I understood why someone who was looking to portray the executive in an unflattering light would consider me an eager ally or a target for catfishing," he'd later write.

But then Enough Sixers sent Detrick the data they had compiled.

There were five accounts: @phila1234567; @AlVic40117560, which listed its name as Eric jr and described itself as a "Basketball lifer" located in "South Philly"; @HonestA34197118, which went by the name of Honest Abe; @Enoughunkownso1, which went by the name of Enoughunkownsources[1]; and @s_bonhams, which went by the name of Still Balling. Enough Sixers told Detrick that over the previous couple of years they had noticed a "bunch of weird tweets" sent to Sixers writers. Enough Sixers said they had worked in artificial intelligence and, through an "open-source data analysis tool," learned that all five accounts shared various characteristics.

For one, they all seemed to follow the same people on Twitter: Sixers players; members of the Sixers front office; Sixers beat reporters; the account of Colangelo's onetime agent and longtime family friend, Warren LeGarie; reporters covering the Toronto Raptors, where Colangelo had previously worked; accounts related to the University of Chicago men's basketball team, where one of Colangelo's sons played.

There was more, too. All five accounts seemed to be interested in the same topics: Sixers basketball, but most notably and specifically the praising of Colangelo—from his basketball decisions, to his acumen, to the size of his shirt collars—as well as the deriding of Hinkie.

"I have no respect for Hinkie's martyrdom bcs it is orchestrated by him behind the curtains via all the bloggers he cultivated with leaks," Enoughunkownsources wrote in November 2017. Eric jr wrote in January 2017, "BC has done nothing but clean up hinkie's mess. Hinkie got great pieces but could [not] make the puzzle work." That February, Eric jr tweeted at a Sixers blog that Ben Simmons's agent "stated that Ben would not have come to Philly, if Sam still here." When a fan on Twitter called Colangelo a "clown," Eric jr replied, "Clown? Why? What did Hinkie build? My gosh the biased insanity." When a Sixers

---

1   Yes, "unknown" was misspelled.

fan posted an image of Hinkie's head superimposed on a dancing body, Enoughunkownsources replied, "I just hate that Gif." And when one account replied to a picture shared by the Sixers' official handle in November 2017 featuring Colangelo in a dress shirt and sweater by saying, "This dude just loves collars," Enoughunkownsources shot back, "That is a normal collar. Move on, find a new slant."

Some of the comments aroused suspicion. "This you, Bryan?," one account once asked Enoughunkownsources.

"No—but thanks for the compliment!" Enoughunkownsources replied. "He is too classy to even engage. Worked with him: he is a class act."

It was clear, in the view of Detrick's source,[2] who the culprit was. "To me, there is no conceivable world where that is not Bryan Colangelo, himself," Enough Sixers told Detrick. "Not his wife, not his son, not his dad."

Detrick began following along and, with the help of editors and staff at the website The Ringer, conducting his own research. The evidence against Colangelo was strong, and also damning. It wasn't just Hinkie the accounts were going after. There were shots taken at a number of players too. Chief among them was Embiid, who'd been publicly poking at Colangelo and praising Hinkie since the latter was ousted and the former was hired.

"Joel is not the future of the franchise," Eric jr wrote in February 2017, "so who cares if he is not 100%, let's exploit him." That same month, with Colangelo being criticized for allowing Embiid to suit up for a late January game against the Houston Rockets with a torn meniscus, Eric jr tweeted at Embiid's official account, "Joel, you are just a kid, but why didn't you tell docs knees hurt before Houston? You costed yrself (&us) 9+ games and play-offs." Eric jr also accused Embiid of concealing the injury so that he could play on national TV.

The accounts often described Embiid as "lazy" and "selfish" in replies to Sixers bloggers and reporters. Eric jr once wrote, "If I were

---

2   As of this writing, the source had never revealed themself to Detrick or the public.

mngt I would step on a ladder and kick his b#**." Enoughunkown-sources once posted, "If I had a medium size ladder I would love to knock some sense in Joel's head right now. He is playing like a toddler having tantrums." Honest Abe said they'd trade Embiid for Knicks big man Kristaps Porzingis in a "heart bit [*sic*]. Such a smarter player."

Embiid wasn't the only player the accounts went after. Nerlens Noel and Jahlil Okafor, two players whom Colangelo had traded, were frequent targets. Both players, along with Embiid, were part of a center logjam that Colangelo inherited; much of his first year on the job was spent trying to clear it up. He came close to dealing Okafor in February 2017 and, believing a trade was imminent, even held him out of a couple of games. But the deal fell through and, according to the accounts, one person was to blame.

"I feel it in my bones, deal was done and Jah did not pass physical," Eric jr replied to a Sixers blogger. "Let's wait & see, only possibility at this point."

The burner accounts spent the next year pillorying Okafor and messaging reporters "hundreds of times," according to Detrick, that Okafor only remained a Sixer because he'd failed a physical, a detail never before reported.[3] "Ask Jah If he passed other team physical?" Eric jr tweeted at Keith Pompey, the *Philadelphia Inquirer*'s Sixers beat writer. "I bet the farm it's what's happened." Months later, Enoughunkownsources tweeted at ESPN's premier NBA reporter, Adrian Wojnarowski, "Nobody wants him. Last year he was traded and sent back because he didn't pass physicals. He asked FO not to let the info out...Still the FO is not leaking the truth to save face, Okafor abusing that. If the truth came out Okafor would be the one looking bad."

Colangelo did eventually deal Okafor—to the Brooklyn Nets along with Nik Stauskas and a future second-round pick in exchange for backup big man Trevor Booker[4]—but not before shipping out Noel, who was dealt in February 2017 to the Dallas Mavericks for Justin

---

3   And not since verified.
4   The Sixers waived Booker the following February.

Anderson, Andrew Bogut, and a pair of future second-round picks. The deal was panned. In April, Still Balling wrote, "Do you remember how Noel ELECTED to have hand surgery at the beginning of the season?...Then he went down south to rehab (did not stay with team and teammates) and was caught playing laser tag instead of being careful?" This, too, had never been reported before.

The one player who seemed to avoid the accounts' wrath was Ben Simmons. This was not a surprise. Colangelo had drafted Simmons just months after being hired. "I am sure it is hard for him 'to process' the fact, that this is now Ben's team," Enoughunkownsources once replied to a Twitter post about Embiid. "So he is acting up. This ego foul is costing us big!"

Convinced that there was a Colangelo connection, and a story to write, Detrick and The Ringer emailed Sixers media relations officials on May 22, thirteen days after the conclusion of the Celtics series. Cleverly, Detrick only shared the names of two of the accounts he'd been monitoring (@phila1234567 and Eric jr), "to see whether the partial disclosure would trigger any changes to the other accounts." A Sixers official told Detrick that he would ask if Colangelo had any information. A few hours later, the three accounts that Detrick hadn't mentioned to the Sixers all switched from public to private and Still Balling began unfollowing other users with connections to Colangelo, such as his son's University of Chicago basketball teammates. The Sixers told Detrick that @phila1234567 did belong to Colangelo, but, they said, he'd told them he knew nothing about Eric jr.

A week later, Detrick reached out to the Sixers "to ask about the seemingly linked nature of all five accounts." The Sixers replied with a statement from Colangelo.

"Like many of my colleagues in sports, I have used social media as a means to keep up with the news," it read. "While I have never posted anything whatsoever on social media, I have used the @Phila1234567 Twitter account referenced in this story to monitor our industry and other current events. This storyline is disturbing to me on many levels, as I am not familiar with any of the other accounts that have been brought to my attention, nor do I know who is behind them or what their motives may be in using them."

At 9:08 that night, Detrick and The Ringer published "The Curious Case of Bryan Colangelo and the Secret Twitter Account." Written cautiously, the article opted to insinuate rather than accuse. The implication, however, was very clear.

"With a 24-win improvement and an exhilarating run to the Eastern Conference semifinals this season, the Sixers were one of the league's feel-good stories. But behind all that could be the story of a team president who has spent the past two years using Twitter to anonymously spar with the media and defend Colangelo's reputation," Detrick wrote in the story's opening section, adding, "Together, these acts, if true, could be severely damaging to Colangelo's organization and amount to a huge breach of trust between him and the people he oversees."

The story blew up, with players, executives, agents, and reporters all reading and sharing. It was picked up by ESPN, the *New York Times*, and the *Washington Post*. Dallas Mavericks owner Mark Cuban and Houston Rockets president Daryl Morey and the official team accounts of Major League Baseball's Colorado Rockies, Tampa Bay Rays, and Oakland Athletics all tweeted jokes. Sixers center Richaun Holmes tweeted out thirty-six Tears of Joy emojis. Embiid got in on the fun too.

His first tweet was simple: a picture of him looking dumbfounded on the night he was drafted along with one word: "Bruh." His next tweet was more direct:

"Joel told me that @samhinkie IS BETTER AND SMARTER THAN YOU @AlVic40117560 #BurnerAccount."

He turned serious early the next morning:

"Fun night on Twitter lmao. All jokes asides I don't believe the story. That would just be insane."

Colangelo was watching a pre-draft workout in an L.A. gym and surrounded by NBA colleagues when the story went live. Gossiping onlookers saw him scrolling down the The Ringer's website on his cell phone while sitting in the bleachers. A few minutes later he got up and left. He spent the night on the phone with players and executives denying responsibility.

"I talked to him and he said that he didn't say that," Embiid told

ESPN that night. "He called me just to deny the story. Gotta believe him until proven otherwise. If true, though, that would be really bad."

The following morning the Sixers announced they had "commenced an independent investigation into the matter," which was conducted by the law firm of Paul, Weiss, Rifkind, Wharton & Garrison. Colangelo, meanwhile, continued insisting that he had no previous knowledge of the accounts. "Someone's out to get me. This is clearly not me," he told ESPN. That night a Sixers fan requested a password recovery for all the accounts and discovered the identity of a likely culprit or accomplice: Three of the accounts had likely been set up by Colangelo's wife, Barbara Bottini.[5]

Paul, Weiss began its investigation on May 30, the day after The Ringer's report. Colangelo surrendered his cell phone and spent hours meeting with the firm's investigators. So did Bottini. She also reset her phone, wiping its data before handing it over. Colangelo repeatedly denied his involvement. Bottini admitted that she had set up four of the accounts. Colangelo pled his case in a meeting with Sixers ownership and CEO Scott O'Neil in New York. He could sense the end was near, telling friends who called to offer words of encouragement that "this is going to be really bad for me."

On June 7, the Sixers released a statement saying they had accepted the resignation of Colangelo. "It has become clear Bryan's relationship with our team and his ability to lead the 76ers moving forward has been compromised," the statement said. Attached was a second statement from Paul, Weiss detailing the findings of its investigation:

"We do not believe that Mr. Colangelo established the Twitter accounts or posted content on those accounts," it read. "The evidence supports the conclusion that Ms. Barbara Bottini, Mr. Colangelo's wife, established the Twitter accounts and posted content on those accounts...Our

---

5   Requesting a password reset for each of the accounts allowed them to see the email addresses and the last two digits of every phone number connected to the accounts. Three of the accounts were connected to the email address bb.bottini@gmail.com, and ended with the numbers 91, which matched a phone number listed for Bottini on a website for Upper Canada College's Parents Organization, and can you believe this is an actual footnote in a book about a professional basketball team?

investigation revealed substantial evidence that Mr. Colangelo was the source of sensitive, non-public, club-related information contained in certain posts to the Twitter accounts. We believe that Mr. Colangelo was careless and in some instances reckless in failing to properly safeguard sensitive, non-public, club-related information."

Colangelo took issue with the law firm's wording. Later that night, reporters were sent a third statement. "I vigorously dispute the allegation that my conduct was in any way reckless," it read. "At no point did I ever purposefully or directly share any sensitive, non-public, club-related information with her. Her actions were a seriously misguided effort to publicly defend and support me, and while I recognize how inappropriate these actions were, she acted independently and without my knowledge or consent. Further, the content she shared was filled with inaccuracies and conjecture which in no way represent my own views or opinions. While this was obviously a mistake, we are a family and we will work through this together."

For the Sixers, though, there was no time to waste. The draft was just fourteen days away and free agency was set to begin ten days after that. Brown was appointed the interim head of basketball operations and the team immediately began searching for a new GM. Like Hinkie before him, The Process had swallowed Colangelo, though that didn't mean he was done trying to help the Sixers achieve their championship dreams.

Chapter 16

STAR HUNTING

Two days after being eliminated by the Celtics, Brett Brown candidly assessed his team's roster. "I think that another high-level free agent is required," he said during an end-of-season press conference in Camden. "I think we need help to win a championship."

The taste of success the previous season—16 straight victories to punctuate the regular season; 52 wins after winning a total of 75 over the previous four years; a playoff berth for the first time since 2012; a playoff series victory for just the second time since 2003; Embiid playing 63 games, more than double his career total entering the season, and proving himself to be a transcendent star; Simmons returning from injury and being named the NBA's 2017–2018 Rookie of the Year—had changed everything. In a single season the Sixers had transformed into one of the most skilled and starry groups in the NBA.

But the Celtics had exposed holes in the foundation, ones the Sixers would need to plug in order to make that next leap. Chief among them was Simmons's inability and unwillingness to shoot from outside. The Celtics prevented him from getting out in transition and driving to the basket. He hit just 47.5 percent of his shots against them after shooting 54.5 during the regular season, and he turned the ball over nearly as frequently as he dished out assists. Boston also shaded off him whenever he didn't have the ball, clogging the lane.

It wasn't just Simmons, though. Embiid's numbers were solid, but the series exhibited just how difficult it was to ride a seven-footer in the faster, more spacious, three-point-centric modern NBA. Redick was almost automatic from deep, but he didn't possess the physical tools to match up with the type of rangy, bouncy wings that the league's top teams all boasted. Covington was an elite defender but limited on offense.

There was no doubt that a team led by Embiid and Simmons would spend the next few regular seasons racking up wins and filling highlight reels. "For the first time since I have been here, there is tremendous clarity on what we have," Brown said that day in Camden. "There's no mystery when you look at what is Ben Simmons's skill package, and there's no mystery of what is Joel Embiid's skill package." But the Sixers had loftier goals, and the combination of expectations, their two stars' budding fame, and the controversial Process that had delivered them to this point would put the entire team under the microscope.

Brown recognized all this, and that the clock was ticking. Embiid was young, but there was no telling how long his body would last. Simmons would be eligible for a mega contract extension in a year, which would edge the Sixers up to the NBA's salary cap line, which meant the Sixers had two off-seasons to make a move before their cap space evaporated. With Markelle Fultz's future now in question, it had grown clear that any help would have to come from outside the organization.

"We are star hunting," Brown would later tell reporters.

———

Jimmy Butler wanted out of Minnesota.

He'd been traded there in June 2017 in what was a monumental deal for the franchise, which was trying to end a thirteen-year playoff drought. Butler was a stud, a three-time All-Star who could both score and defend, and he was joining a group with an exciting core of young players and, in Tom Thibodeau, a high-profile coach. For the first time in more than a decade, people outside of Minnesota cared about its professional basketball team. *Sports Illustrated* even splashed a photo of Butler across the cover of its season preview issue.

On the court, Butler did everything asked of him, leading the Timberwolves in scoring that year and carrying them into the playoffs. But they were eliminated in the first round and he was set to be a free agent in the summer of 2019. Over the year he had recognized that the Timberwolves were not a team and Minnesota was not a place where he wanted to be long-term. One problem was that he'd already handed max deals to two former No. 1 picks—Karl-Anthony Towns and Andrew Wiggins—limiting how much money Butler could make and when he could make it. But he also thought Towns was soft and Wiggins was lazy, and he had no patience for such apathy. It was only because of hard work that he'd made it this far.

His father had left his mom when Butler was an infant. His mom had kicked him out of her Houston suburb home when he was just thirteen. "I don't like the look of you. You gotta go," he recalled being her last words to him.[1] He spent the next four years couch surfing before a friend's family finally took him in. By the end of high school he had just one scholarship offer, to a junior college in Texas, where he spent a year before landing at Marquette University. Even there it took a year for him to crack the starting lineup. He kept working, though, and grew into an NBA prospect, and the Chicago Bulls selected him with the 30th pick in 2011. Butler played less than 10 minutes per game as a rookie, but he worked hard and played defense, the two things the hard-nosed and fiery Thibodeau valued most. Within two years Butler had become the team's starting shooting guard. He'd defend the opponents' top wing scorer and rarely come out of games. Little by little, his offense developed, too (he went from averaging 2.6 points per game, to 8.6, to 13.1, to 20.9, to 23.9), and with that rise came stardom, and with it a belief that he could do and say whatever

---

1   "Please, I know you're going to write something. I'm just asking you, don't write it in a way that makes people feel sorry for me," Butler told ESPN's Chad Ford in that same interview. "I hate that. There's nothing to feel sorry about. I love what happened to me. It made me who I am. I'm grateful for the challenges I've faced. Please, don't make them feel sorry for me."

he wanted. He considered himself an A-lister, and grew jealous of the way Bulls point guard Derrick Rose, a Chicago native and former MVP who had been diminished by a series of injuries, received top billing. He clashed with some of his older teammates, believing they still viewed him as the scrappy kid off the bench.

The Bulls fired Thibodeau after falling to LeBron's Cavs in the second round of the 2015 playoffs and replaced him with Fred Hoiberg, a forty-two-year-old former NBA guard and college coach who was Thibodeau's antithesis. He prioritized offense. He was reserved. Butler didn't respect him as a coach, and he hated his playbook. "It was either, 'We're going to build the team around me for a little bit and allow me to distribute the basketball, iso[lation] in pick-and-roll. Or you go with Fred,'" Butler recalled. "Go up and down, shoot a lot of threes, that type of stuff." Butler, who received a five-year, $95 million contract extension that summer, made his displeasure known. He also began questioning his younger teammates' desire to win, both in public and private.

The Bulls sided with Hoiberg and sent Butler to Minnesota, reuniting him with Thibodeau. "I'm so happy to be here," Butler said at his introductory press conference in June 2017, before sharing his phone number so any critic "who has anything to say to me" could voice their complaints. "These young guys are really really really talented," he added, "and I'm just here to push them to the best of my abilities."

But Towns and Wiggins weren't interested in being pushed, and not in the way Butler preferred. This only frustrated Butler even more. He called them "pussies." He threatened to sleep with Towns's girlfriend (using more colorful words). He'd body up to them and jut his face close to theirs. "To tell you the truth, fear will make you do a lot of things that you don't know that you could do," he told The Athletic that January. "So if I strike fear in somebody and they know I'm not playing around, they're going to do it. But if you just talk to them softly and all of that, the majority of the time it don't work." He'd always oscillated between urges. Sometimes winning was what mattered most, other times it was the spotlight. Whenever he had one he always seemed to crave the other. In Minnesota he had the spotlight, but he was twenty-eight, with a history of minor knee injuries and thousands of minutes on his odometer. He worried that "Minnesota's window didn't match his," his agent, Bernie Lee, said. "He didn't have four to five years to figure it out."

In February 2018, Butler earned an All-Star nod, and in the draft to divide up teams for the game he was selected by Stephen Curry. Butler joined the rest of his teammates in L.A. that weekend, a group that included Embiid. It was his first time interacting with the Sixers' star, and he was impressed by Embiid's skills and his demeanor. "That's a guy I'd love to play with," he told Lee. Embiid even appeared open to Butler's leadership style. At one point during the game, Butler noticed Embiid fail to pass the ball out of a double-team. After an ensuing timeout, he leapt up from the bench to cut him off.

"You're on the floor with four other All-Stars," he told him. Embiid's eyes met Butler's. "Pass that ball out."

From his seat across the Staples Center court, Bryan Colangelo watched the scene unfold. He also noticed Lee, a close friend of his, eyeing the interaction from behind the bench. Colangelo took out his phone.

"I've never seen Joel listen to someone like that," Lee recalled Colangelo texting him.

A little over two months later, the Timberwolves were eliminated by the Houston Rockets in the first round of the playoffs. "I'm done here," Butler told Lee after a series-ending Game 5 loss. Lee told him to take some time to think. Butler agreed and flew home—separate from the team—and a few days later called Lee to tell him he was sure. On April 29, Lee called the Timberwolves to pass along the message but kept the request quiet. Both he and Butler loved and respected Thibodeau. They wanted to work together and figure out a solution that helped all parties. But Minnesota, and particularly Thibodeau, wasn't interested in a trade. Thibodeau believed that getting Butler back into the gym with the team and focused on the upcoming season could prompt a change of heart.

Lee and the Timberwolves went back and forth all summer. On August 17, Lee's wife threw him a surprise fortieth birthday party in his hometown of Toronto. He was greeted by a bunch of friends seated around a table, a group that included Butler, who had chartered a plane from L.A., and Colangelo, a little over two months removed from the Twitter scandal that had forced him to resign. With the drinks flowing, Butler turned to Colangelo.

"Tell me about Philly," Lee recalled him saying.

Colangelo looked at him. "If you go there, you're going to win a championship."

The two chatted for a while, and the group spent the rest of the night drinking and eating and laughing. But the chat with Colangelo stuck with Butler. At breakfast the next morning he had a question for Lee: "What do you think about Philly?" He posed that same question to Colangelo on a Sunday morning a couple months later, at the NBA Players Association's midtown headquarters. Colangelo had come up from his downtown apartment to spend some time with Lee. There, he shared some advice with Butler. The Sixers, he told him, could give him everything he was looking for.

Despite their lofty ambitions, the Sixers entered the season with the same core of players that had fallen to Boston the previous postseason. All-Star forward Paul George, a free agent, re-signed with Oklahoma City without meeting any other teams. LeBron James, also a free agent, allowed his representatives to meet with Sixers' ownership in L.A.—but by then he'd already decided he'd be joining the Lakers. All-Star forward Kawhi Leonard was available, but the Sixers refused to part with Simmons or Embiid, and the San Antonio Spurs sent him to Toronto.

Sixers managing partner Josh Harris went star hunting to replace Colangelo as well, and, despite telling reporters at Summer League that there'd be "a line out the door" of interested candidates,[2] failed there too. He tried prying Bob Myers (architect of the Warriors dynasty) away from Golden State and Daryl Morey (ironically, Sam Hinkie's former boss and mentor) away from Houston. Morey met with ownership, but

---

2   He also, strangely, referred to The Process as "a science project that had its benefits."

passed on the offer. The Sixers chased a few other sitting GMs, most of whom were either not interested or were not granted permission to interview by their employers.

Others pursued by the Sixers were wary of the team's existing management structure. For one, Harris made clear that he expected whoever was hired to inherit the executives Colangelo had left behind. It was also known around the league that Harris and his partners expected to be involved and consulted in basketball decisions, and that the power vacuum created by the absence of both Jerry and Bryan Colangelo had provided them even more room to operate. On draft night, for example, the Sixers had traded No. 10 pick Mikal Bridges, a wing player considered to be NBA-ready, to the Phoenix Suns in exchange for a younger, rawer prospect named Zhaire Smith and a future first-round pick,[3] at the behest of minority owner David Heller. The search continued throughout August and into September. On September 18, with training camp just five days away, reporters were informed that Elton Brand, the team's recently promoted former G League GM, just thirty-nine and two years removed from wearing a Sixers uniform, was getting the job.[4]

"He's smart, hardworking, and represents everything we aspire to be as an organization. It's a players' league and Elton is universally respected," Harris said. "He has a remarkable understanding of the game. He knows how players feel and react, he knows what's important to them. He's the perfect general manager for today's NBA, where relationships throughout the NBA ecosystem, creating a desirable free agent destination and driving a team-centric culture, are paramount.

"He will be incredible, in not only helping our young core to develop but also in recruiting other players to our program," he added. Unlike Hinkie and Colangelo, Brand was not given the title of team president. Harris made clear that Brand would be reporting to him. Quietly, the

---

3 A 2021 Miami Heat pick, which was unprotected.
4 Joel Embiid's reaction? "As soon as I heard the news, I just thought about how two years ago I was dunking on him...I just remember dunking on him really bad."

Sixers announced another promotion the same day. Alex Rucker, the team's senior vice president of analytics and strategy, was elevated to executive vice president of basketball operations. Rucker, a lawyer and former Navy officer who came to Philadelphia from Toronto, already had more clout than many of his analytics-focused peers. The year before, the Sixers had granted his department the power to draw up an in-game substitution plan for Brown to follow. Brown was allowed to improvise, but the basic template was constructed by Rucker's staff. Now he was leapfrogging a pair of colleagues, Ned Cohen and Marc Eversley, on the org chart, giving Harris a fellow data-driven executive in every meeting. Brand would be the face of management and officially billed as the team's top decision maker, but Rucker would also have Harris's ear.

In the meantime, the Sixers had a season to prepare for. Having struck out on all their primary off-season targets, Brown decided to replace Redick in the starting lineup with Fultz. "It is our goal to go play in an NBA final [this year]," he told reporters. He believed boosting Fultz's confidence and harnessing the talent that had launched him to the top of draft boards presented the Sixers with their best shot at doing so.

It had been a strange summer for Fultz. He'd trained with Drew Hanlen, the skills coach who also worked with Embiid. Hanlen spent the summer hyping up Fultz's progress on social media, but never shared video of Fultz's supposedly reworked shot. He also became the latest person close to Fultz to attribute the shooting breakdown to something beyond a physical injury. "Markelle, obviously, he had one of the most documented cases of kind of the yips of basketball in recent years," Hanlen told the *Talking Schmidt Podcast* in June, "where he completely forgot how to shoot and had multiple hitches in his shot."

During the team's media day, in September, Fultz was asked about Hanlen's comments. "I think it was a mis-term in words, what happened last year was an injury. Let me get that straight," Fultz told reporters. "It was an injury that happened that didn't allow me to go through the certain paths that I needed to, to shoot the ball. Just like any normal person, when you're used to doing something the same way each and every day and something happens, of course, you're going to start thinking about it. It's just normal."

The Sixers did everything they could to boost Fultz's confidence. He was drilling threes in practice, Brand told ESPN's Zach Lowe. He took more than 150,000 shots over the summer,[5] Brown claimed Hanlen told him. None of it mattered. If left open Fultz could push in an occasional corner three, but his shot remained broken. Brown kept him in the starting lineup, but, in a rarely seen move, would begin each second half with Fultz on the bench.

The Sixers, meanwhile, were regressing. Simmons feasted on poor teams, but he showed little improvement from the previous year and often struggled against top-tier opponents. His work ethic had become a concern. He spent little time in the gym outside of practices. He'd goof around when coaches, including Brown, worked with him on his free throws, sometimes flippantly launching the ball high into the air instead of attempting a normal shot. He also recognized, like Embiid and other Sixers before him, that his talent gave him the power to bully the team's coaching staff and management. Over the summer he informed Brown that one of his half brothers, Liam, a former low-level NCAA Division I assistant, would take over as his primary shooting coach, despite the progress he made under the tutelage of Sixers shooting coach John Townsend. Simmons had made 71 percent of his free throws during the 2018 playoffs but now had fallen back below 60 percent. This, coupled with his near-absolute aversion to jump shots—he didn't attempt a three until the Sixers' 49th game of the season—left the coaching staff frustrated.

"Name me one area where Ben Simmons has improved," Jim O'Brien, a longtime NBA coach and former Sixers assistant who was serving as a "special adviser" to Brown, asked during an early-season coaches' meeting. The room went silent for a few seconds before one assistant tepidly offered a response: "Working out?"

The relationship between Simmons and Embiid was also

---

5   An amount that would mean Fultz took about 1,500 every day, for three straight months, with no days off.

deteriorating. There were no blowups or fights, but the little eye rolls were growing more frequent, behind closed doors but also during games. "It's not like their games entirely complemented each other," Brown said. Both wanted the offense to run through them. Simmons wanted more pick-and-rolls. Embiid wanted more post touches. Simmons was best when playing without a big man so that the paint could be left open. Embiid was best when surrounded by shooters who could spread the floor. The combination gave the Sixers' offense a round-peg-in-a-square-hole feel.

Their personalities didn't mesh either. Simmons was quiet, and behind the scenes Embiid mostly kept to himself. Both players wanted to be stars and lusted for the spotlight. Embiid was the social media sensation. Simmons over the summer had begun dating Kendall Jenner. Brown was aware of the dynamic. At least once he asked his PR team to post clips of Embiid and Simmons interacting on the team's social media channels, an effort to change the perception. He even summoned both into his office for a number of private meetings.

"You're gonna be teammates, I hope, for a very long time and at some point that admission needs to rule the day," he recalled telling them. "You don't have to go have pizza with each other every single night or hang out with each other. That's not it. It's what goes on between the lines [that matters]."

Getting there was taking longer than he hoped. During a November 4 game against the Brooklyn Nets, Simmons bumped into Embiid on three different occasions while going for rebounds. Embiid grimaced after each collision. The two barely communicated all game and the Sixers lost by 25, falling to 6–5. It had become clear that the Sixers were in trouble and that Fultz was certainly not the answer; and that if Harris, Brand, and Brown planned on fulfilling the team's preseason expectations they'd need to find some help.

———

The Timberwolves weren't budging, so Lee and Butler came up with a new strategy. Butler met with Thibodeau in mid-September, the week before training camp, and told him that he'd be opting out of his contract the following summer and that he'd like to be traded before that. Thibodeau said he couldn't trade Butler. He wanted—and, for his job security, possibly needed—to make the playoffs,[6] and couldn't do so without him. The meeting was leaked to multiple reporters. Thibodeau was flooded with trade calls. He rebuffed all inquiries. More gossip trickled into the media. Butler became the biggest story in the NBA. He skipped Media Day, and didn't show up to training camp. The Timberwolves continued receiving calls. First they declined to make specific requests. Then the requests became outlandish; Brand was told he could have Butler for *both* Simmons and Embiid the first time he called.

Butler skipped more practices, using the court at a local Life Time gym to keep in shape instead. He continued leaning on Lee, who continued leaning on the Timberwolves. Team owner Glen Taylor gave Thibodeau the green light to make a deal. He came close. In early October, he and the Miami Heat agreed to a trade centered around guard Josh Richardson. The teams were set to share medical reports—typically the signal of a done deal—before Thibodeau demanded additional draft picks.

Butler decided to take matters into his own hands. He was frustrated, and growing impatient. The following week he arrived late for a practice and subbed himself into a scrimmage and onto the third team. He wanted to play against, not with, the starters. His team didn't lose a single game, and Butler used the practice as an opportunity to share his candid thoughts.

"You fucking need me, Scott, you can't win without me," he shouted at Timberwolves general manager Scott Layden. He roared, "He can't do shit against me!" when guarding Towns. "They ain't shit! They soft!" he yelled about Wiggins and Towns. He ended the practice by walking straight out of the gym, skipping the group stretching period, and meeting ESPN's Rachel Nichols for a one-on-one interview that was set to be aired that evening on *SportsCenter.* By then, the details

---

6   He'd be fired that January with the Timberwolves 19–21.

of the practice had leaked out, ginning up all sorts of buzz for the segment.

"A lot of it is true," Butler said when asked about the reports. "I haven't played basketball in so long. I'm so passionate. I don't do it for any reason but to compete. All my emotions came out in one time. Was it the right way? No! But I can't control that when I'm out there competing. That's raw me, me at my finest, me at my purest. Inside the lines."

Nichols asked him about the back-and-forth with Towns.

"Am I being tough on him? Yeah, that's who I am," Butler replied. "I'm not the most talented player on the team. Who is the most talented player on our team—KAT. Who is the most God-gifted player on our team—Wiggs. Who plays the hardest? Me!"

He added later, "I think that's the part everybody doesn't see. I'm not going to say no names. I'm going to be honest: If your No. 1 priority isn't winning, people can tell. That's the battle. Now there is a problem between people. That's where the disconnect is."

Thibodeau canceled the next day's practice and media availability. But the outburst and subsequent press hadn't moved him. Incoming proposals were rejected. Butler returned to practice a few days later and suited up for the Timberwolves' regular-season opener, as well as nine of their next 11 games, with Thibodeau often pleading with him on game days to play. Lee kept pushing the Timberwolves and searching for new homes, and in late October, the Sixers traveled to Toronto for a game against the Raptors. That morning, Brand met Lee for breakfast at the Ritz-Carlton downtown. Brand was upfront. Since being promoted he'd made a point of tightening his inner circle and controlling what Sixers information was shared with the public.

"I don't deal with leaks," he told Lee.

Lee told him he understood. He explained why the situation was playing out publicly, how he and Butler felt that the Timberwolves had left them no choice. He and Brand spoke for about an hour. Lee told Brand that the Sixers were exactly what Butler was looking for—a team with young players ready to win and capable of carrying the load but who just needed a little help reaching that next level.

The Timberwolves left for a West Coast road trip two days later.

Butler played 39 minutes in a November 5 loss to the Clippers and 43 minutes in a loss two nights later to the Lakers. In Sacramento two nights after that, at halftime and having played 19 of the game's first 24 minutes, Butler called Lee.

"This is the last half I'm playing for the Timberwolves," he told him. "I can't keep doing this. This shit has gone on long enough."

Lee called Taylor and passed along the message. The Timberwolves lost by 11, their fifth loss in a row. That night Butler gave a wide-ranging, meandering interview to The Athletic, saying "that shit has to stop" when asked about the amount of minutes he was playing and then, when asked to clarify, responding, "I just want to win, I'll do whatever it takes." That same night, Lee called Brand, urging him to move forward. Sixers managing partner Josh Harris called Taylor, re-visiting a discussion that began during the league's board of governors meetings in September. The two reached an agreement: the Sixers would send Robert Covington, Dario Šarić, Jerryd Bayless, and a 2022 second-round pick to Minnesota in exchange for Butler and injured rookie Justin Patton. It was a haul for the Sixers. They'd acquired that much-needed third star, one who boasted the exact skills they were lacking, and had done so without surrendering any key assets. Butler could create his own shot late in games and space the floor with his jumper and defend opposing wings. If things worked out—and Brand believed they would—the Sixers would sign him to a five-year, $190 million contract the upcoming summer. If things didn't, and if the drama that had followed Butler from Chicago to Minnesota followed him again to Philadelphia, the Sixers could simply cut bait and use cap space to move on.

Butler flew back to Minnesota. Harris and Brand met him there, and the three of them, plus Lee, took a private jet back to Philadelphia for physicals and a press conference. Brand asked Butler if he was really that difficult, and for his view of what had gone wrong in Minnesota. Butler answered the questions the way he always did. He explained how all he wanted to do was win, and he was engaging and funny, the way he always was. Everyone knew the transition could be messy, that he was joining a team with two stars and an infrastructure already in place. But Brand and Butler had clicked, and they walked off the plane agreeing to maintain constant communication, whether things were good or bad.

It took a few days for the NBA to make the trade official, but on November 13, Butler finally joined the Sixers, who were in Orlando. He met the team at the hotel where they were staying. Embiid was on his way to a tennis court and invited Butler to join. The two spent a couple of hours "shooting the shit," according to Lee, who had tagged along. Butler made his debut the following night. "When you look in the rearview mirror and sort of look where we were as an organization and to be able to have the wherewithal and resources to attract somebody like Jimmy Butler, it's a very exciting day for the city and program," Brown told a throng of reporters before the game. He added that "Sam Hinkie deserves a lot of credit," and then explained what it was he thought Butler could bring to his team: "When you look up at the clock and its 94–94 and there's, like, six, seven minutes left in the game, the notion of equal opportunity, move-pass, isn't there for me. It's put your best players in a situation with the ball." He and his staff had learned this the previous spring in the playoffs against the Celtics. Butler, he said, gave the Sixers "something they hadn't had before."

In the visitors' locker room a few feet away, Butler was sitting in front of the two cubbies prepared for him by the team's training staff—an indulgence provided for him and no one else—and reading *Unfu*k Yourself: Get Out of Your Head and Into Your Life*. Around forty-five minutes later he was on the floor and helping the Sixers grab a 16-point fourth-quarter lead. But a 19–0 Magic run erased that deficit, and they won, 111–106. Butler played well, finishing with 14 points, but took just two shots in the fourth quarter and spent most of crunch time watching the action from the court's weak side.

"It's going to take time," Brown said afterward. But he wasn't going to let a tough loss ruin the moment. "In general, you see what you have in him," he added. "It's incredibly exciting."

———

Initially, Butler provided the Sixers a boost. They responded to the Magic loss with 10 wins over their next 12 games, two of them thanks to Butler drilling step-back, game-winning threes. He had become their closer, but he was also making a point of taking a backseat to Embiid and Simmons and doing his best to fit into the Sixers' pass-happy offense, the exact type of offense he'd protested when it was instituted by Fred Hoiberg back in Chicago. "When he first came here, I was caught off guard with how sort of complementary [he was]," Brown said.

But the ways in which Brown was trying to integrate Butler irked Embiid. "I haven't been myself lately, I think it's mainly because of the way I've been used, which is I'm being used as a spacer, I guess, a stretch five," he told the *Philadelphia Inquirer* before a December 7 win in Detroit. He had missed 21 of 30 shots in his previous two games and was also angry at Brown for insisting that he take that evening's game off for rest (he was averaging four more minutes per game than he had the previous season). "It seems like the past couple games, like with the way I play, our setup, [Brown] always has me starting on the perimeter and it just really frustrates me."

Butler was asked about Embiid's comments at Sixers practice the next day. He brushed them off. "I know where his heart is, man," he said. "I can feel for him. It's new for myself. It's new to him. It's new to everybody. But we're okay. I know he wants to win. He's frustrated. As our best player, I can understand him being frustrated. We'll figure out ways to make sure he's successful."

The following week, Simmons decided to poke at Brown and Embiid. The Sixers had lost at home to the Nets, but rookie sniper Landry Shamet had drilled three triples late in the fourth quarter, and after the game a reporter asked Simmons what he thought of the display.

"That we have multiple guys that can step up and play, and I think tonight we tried to go through one way too much," Simmons replied. "I think the way we've been playing in past games, we've been playing together. And I think we need to do more of that." Later that month, after a Christmas Day loss to the Celtics, Embiid groused to reporters, "The ball didn't find me in the fourth quarter and overtime, so, in those situations, I've got to show up, but I also have to be put in the right situations to be able to help this team. I felt like I wasn't in the right situation." He was asked why he thought that was. "Don't know, got to ask Coach," he tersely replied.

Brown had spent more than five years trying to build a culture. The son of a pair of teachers, he believed curiosity and education forged team unity. He led regular discussions on current events and instituted monthly team breakfasts where players were required to present on a topics of interest. (Simmons talked about Australian wildlife; Redick detailed the belief among certain scientists that we're all living in a *Matrix*-like simulation.) He loved teaching young players the intricacies of the game, like he had back when he was an assistant coach and like he had during his first few seasons in Philadelphia when wins and losses weren't of concern.

But things were different now. *The Sixers* were different. There were expectations, and with them came stakes, and with those came pressure, and with the pressure came all sorts of new feelings, and there were now big egos involved, and sacrifices to be made, and decisions, too, and none of them were easy, and each would trigger a dozen more, and just one wrong one could undermine everything Brown had worked so hard for.

Embiid was griping. Simmons was grumbling. Butler, after a brief honeymoon period, was grousing. He protested Brown's egalitarian offense by passing up nearly every shooting opportunity that arose off ball movement. He questioned Brown's decisions. Sometimes he ignored play designs.

Opposing teams, sensing the discord, began inquiring with Brand whether Butler was again available. Brown did his best to keep the fissures from revealing themselves, and publicly preached patience and optimism. "We're coming together," he told reporters after a New Year's Day road victory over the Clippers. "We have a new opportunity. You don't just click your heels and throw Jimmy Butler in and every-body's going to be playing the same way and style." But behind the scenes he was losing control of both his team and the narrative.

On January 4, ESPN published a report stating that Butler had "ag-gressively challenged" Brown on "his role in the offense." It claimed that Butler had been "vocal in his contesting of Brown and his system, including a recent film session in Portland" five days earlier "that some witnesses considered 'disrespectful' and beyond normal player-coach discourse." The report went viral. "You May Be Shocked to Learn Which 76er Is Reportedly Causing Problems Behind the Scenes," Deadspin quipped in its headline.

The next day, prior to a home game against the Mavericks, Brown put on his flak hat and started spinning. "In that film session that was referenced, I didn't feel like any of that crossed the line. And if it did, it would've been dealt with quickly," he said. He'd come into training camp sporting a professorial gray beard, and on chaotic days like this it made him look haggard. "People speculating about an argument or some type of 'aggressive disagreement'—if it were I would own it. I think that from his standpoint, that is unfair." Brown did, however, acknowledge that Butler has asked for "more pick-and-rolls."

Butler didn't play that night, and so reporters had to wait until the team's next practice to hear his response. That came two days later. "I don't think any part of it was confrontational," he said. "I think it was just a player-to-coach talk, a coach-to-player talk, it just so happened to be in front of everybody." Butler didn't dive into many more details, but told people close to him that he was shocked by the tone of the report. Brown, he said, had asked at the end of the film session if anyone had anything to add. Butler figured this was an open invitation, and so he spoke up and suggested the team run more pick-and-rolls, for him, yes, but also for backup point guard T. J. McConnell. He told associates that Brown had responded by saying Butler had a good point, and that he'd look into it, to which Butler pushed back.

"Well let's settle this right now," he replied. "Why don't we do more pick-and-rolls?" He didn't think he had crossed a line, and if Brown had felt aggrieved Butler hadn't noticed. He and some associates met with Jordan Brand at the team hotel later that day. Butler didn't mention the film session or the back-and-forth with Brown. He didn't think there was anything to share.

But it was clear that not everyone on the team shared Brown's belief. Someone in the locker room, frustrated by Butler, had passed along the story to ESPN, and described it in a certain tone, and other sources had verified it, further enhancing the microscope over the team. Brown wasn't sure how to respond. But, despite often professing otherwise, he was aware of the noise surrounding his team—after every game and before every press conference he'd have a flak update him on the latest NBA news and notes—and looking for people to blame, and not just for that report. The day of the argument with Butler, during the same film session but before any details had been reported, he'd noticed Serena Winters, the team's TV sideline reporter, working inside the gym before the media had been allowed in. This was standard procedure for Winters, and other members of the team's TV and radio crews, yet Brown, upon seeing her, unleashed a tirade—"What the fuck are you doing in here?! Get the fuck out!"—that many in the room found troubling.[7]

The Sixers closed January with a pair of victories, bumping their record up to an impressive 34–18, just four games out of first place. But something still seemed off, and not just the team's chemistry. Their defense was middling. Opposing point guards routinely torched them. "We seem to make every guard look like a Hall of Famer," Embiid said. The offense still looked clunky. And they still struggled when facing off against the league's top units.

On February 5, the Toronto Raptors, one of the two teams ahead of the Sixers in the Eastern Conference standings, came to Philadelphia, and jumped out to a mid-first-quarter lead thanks to an 8–0 run. Some scattered boos broke out, and one fan shouted at Brand, who spent the first half of every game seated on the baseline among scouts and media, for help. "Anthony Davis is available. Go get him, Elton!" the fan yelled, a reference to the New Orleans Pelicans superstar who had recently demanded a trade. More requests rained down. Brand turned around and briefly smiled. With the first half winding down, and the Sixers still trailing, Brand rose from his seat to head back toward the team offices. "Make a move, Elton!" the fan shouted, this time louder. Frustrated, Brand glanced up into the stands.

"I got you," he shouted back.

The Sixers lost that night. After the game Brown was pulled into

---

7   Lest anyone think Winters was the one who shared this story, she declined to comment, both on and off the record.

a room in the Wells Fargo Center. Brand, Harris, his partner David Blitzer, CEO Scott O'Neil, and Rucker were already seated. Brown was informed that the Sixers had an opportunity to acquire Tobias Harris, a sweet-shooting, well-liked 6-foot-9 forward who was averaging a career-best 20.9 points per game for the Los Angeles Clippers. Harris was a good fit for the Sixers. His shooting could space the floor for Simmons and Embiid. He was comfortable playing within a system. His size would give the Sixers one of the league's biggest lineups and trigger all sorts of matchup problems for opponents. But there were a couple of catches. One was that Tobias Harris, like Butler, would be a free agent in the summer. The other was that obtaining him would cost the Sixers Shamet, just twenty-one years old and on a cheap rookie deal, and also an unprotected 2021 first-round pick belonging to the Miami Heat, their most valuable trade asset. It was a lot to give up—more, even, than they had surrendered for Butler, a four-time All-Star—for a player who could bolt in a few months. And if they did bring Tobias Harris back, they'd likely have to do so on a max deal, which, combined with the rest of their salaries, would leave them little flexibility to improve the roster.

The group went around the room. "The assets you give up, we've all worked hard to accumulate over our years, and so it's not discussed lightly, there's tremendous thought," Brown recalled. "But at the end of the day it was a unanimous thumbs-up." Brand spent the rest of the night negotiating with the Clippers. At around 1:30 the following morning, the Clippers informed Torrel Harris, Tobias's father and agent, that Tobias had been traded to the Sixers. Torrel spoke to Brand. "He let us know that he planned on giving Tobias a max deal," said a person familiar with the conversation.

Brand made a few more moves before the trade deadline to bolster the team's depth. One of them was dumping Fultz onto the Orlando Magic in exchange for reserve Jonathan Simmons and a pair of late draft picks. Fultz hadn't played since November. His shot had short-circuited once again, and after Brown had played T. J. McConnell over him in a game against the Phoenix Suns his mother had berated Sixers assistant general manager Ned Cohen. The following morning, Fultz's agent, Raymond Brothers, notified The Athletic's David Aldridge that

Fultz would see a shoulder specialist and that he would not participate in any games or practices until then. The Sixers learned of the news via Twitter. Fultz visited around ten specialists (none affiliated with the Sixers), and in December was diagnosed with a nerve disorder called thoracic outlet syndrome. It was reported that he'd miss three to six weeks, but by then the Sixers were ready to move on.

On the Friday morning after the trade deadline, Brand held a press conference to explain his rationale for the moves. "We believe we're in a position to contend now," he said in his opening statement.

"The goal was to seize the moment," he said in response to a question.

"The window is now."

———

Josh Harris had been more involved in the team's basketball operations than ever before. He'd negotiated the Butler trade. He often met with Brand after games. He and his partners bought out David Heller, the minority owner who'd relished playing GM. Occasionally Harris would stand to the side during Brown's postgame press conferences, stat sheet in hand. But in March, he decided to step out from the shadows. During the annual MIT Sloan Sports Analytics Conference, he participated alongside ESPN's Jackie MacMullan, New England Patriots president Jonathan Kraft, and entertainment executive Casey Wasserman in a panel titled "Creating a Sports Legacy." "Making a franchise successful involves a lot of people," Harris said during the panel. "Certainly ownership is front and center in that. Players understand ultimately who controls the club and calls the shots." He also made news when, in an interview with MacMullan afterward, he said that another early-playoff exit would be "very problematic," adding, "We'd be unhappy. I'd be unhappy." The comments were taken as a warning shot at Brown, whom many people around the NBA believed would be canned if the Sixers didn't advance further than they had the previous season.

Despite all the bickering and shuffling, the Sixers finished 51–31, the third-best record in the East. An hour before their playoff opener against the Brooklyn Nets, in April, Harris decided to hold a state-of-the-union. Early in his press conference he was given the chance to remove the guillotine hovering over his head coach.

"Look, we have a lot of confidence in Brett. We're glad that he is leading us into the playoffs and we're focused on the Nets," Harris said. "We're focused on winning this series. And that's what we're here to talk about today." But reporters, uninterested in hearing Harris's thoughts on the Nets' pick-and-roll defense, pressed on.

"Right now, I think we're supportive of Brett," Harris added, declining to flatly state that Brown's job was not in jeopardy. "And we think he is the right leader to take us where we need to go in the playoffs. And I am focused on the Brooklyn Nets. He's focused on the Brooklyn Nets."

He was right about the team's talent. Tobias Harris's shot deserted him after coming to Philadelphia. But his presence opened up the floor, and the quintet of him, Embiid, Simmons, Butler, and Redick had outscored opponents by more than 19 points per 100 possessions in the minutes they'd played together, a mark that only two five-man units (among those that had played at least 150 minutes) had outperformed. The problem was that group had only played 161 minutes together, and only in 10 games, and mostly because its centerpiece couldn't stay on the floor.

Embiid had entered the season healthy for the first time in his NBA career. He had lofty aspirations—his goal, he said, was to be named both MVP and Defensive Player of the Year—and he was also eager to prove that he wasn't fragile, that he could carry a team. He played a ton of minutes early on, repeatedly scoffing at the notion that he could benefit from some extra rest. "If these guys tell me I have to take a day off, I might kill 'em," he said after playing 39 minutes in an overtime win on November 9. He followed that up by logging another 39 minutes in Memphis the next night.

He was playing the best basketball of his career and was in the MVP conversation, but in February he began experiencing tendinitis in his left knee, the same knee in which he had suffered a torn meniscus two years earlier. He missed the team's first eight games after the All-Star break, and five of their final seven, and 14 of their final 24. The time off killed his conditioning. Embiid, who'd always struggled with injury rehab and who was never one to worry about nutrition—rookie teammates were instructed to bring a Chick-fil-A order of four spicy chicken sandwiches, four orders of fries, and four cookies-and-cream milkshakes to him before every team flight[8]—ballooned to around 300 pounds (he weighed 240 coming out of college). Worse, the Sixers didn't seem to have any idea when, or if, he'd fully recover. A few hours before the team's second-to-last game of the regular season, in Miami, Brown berated the team's medical staff over Embiid's poor conditioning and health.

"We're all going to get fired because Joel's out of shape!" he shouted.

That night, Embiid had a Sixers security guard pick him up Krispy Kreme donuts for the team flight.[9]

It was assumed that Embiid was biding his time so that he could be at his best for the playoffs. But even that was now in question, with Brand telling reporters before the final game of the regular season that there was a chance Embiid wouldn't be ready. This seemed to be news to Brown, who told reporters he expected "all our starters to be available, if somebody tells me something else, so be it." This was met with a series of follow-ups. "The club will make the statement in a clearer way than I guess I have about Joel," Brown replied. "I'm done with the Joel questions. We'll put out something that's fair."

Embiid did suit up for Game 1. But he only played 24 minutes, and the Nets caught fire from deep, and their speedy guards ran circles around the Sixers' bigs, and they held Simmons to just nine points and three assists by mimicking the Celtics' strategy. The game's final buzzer was drowned out by a mix of boos at *Brooook-lyn* chants as the Nets, who had finished the season nine games behind the Sixers, walked off the Wells Fargo Center court with a 111–102 victory and 1–0 series lead.

The early part of Game 2 didn't offer much solace. The Sixers

---

8   Embiid would later claim that the order wasn't for him to eat. "As a rookie you have to make them work," he told ESPN's Zach Lowe. "You try to find ways to get them to do more than they should. I don't drink milkshakes."

9   A representative for Embiid denied this claim.

opened up a 13-point lead in the second quarter, but a series of mis-
cues enabled the Nets to close the gap. With a little over three minutes
left in the half, Tobias Harris, ignoring the defensive scheme, ducked
under a ball screen, allowing Nets point guard Spencer Dinwiddie to
walk into an open three. Furious, Brown called a timeout. He stomped
onto the court and barked at Harris. By the end of the first half Brown
had seen enough. He entered the locker room and unleashed a barrage
of curses. "It was fiery," Harris said. The Sixers came out in the third
quarter and reeled off 14 straight points. Embiid was able to rest for
nearly the entire fourth quarter, and the Sixers evened the series with a
convincing 145–123 win. After the game, Brown's players credited him
for awakening them from their slumber.

"I love that shit," reserve forward Mike Scott said. "I love when
people get cussed out, yelled at, and say, 'You can't do it, it's your fault.'
I'm all for it."

"Shocked me a little bit to tell you the truth," added Butler. "But I
like it, that's the type of energy I love. He just made sure everybody
did their job, letting them know you can't have it, it's not winning
basketball."

The Sixers took a 2-1 series lead behind a monster performance
from Simmons (31 points, nine assists) in a 131–115 win in Brooklyn.
They eked out a close win in Game 4 (112–108) thanks to a 31-point,
16-rebound, seven-assist, six-block night from Embiid. A 25–3 run to
open Game 5 delivered them the series.

"We think we can win it all," Embiid told reporters after the game.
He wore a black hoodie with a cartoon image of his girlfriend, *Sports
Illustrated* swimsuit model Anne de Paula, plastered on the front.

"I didn't finish up the regular season, so just getting my rhythm and
getting healthier and just doing the right things I think is working out
well," he added. "Still got a long way to go, but as long as I'm alive, I've
got to keep pushing." He'd been waking up at 5 a.m. every morning so
that he could undergo six sessions of treatment every day, and he was
finally looking like himself. Bullying the Nets in the post. Flying down
the lane for slams. Bouncing around on defense.

"I feel like this team is better than last year's team," Embiid said.
"Going into this [second-round] series, it's kind of different. I've seen

it, this is my second time being here. Last year, we were kind of over-confident." He stepped off the podium and gingerly walked alongside his agent back toward the locker room. Kawhi Leonard and the 58-win Raptors were waiting.

Silence filled the visitors' locker room in Toronto's Scotiabank Arena. Embiid, emerging from a trainers' area in the back, staggered across the carpeted floor and took a seat. Tip-off for Game 7 was less than an hour away. The Sixers were facing a superior Raptors team—they had won seven more games than the Sixers in the regular season (58) despite Leonard missing 22 of them—and neither of their two corner-stones were living up to their respective billings. And yet here they were, just three years removed from their 10-win season and about to take the court with the chance to advance to the conference finals.

A lot of the credit belonged to Brown. It had been a trying season for him, one full of egos and trades—"I feel like this is the third team I've coached this season," he said after the Tobias Harris deal—and questions about his job status. Many around the NBA wondered whether he could survive a second consecutive second-round defeat. Brown responded by coaching the best series of his life.

After spending years building an offensive system heavy on ball movement—"Pass is king," he'd say—and light on one-on-one action and pick-and-rolls, he tweaked his playbook, something coaches are typically loath to do. He recognized that playoff basketball was a different game, and that playoff defenses were locked in to opposing tendencies and schemes, and that often the best way to score against a playoff defense was to hand your best player the ball and get out of the way. So Brown did exactly that. He took the ball from Simmons's hands and gave it to Butler. With the change came a new pick-and-roll-heavy scheme and with that a number of monster Butler performances.

"This was James Butler. That was the adult in the gym," Brown said after Butler's 30-point, 11-rebound, five-assist night in Game 2, offering his highest level of compliment. Butler, upon being informed of the quote and never one to cut a coach a break, issued a correction.

"My name isn't James," he said. "It's literally Jimmy."

Brown had also made some savvy adjustments to the Sixers' defense. In Game 2 he shifted Embiid onto Toronto's second-best player, Pascal Siakam. In Game 3 he tasked Simmons, who was spending more time without the ball and exerting less energy on offense, with chasing Leonard around. The moves helped limit Siakam and slow Leonard just enough—the 29 points he scored in Game 6 were nearly four below his series average—to keep the Sixers afloat.

But Brown's biggest challenge was managing Embiid's playing time. The Sixers backup centers were too slow, and thus easily exploited, and their backup forwards were too small, and thus easily pushed around, and whenever Embiid left the floor the Sixers' defense cratered and the offense stalled. But tendinitis had continued plaguing his left knee, and he'd also battled a series of stomach viruses and infections early in the series that left him vomiting and in need of occasional IVs. "If you've had the shits before, you'd know how it feels," he said after Game 2. The shits had sapped his already poor conditioning, leaving Brown even less room to maneuver. But this was a Game 7. Embiid knew his breaks would be limited.

Sitting in front of his locker, with the clock to tip-off ticking down, he carefully tugged at the laces of his Under Armour sneakers. Simmons, having just completed his warm-up, bounded into the room. "You ready, Jo?" he asked. The two had grown closer over the season's final months. Brown's private sessions had helped, and they'd matured, and the additions of Butler and Tobias Harris meant *everyone* was now sacrificing and *everyone* was chasing a greater goal.

Embiid removed one headphone from his left ear and looked up at Simmons, seated a few feet away. Simmons repeated the question. Embiid nodded.

———

The two teams traded jabs through the first three quarters. Leonard racked up 26 points. Embiid barely left the floor and the Sixers' defense smothered Leonard's teammates. Both teams had averaged more than 114 points per game in the regular season but on this night neither team would come close to those respective marks. Entering the fourth quarter the Raptors clung to a 67–64 lead.

The quarter opened with Leonard finally receiving help. Raptors center Marc Gasol canned a three. Two possessions later Raptors big man Serge Ibaka added another. With 9:37 remaining, the Raptors led, 73–68.

Two possessions later, with the game slipping away, Brown called for Embiid to set a high screen for Butler. Butler dribbled left. The Raptors switched it (Gasol, who was guarding Embiid, and Leonard, who was guarding Butler, swapped men so as to not leave any creases), gifting the Sixers the matchup they wanted. Butler stepped back and flicked a three over the bigger and slower Gasol, cutting the lead to two. Leonard responded with another smooth pull-up. The Sixers went back to the Embiid-Butler pick-and-roll. Butler weaved into the paint and splashed another step-back. With 7:35 left, Embiid buried a three, giving the Sixers their first lead of the quarter, 76–75. An off-balance Lowry fadeaway put the Raptors back up by one. Brown called for another Butler-Embiid pick-and-roll. The Raptors trapped it. Butler hit Embiid, who hit Simmons, who banked a righty floater off the glass.

78–77, Sixers, 6:50 left.

Now it was the Raptors' turn. Two offensive rebounds set up Leonard for a rare wide-open look from the top of the arc. He followed that up with another stop-and-pop, then a floater over Simmons while being fouled. The free throw gave him 36 points for the night and Toronto an 85–80 lead with just 4:48 left.

The 20,917 fans packed into Scotiabank rose to their feet.

With the game and his season and possibly his job on the line, Brown went back to the pick-and-roll, the play that had carried him all quarter and series. Butler drew a foul and hit both free throws. Simmons dished and screened to a whirling Redick for a one-and-one, tying the game at 85 with 3:27 left.

Ibaka missed an open look from the corner. Brown called a time-out to draw up a play. The Sixers swung the ball around, but Embiid passed up an open three, leading to a shot clock violation. Leonard responded with a brick. The Sixers responded with another near shot clock violation. Leonard slithered around a screen and, with his right toes touching the three-point line, drilled a jumper.

87–85, Raptors, 1:41 remaining.

Brown signaled for another timeout. The ball was again given to Butler, who looked for a curling Redick. The Raptors sniffed it out. With the shot clock winding down for the third straight possession, Lowry picked off an off-balance pass from Harris. He hit teammate Pascal Siakam streaking down the floor.

89–85, 1:14 left.

Butler attacked again, drawing another foul. He hit one of two free throws.

89–86, 0:59 remaining.

Leonard missed a fadeaway, but Ibaka grabbed the offensive re-bound. Toronto called timeout. Leonard dribbled out the clock and clanked a fadeaway three off the rim. Another Sixers timeout. A dribble-handoff between Redick and Embiid left the 6-foot-1 Lowry on the larger Embiid. Embiid lowered his shoulder and plowed through him. Lowry poked the ball away. Embiid recovered it and drew a foul. He hit both free throws.

89–88, Raptors, 12 seconds left.

Redick intentionally fouled Leonard. Leonard stepped to the line for two free throws.

He hit the first.

The second shot clanked off the front of the rim.

Harris grabbed it. He tossed the ball ahead to Butler. Butler saw an opening and powered ahead. He floated the ball up over Ibaka and off the glass, the Sixers' first field goal in more than three minutes.

Tie game, 4.2 seconds left.

A stunned silence fell over Scotiabank Arena.

The Raptors called timeout.

Raptors head coach Nick Nurse took out his clipboard. Lowry was to cut down from half-court to the corner; Leonard was to pop out to the perimeter off a Siakam screen. Sitting on the bench listening to Nurse, Leonard thought about the three he'd recently missed, and how it had come up short, and reminded himself to put more arc on his next look.

Leonard caught the ball about 30 feet from the basket, his toes pointed to the opposite baseline. Simmons inched up to his right hip. Leonard turned toward his left shoulder. He knew he had time for four dribbles. He shifted into a sprinter's stance. He extended his left arm into Simmons's thigh and gently pushed off. He dribbled once with his right hand.

2.9 seconds left.

Embiid, watching from the top of the three-point arc, abandoned his man and scuttled toward the right sideline to cut Leonard off. Leonard dipped even lower. He took another dribble. Simmons shuffled with him, his right hand glued to Leonard's left hip. Embiid, looking to trap Leonard with Simmons, slid over. Leonard squared his shoulders and slowed for a moment, like a running back reading the terrain in front of him. He pounded the ball onto the hardwood again, and took a big, long step, leaving Simmons behind. Now it was just him and Embiid.

1.8 seconds.

Another dribble. Leonard pushed toward the right corner. He stopped and planted his feet.

0.9 seconds.

Embiid lurked just a few inches away. Leonard bent his knees. He rose up. Embiid rose with him, his right arm extended as far as the ligaments would allow. Leonard tilted his body toward the sideline. He launched a rainbow, his 39th shot of the game, the most ever taken by a player through four quarters of a Game 7.

The buzzer sounded, signaling the end of regulation. The shot was short. The ball caromed off the front of the rim. The game looked headed for overtime. Three hundred and thirty-six minutes over 16 days hadn't been enough to determine a victor.

Instead of falling to the ground, the ball bounced high into the air.

Leonard, just inches in front of the Raptors bench, squatted like a catcher. Embiid leaned over him, mouth agape and eyes fixed on the ball as it tumbled back toward the rim. It landed on the front of the iron and shot up. The topspin generated by the bounce spun the ball 18 inches forward, to the opposite end of the rim. It bounced again, this time softly, and on the fourth bounce gently kissed the rim once more before dropping through the net, the first ever Game 7 buzzer-beater in NBA history.

Scotiabank Arena exploded.

Embiid, shaken and stunned, collapsed into the arms of the first man he saw, not caring that they belonged to his opponent, Marc Gasol. His eyes welled. T. J. McConnell guided him back to the locker room. Tears streaked down Embiid's face, which was contorted and twisted from emotion. He'd given all of himself, playing all but two minutes and 48 seconds and he'd played well (21 points on 6-of-18 shooting, 11 rebounds, four assists, three blocks), but he also thought he was capable of more, that he could have been better. His body had betrayed him and now he felt like he'd betrayed his teammates.

His girlfriend met him outside the locker room. She caressed his cheeks. She wiped tears out of his eyes. He looked small, with his shoulders dipped and his head dropped. She wrapped her arms around his neck and pulled him in tight.

"Have you ever lost a Game 7?" he asked Brand a few minutes later outside the locker room.

Embiid showered. He picked at a Tupperware dish filled with cut-up orange slices. The room was silent. A few lockers away, Butler, post-shower, studied a box score with a towel wrapped around his waist. McConnell stared at his phone, eyes bloodshot.

At the podium, Embiid was asked by a reporter to describe what he was feeling.

"I don't know, I mean, I don't know. Game 7. Losing a game that way. Last shot, after a hard-fought game. I feel like we had a chance, a lot of things are going through your mind," he offered.

"It sucks. I don't know, I can't explain it, it just sucks."

A month later the Raptors knocked off the two-time defending champion Golden State Warriors in the NBA Finals. The Sixers, having lost on a bounce in a Game 7, had come closer to beating them than anyone else.

Chapter 17

THE RESULTS

The Sixers held exit meetings in Philadelphia the day after the Game 7 loss. The defeat remained raw, but there were so many questions to address. Would Brett Brown be back? Also what about free agents like Jimmy Butler, Tobias Harris, and J.J. Redick, and did they even want to return, and if they did was Josh Harris willing to spend the money to sign them? And would Ben Simmons ever learn to shoot and would Embiid ever start taking care of his body the way other MVP candidates do and did he and Simmons get along and what would Elton Brand do in his first off-season as GM?

Embiid was one of the first to address reporters. He was asked how he felt about Brown as a coach.

"I heard about all these rumors and I thought it was bullshit," he said. "He's done a fantastic job. He's been there through everything, and this year, I think he grew even more as a coach. He learned, we all learned, it's hard when you've got five guys that can score the ball and do a lot of things on the basketball court."

He added, "He's an amazing coach, a better person, and I got a lot of love for him."

Embiid spent the next twelve minutes answering questions about how he could improve. His responses sounded different than in the past. They were mature. Introspective. He sounded like someone who had just discovered how much more learning he had to do, and who was eager to get started. His regular-season marks of 27.5 points per game and 48.4 percent shooting had plummeted to 20.2 and 42.8 in the playoffs, and he didn't offer excuses. He talked about the specific ways—rolling to the basket, scoring outside of the post—in which he needed to expand his game. He acknowledged the need to take better care of his body so that he could be in better condition come playoff time. He expressed a willingness to sit when the Sixers played on consecutive nights. He said the season had taught him that winning, real winning, required real sacrifices.

The rest of the morning played out as expected. Tobias Harris and Butler both said they'd like to return, but that no decision had yet been made. Simmons, who during the Raptors series had told ESPN's Zach Lowe that his role was "definitely not" to spend chunks of games stationed around the basket and off the ball, refused to concede that he needed to work on his jumper. "I think for me, I just want to get better all around and just become a better, more efficient player and just keep growing as just a better player," he said.

Later that night, Josh Harris put the Brown rumors to rest. He informed ESPN's Adrian Wojnarowski that Brown would be returning, and that the two of them and Brand had already begun planning the team's off-season.

"I think a lot's been made about this in the press, and truthfully you can't believe what you're reading or what you're hearing," Harris told reporters the next day, seemingly forgetting that much of what was read and heard were words he had uttered. "Brett's job was never in jeopardy. We were very focused on the playoffs, and yeah, we declined to get into a lot of questions that people were asking us, but I have a great relationship with Brett. He's been our coach for six years. I've talked with him constantly through the playoffs, including last night in terms of planning for the future. We have been and continue to be excited that Brett is leading us." He added that "a lot of noise in the press" was "probably kicked up by our competitors."

Brown had endured so much since coming to Philadelphia. The ride wasn't always smooth, and there had been valid questions raised along the way. "This is my sixth year in Philadelphia. I have been fired every one of these years," he joked to reporters during his press conference. "Every single one of these years, somebody has me not coming back, and it will happen again next year, early. This is just the way it works in my industry, in this city." He'd been hired to lead a losing team, and now, 314 regular-season losses and three GMs later, he'd proven that he could lead a winning one too. He'd juggled schemes. He'd mixed rotations. He'd outmaneuvered opposing coaches. He'd united clashing players. He'd almost beaten the champs.

Sitting there, two days removed from a heartbreaking loss, coming off back-to-back 50-win seasons, and with his future bright, Brown, hair now all gray and face bearded—fans would joke that he'd aged like a president—marveled at how far he and the Sixers had come.

"When I put my rearview mirror hat on and I remember going to PCOM, we were at PCOM. Think about that. I had one court," he said. "I wouldn't even go down to my players' locker room. I was ashamed."

Two months later, on a Friday in July, Josh Harris and Brand were back in the same room and once again looking out at dozens of reporters. The Sixers had spent the previous month tweaking their roster, first in the draft, then in free agency, and now it was time to celebrate the off-season.

"I'm excited to welcome all the gentlemen on this dais," Josh Harris said, sitting front and center once again, between Brand and six players.

The moves had been mostly finalized thirteen days earlier, on the last day in June. Tobias Harris was signed to a five-year (near-max) $180 million deal. Butler, whom Brown had lobbied not to re-sign, was sent to the Miami Heat as part of a sign-and-trade. In return the Sixers received Josh Richardson, a twenty-five-year-old, 6-foot-6 defensive stud who had averaged 16.6 points per game the previous season and who, with two years and just over $20 million left on his contract, was signed to one of the league's most team-friendly deals. With the extra cap room, and by letting Redick walk, the Sixers were able to throw a four-year, $109 million deal at five-time All-Star Al Horford and pry him away from the Celtics. They were also close to announcing a five-year, $170 million extension for Simmons.

"In addition to having Joel and Ben, two of the brightest stars in the NBA, we're moving forward with an elite starting five, an elite core," Harris said, speaking like the chief basketball decision maker that he now was. The days of him describing the Sixers as "a really exciting business opportunity," like he had during his introductory press conference after buying the team in 2011, were long gone. He'd made good on his investment—*Forbes* valued the Sixers at $1.7 billion in 2019, nearly four times the $280 million he and his partners had paid for them back in 2011—but now was interested in something else.

"I will, and we will work tirelessly and do everything we have to do and be all in on delivering a championship to the city of Philly," he said.

Six years after Sam Hinkie's arrival, the Sixers were close to achieving this goal. So much had transpired since then. Some highs and so many lows. There were All-Stars traded away and losing streaks and injured lottery picks and more losing streaks and happy fans and angry fans and more veterans traded away and so many second-round picks and more injured lottery picks and more losing streaks and more veterans traded away and TMZ clips and angry agents and more losing streaks and coups and manifestos and even happier fans and even angrier fans and Joel "The Process" Embiid and mysterious shoulder injuries and burner Twitter accounts and playoff wins and playoffs losses and more playoff wins and more playoff losses and while it hadn't exactly gone according to Hinkie's plan, here, six years later, his vision had been fulfilled.

The roster was locked in. Hinkie had planned for all the losing to net the Sixers multiple stars—they now had Ben Simmons and Joel Embiid. Hinkie had planned for all the accumulated assets and cap flexibility to net them high-level free agents—they now had Al Horford and Tobias Harris. There had been bumps along the way, and casualties along the path, and mistakes, so many mistakes. Nerlens Noel, Jahlil Okafor, and Michael Carter-Williams—young men who were given millions of dollars and little direction—were barely hanging on to NBA careers. Dozens of other had come and gone. Hinkie had lost his job and possibly his NBA future. But he had been hired to build a championship-level basketball team and the Sixers had become exactly that. In exchange for three years of losing (plus one in Bryan Colangelo–designed purgatory), they had received the previous two 50-win seasons plus a team with Embiid, Simmons, Harris, and Horford all signed for at least four more years. Maybe they'd win a title. Maybe they'd win two. Maybe they'd never make it to the Finals. Maybe Embiid would break down. Such things were results, and results were determined by things like luck and bounces and other areas outside of human control. All you could do was position yourself properly and trust the process. Hinkie had. And now his Process was complete.

EPILOGUE

In February 2019, I finally met Sam Hinkie.

It was a Thursday night in Boston and I, like a few thousand others, had come to town for MIT's Sloan Sports Analytics Conference, which was slated to begin the next morning.

The conference in many ways had become a testament to Hinkie's impact. The first one was held in 2007—back when applying data to sports decisions was still viewed as radical. The inaugural Sloan Conference took place in MIT's classrooms and had around 175 attendees. Its keynote speakers were J. P. Ricciardi, then the general manager for Major League Baseball's Toronto Blue Jays, and Jamie McCourt, the co-owner, president, and CEO of the Los Angeles Dodgers. Eleven years later, the conference had taken over Boston Convention and Exhibition Center so that it could fit its nearly 3,500 attendees. Its keynote speaker was Barack Obama. It had become an event circled on NBA calendars, which was why I was there. Few weekends offer more opportunity to network and gossip with friends and sources from around the league.

The night before the conference, an NBA friend of mine invited me to meet him at a bar outside TD Garden. I found him in a corner, where a TV playing a Sixers–Oklahoma City Thunder game was hanging from the ceiling. We watched the Sixers, thanks to 32 points from Tobias Harris, hold on to a four-point win, their 40th of the season.

"How's the book coming?" my friend asked.

"I'm still trying to find a way to speak with Sam," I told him. I showed him the text I'd sent to Hinkie the previous day, telling him that I'd be in Boston for Sloan and asking if he'd be there too.

"He never responded," I said.

"You know he's here?"

My eyes grew big. I had hoped that I'd run into him over the weekend, and kind of assumed I would. But I also figured if and when I did it'd be outside at a panel and he'd be frantically scribbling down notes too complex for a simple plebeian like me to understand.

"Right there," my friend said, pointing to a corner on the other end of the bar, and there Hinkie was, sitting at table with a small group of men and picking at a sandwich and fries. I'd heard about his new look—the shaved head, the sleek beard, the blazers in colors other than navy—but seeing it in person was jarring. The accountant-like garb had been traded in for a look you'd find in a J. Crew catalog.

I ambled over, sort of nervous but ready for my Ahab moment.

"Sam," I said.

He looked up. At Sloan, Hinkie was a rock star, or as my friend put it later, "one of the conference's OGs." He'd participated in a panel the previous year and received a larger ovation than Obama. He was used to strangers introducing themselves as admirers and asking to shake his hand.

This was not that.

"Yaron Weitzman," I said and extended my hand.

I searched his eyes for some sort of recognition. I knew he didn't necessarily want to talk with me, but I figured we'd at least share some laughs about the nature of our strange relationship.

"Oh, hello," he said. We shook hands. I asked if I could sit down. "Sure," he said. We spoke for about five minutes. I told him it was my first time at Sloan. We exchanged some banal small talk. He wasn't rude, but I did most of the heavy lifting. Sensing the conversation dwindling, I went to one of my go-to moves, one I pull out nearly every time I interview a fellow father.

"Yeah, I'm excited to be here but it's tough to leave the kids at home, you know?"

"You have kids?" Hinkie asked.

That bought me a few more minutes. We exchanged some possibly not quite #2019-approved jokes about dealing with wives when away on work trips. "Never tell them how well you slept," he said. I told him I'd learned that lesson early on. One of his friends seated at the table, an assistant GM for another NBA team, asked me how many kids I have. I told him two, and that I was happy with that but that my wife is from a family of four and wanted a big family.

"I have three," he said. "Get a vasectomy."

I laughed. He looked at me.

"I'm not kidding."

Hinkie had moved on to a conversation with another person at the other end of the table. I tried waiting him out. Then he got up.

"Nice to meet you," he said. "Enjoy the conference."

I spent the next ten or so minutes talking to the assistant GM. I told him about the book I was writing.

"What Sam did, the principles he showed, the loyalty to those principles, it takes a really special person," he said.

I ran into Hinkie a few times over the next two days. Once was on the way out from a panel where Josh Harris, the Sixers' managing partner and the man who had both hired and turned on Hinkie, answered questions about the ways the Sixers used data and analytics to gain a competitive edge. The second time was in the lobby after I had watched Sixers CEO Scott O'Neil, one of the people who had pushed Hinkie out, sit onstage and talk about all the revolutionary ideas the imaginative Sixers, no longer associated with mediocrity or losing, were now putting into action. "The 76ers, according to *Forbes*, have increased in value over 40 percent a year in each of the last two years," O'Neil said, adding, "We built an innovation lab. We have a venture fund. We are looking at a real estate project. We're looking at all types of different businesses." They'd also filed a trademark claim in September for "Trust The Process."

There was something ironic about the whole thing, about the image of Hinkie quietly wandering the halls while his former bosses and colleagues, reaping the benefits of his Process, all took victory laps. At one point, figuring I'd take my shot, I said so to Hinkie. He pursed his lips and politely nodded.

The last time I saw him was on the Saturday night a few hours after the conclusion of the conference, once again at a bar, this time one tucked into the Marriott Copley Square. I offered to buy him a beer. He passed. "Well, it was nice meeting you," I said. I told him that I hoped one day we'd get to have a real conversation. He nodded.

"Don't forget, don't tell your wife how much you slept," he said.

The Sixers were playing again that night, this time against the two-time defending champion Warriors. Joel Embiid, battling tendinitis, was sitting out, as was Warriors sharpshooter Klay Thompson. But it was a prime-time game, one featuring two high-profile teams, and the score was close. Most of the NBA people in bar had their eyes glued to the giant TV plastered to one of the walls.

Not Hinkie, though. Watching him, you'd never know he was the one who laid the infrastructure for the Sixers to become a team that could go toe-to-toe with a dynasty. He was paying attention but looked no different than everyone else in the room. He was more than happy to talk shop with friends.

"Is MCW [Michael Carter-Williams] still in the league?" he asked one.

Later he gave Houston Rockets general counsel Rafael Stone, a former colleague of his, a big hello. Earlier that day Stone had participated in a panel with Evan Wasch, an NBA executive. The panel was about one of the battles inherent in professional sports—the push-and-pull between teams whose priorities are to win and leagues whose priorities are to make money. In his position as senior vice president of basketball strategy and analytics for the NBA, Wasch is tasked with helping the league manage the balance. He was, for example, at the forefront of the NBA's decision in September 2017 to flatten the lottery odds, a move done to discourage future Process-like plans.

"Hopefully it will stop fans in those markets from rooting for their teams to perform poorly," NBA commissioner Adam Silver told ESPN in June when asked about the change. "Because that race to the bottom is just destructive, I think for everyone."

During the panel, Stone spoke about the ways he and his staff go about combing the NBA's rules and Collective Bargaining Agreement for cracks. "These guys are much smarter than me, much smarter than anybody in the league, they're going to find the loopholes," he said. The comment had annoyed Wasch, and the back-and-forth had made it back to Hinkie.

"Way to use your powers for good!" he said while greeting Stone. A big smile popped up from under his beard. "Stick it to the NBA a little."

The line generated some laughs, but as the Sixers-Warriors game entered the fourth quarter the side conversations died down. The two teams traded baskets. The Warriors led. The Sixers led. The Warriors led. The Sixers led. Standing in the middle of them all was Hinkie. Watching his former team and surrounded by friends and followers, he looked like a man content.

ACKNOWLEDGMENTS

The first person I spoke to about this book, and who turned the possibility into a reality, was my friend (and I believe, if I have my family tree right, also my fourth cousin through marriage) Mike Klein, so I'll start my thanks with him. Mike sent the idea to his CAA colleague, the awesome Anthony Mattero, who not only was incredibly enthusiastic and supportive from the start, but remained so even after getting me a book deal. Anthony was a great sounding board and, despite it occasionally making his life more difficult, ally throughout the entire process. (Can I still say "no pun intended," or do I have to retire that joke?) A writer could not ask for anything more from an agent. Thank you.

Thank you to my wonderful editor, Sean Desmond, and the rest of the folks at Twelve who took a shot on me and shared their support and knowledge.

A huge thank-you to all the people who spoke to me for this book, whether on the record or on background. And an even bigger thank-you (what's bigger than huge?) to those sources who became go-tos throughout my reporting process, be it for clarifications, explanations, or just to share thoughts. I don't think it would be possible to write a book like this without finding at least a few individuals willing to play this role.

Along that same line, thank you to T. J. McConnell for patiently fielding my random Process-era questions during dozens of pregame media availabilities last season.

Thank you to Daniel Lubofsky and Jordan Teigman for all the transcribing and research help. Without it, I'm not sure what I would have done. Both are smart, incredibly hardworking, and deserving of bigger and better professional opportunities. Consider this my letter of recommendation. The same goes for David Samuels, a recent high school graduate who came on at the end and is so far ahead of where I was at that age it's scary. Also, big thanks to Jack Cassidy, a fact-checking wiz whom anyone writing a book should hire, and to Lori Soderlind, for her advisement, editing, and support, and to my friend and officemate Eitan Nidam, for tolerating all the phone calls and providing me with a clean and quiet workspace.

Thank you to Michael Pina, and especially James Herbert and Mike Vorkunov, for all the editing and thoughts. The amount of time you devoted to helping me with this—I don't even know what to say. This is a cutthroat and often lonely profession, and I'm lucky to have friends like you, for projects like this but also to help navigate this crazy industry. More important, if not for you, I'd have no one to hear my gripes about all those writers getting more praise and opportunities than me.

Thank you to the fine veterans of the Knicks beat, Marc Berman, Stef Bondy, Steve Popper, Frank Isola, Chris Iseman, and Ian Begley, and I guess I'll throw in Al Iannazzone, too, for teaching me how to be an NBA reporter, and for all the laughs.

Thank you to the members of the Sixers beat who took me in during the 2018–2019 season, primarily Keith Pompey, Derek Bodner, Rich Hofmann, and Kyle Neubeck. Covering the Sixers is a tough gig (unless you work for ESPN and get that red carpet treatment), and I hope fans appreciate all the work these reporters do on their behalf. They're lucky to have them. I certainly was.

To everyone at *SLAM*, both past and present. I'll start with Tzvi Twersky, who essentially got me my first internship with *SLAM* back when I was just out of college and knew nothing, and who's been a friend and incredible resource ever since. A big thank-you also goes to Susan Price, Ryne Nelson, Abe Schwadron (#TDdaily, #size9.5), and

Adam Figman, *SLAM*'s brilliant editor in chief. #SLAMisFam is real and I consider myself lucky to be a part of that magazine's incredible history. More than that, if not for the opportunity *SLAM* gave me I'd probably still be covering Westchester high school cheerleading, and let me tell you—those parents were *mean*.

Thank you to Ian Blair, Matt Sullivan, Paul Forrester, and the rest of my Bleacher Report colleagues, also past and present. Most of all, a big thank-you to Chris Trenchard, B/R's brilliant NBA editor. None of *this*—the book, but also my career—would be possible without him. It's hard to describe how awesome it is to have an editor who you know has confidence in you, your work, and your ability to execute, who's always looking for opportunities for *you*. Chris is all that, and also a friend. I'm lucky to have found him, though I guess should be thanking Adam Morrison and his not-quite apocalypse bunker for bringing us together.

A major (I'm running out of synonyms for *huge*) thank-you to Howard Beck. Anyone who follows the NBA is familiar with Howard's work. He is without a doubt one of the best reporters and writers covering the sport. What you might not know, though, is that he's also one of the kindest, most genuine, and most generous people—with his time, resources, and thoughts—you'll find in the profession. I consider myself lucky to count him as a colleague, a mentor, and, most importantly, a friend.

There are three people whom I feel I owe almost everything I have professionally. The first is Jonathan Tropper, who encouraged my writing and pursuing of this profession in a community where many scoffed. More telling, though, is how generous he is with his contacts, and how eager he's always been to help me out. It's a rare trait among those who've *made it*. I'm lucky to count him as a friend. I'll also be forever grateful to him for introducing me to Jeff Pearlman. Jeff taught me everything I know: how to write, report, interview, make calls, make more calls, make more calls after that, and, well, how to write a book about a sports team, which no one does better than him. I was a junior in college the first time I met Jeff. I knew nothing, and he had no reason to help me. We spoke for three hours and the meeting changed my life. Ever since, Jeff has been an incredible role model, mentor, and friend. It would take a thousand words to properly express my gratitude.

Then there's Ben Osborne, my former editor at *SLAM*, the current editor in chief at Bleacher Report, and the person who has given me more professionally than anyone else. Opportunities, confidence, support, paychecks, advice, friendship...the list goes on and on. Ben, I don't even know what to say, so I'll just go with this: Neither this book nor my career exists without you. Thank you for everything. Once again, I am forever grateful.

If it takes a village to raise a kid, then it takes two to raise two kids, especially when they're both under two, and it probably takes another two to raise those two when one of the two parents is writing a book and away half the time. What I mean to say is the year it took to write this book was the most trying of my life, and that this book does not happen if not for my amazing family.

First, I owe a special thank-you to my wonderful sister-in-law, Marielle, and her husband, Shlomie, for all the babysitting help and just overall support. Thank you to the rest of my wife's family: Corey and Sammy (though would a few more visits to Riverdale for babysitting have killed you guys?), and especially Savta, for all the support and encouragement. And of course to my wife's parents, Marla and Avri. It took about fifteen months to write this book, and I don't think Micole and I would have survived without you in our lives. We don't choose our in-laws, but if given the choice I'd choose you both every time.

To my family: Nani, Popi, Sabba, Savta, Rebecca—your love and support throughout the years means more than you could ever know.

To Ilan, my brother, editor, commissioner, fellow #RideorDie-er, occasional therapist, and best friend. You know how much you mean to me, and how much you've done for me, and how much I appreciate it, but I'll say it anyway. When I write, you're the audience I have in mind. Thank you for everything.

To my parents, who, well—I don't even know where to start. If not for all your support—emotional, financial, and everything in between—I'd never have been able to pursue a career in this crazy field. You're two of the hardest workers I know, which not only served as an example to emulate, but also afforded me all sorts of opportunities and privileges that so many others don't receive. I am forever grateful and appreciative. Please consider this my way-too-short thank-you for everything.

To Maayan and Lior, you don't always make it easy, but you certainly make it fun. It will be a bit before either of you can read this, and I'm sure you'll both find it inferior to *Llama Llama Red Pajama*. It's okay. Just know that you both bring more meaning to my life than I ever knew was possible. I hope one day this book makes you proud.

And last but certainly not least, Micole. I could go on and on, but instead I'll keep it short and simple. None of this happens without you, and I don't just mean because someone has to watch the kids while I'm enjoying the confines of a Courtyard. If partners were doled out via a draft, I'd tank for you. Thank you for everything. I love you more than you could ever know.

NOTES AND SOURCES

The book is primarily based on interviews conducted with nearly 175 people. In lieu of interviewing Sam Hinkie, I relied on two long-form podcast interviews that he'd previously conducted: the April 5, 2016, episode of *The Lowe Post* with ESPN's Zach Lowe, and the May 22, 2018, episode of Patrick O'Shaughnessy's *Invest Like the Best*. The majority of Hinkie's quotes are from those conversations. I also drew upon press conferences archived on NBA.com and YouTube and the archives of the *Philadelphia Inquirer*, The Athletic, and PhillyVoice.

Below is not quite a full bibliography, but a list of the sources that I drew upon most.

Aldridge, David. "Careful Steps and New-Age Stats Fuel Hinkie's Rebuild in Philly." NBA.com, July 15, 2013.
———. "Sixers, New Coach Brown Gamble on Each Other in Rebuild Effort." NBA.com, October 21, 2013.
Arnovitz, Kevin. "The Future Is Bright for the 76ers, but Was the Process Worth It?" ESPN, May 9, 2018.
———. "Inside the NBA's Foodie Franchise." ESPN, March 3, 2018.
———. "Pythons and PowerPoints: How the Sixers Cracked the Culture Code." ESPN, April 9, 2018.
Babb, Kent. "Markelle Fultz Never Forgets." *Washington Post*, June 22, 2017.
———. *Not a Game: The Incredible Rise and Unthinkable Fall of Allen Iverson.* New York: Atria, 2015.
Ballard, Chris. "After The Process: Meet Sam Hinkie 2.0," *Sports Illustrated*, August 21, 2012.
———. "The Smartest Basketball Mind Outside the NBA." *Sports Illustrated*, March 3, 2018.
Baskin, Ben. "Philly Freedom: Behind the Scenes of Meek Mill's Release." *Sports Illustrated*, April 25, 2018.
Bodner, Derek. "Meet Sachin Gupta, the Driving Force Behind Many of Sam Hinkie's Trades." *Philadelphia* magazine, January 31, 2017.
Brenner, Jordan. "How the Process Failed Jahlil Okafor." SB Nation, October 11, 2017.

————. "The Man Who Just Can't Win: Sam Hinkie (Finally) Speaks." ESPN, June 29, 2016.

Buckner, Candace. "From No. 1 Draft Pick to Basketball's Biggest Enigma: No One Knows What's Up with Markelle Fultz." *Washington Post*, December 14, 2018.

Carey, David. "Apollo Fueled by $9.6 Billion Profit on Debt Beats Peers." Bloomberg, June 24, 2013.

Carter-Williams, Michael. "Don't Talk to Me About Tanking." The Players' Tribune, November 13, 2014.

Davis, John. "In the Hot Seat." *Arizona Republic*, November 26, 1997.

Detrick, Ben. "The Curious Case of Bryan Colangelo and the Secret Twitter Account." The Ringer, May 29, 2018.

Dodd, Rustin. "Lions, Brownies and Baby JOJO: The Amusing Stories from Joel Embiid's One Season at Kansas." The Athletic, April 25, 2019.

Embiid, Joel. "It's Story Time." The Players' Tribune, August 31, 2018.

Fagan, Kate. "Those Who Know Him Say Joshua Harris, Soon-to-Be Sixers Owner, Lives for Competition and Success." *Philadelphia Inquirer*, August 2, 2011.

Fischer, Jake. "Despite Tough On-Court Season, 76ers' Sales Staff Finds Success." *Sports Illustrated*, March 19, 2016.

Forde, Pat. "How Markelle Fultz Rose from Obscurity to Top NBA Draft Prospect (and Trick-Shot Expert)." Yahoo! Sports, November 2, 2016.

Forgrave, Reid. "Duke's Jahlil Okafor, His Father Rose Together from Tragedy." Fox Sports, February 23, 2015.

Fultz, Markelle. "What's Up, Philly?" The Players' Tribune, June 23, 2017.

Geltzeiler, Brian. "Covert Dealings, Embiid's Attitude Are Undermining Philadelphia's 'Process.'" The Cauldron, October 25, 2015.

Giambusso, David, and Craig Wolff. "Likely New Owner of the N.J. Devils Seen as a Builder, Not a Destroyer." *Star-Ledger*, August 11, 2013.

Gold, Jonathan. "Living in Australia, Brett Brown Once Stole Eggs from an Emu's Nest for an Omelet." ESPN, April 23, 2019.

Gonzales, John. "Trust and the Process." The Ringer, February 15, 2017.

————. "What's Next for Sam Hinkie?" The Ringer, March 5, 2018.

Haberstroh, Tom. "'Trusting the Process': The Sixers' Plan to Get Joel Embiid Healthy." ESPN, March 10, 2016.

Herbert, James. "Brett Brown's Process: How 76ers Coach Uses Schoolteacher Tactics with Young Team." CBS Sports, January 2, 2018.

————. "With the 76ers in the NBA Playoffs, The Process' Preeminent Podcast Must Learn How to Win." CBS Sports, April 13, 2018.

Himmelsbach, Adam. "Markelle Fultz Was Once Cut from His High School Team. Now He's the NBA Draft Top Prospect." *Boston Globe*, June 6, 2017.

Hofmanb, Rich. "From Australia to the Sixers: Brett Brown Coaching Dave and Ben Simmons a Full-Circle Family Affair." The Athletic, December 24, 2018.

Jenkins, Lee. "76ers' Joel Embiid: I'm The Process." *Sports Illustrated*, October 16, 2016.

Johnson, Chris. "Rapid Rise: How Markelle Fultz Went from Jayvee to Top 25 in Two Years." *Sports Illustrated*, June 17, 2015.

King, Jason. "Meet Kansas' Joel Embiid, a Cameroon Native Blossoming into a Top NBA Prospect." Bleacher Report, December 17, 2013.

Kosman, Josh. *The Buyout of America: How Private Equity Will Cause the Next Great Credit Crisis.* New York: Portfolio, 2010.

Lake, Deborah. "Our Hero." *Phoenix New Times*, March 26, 1988.

Lee, Michael. "'He's a Natural for It': Elton Brand Tries to Complete the Process in Philly." The Athletic, January 17, 2019.

Lewis, Michael. "The No-Stats All-Star." *New York Times*, February 13, 2009.

Lowe, Zach. "The Hinkie Chronicles' Latest Chapter." ESPN, December 11, 2015.

———. "The Ignored Evolution of the Sixers." *Grantland*, December 16, 2014.

———. "Sam Hinkie." *The Lowe Post* podcast, ESPN, April 5, 2016.

———. "The Sixers' Extreme Plan to Run Everything Through Their Two Stars." ESPN, May 8, 2018.

———. "A Tale of Two Cities." *Grantland*, July 14, 2015.

MacMullan, Jackie. "Cameroon Calling." ESPN, May 8, 2017.

Maese, Rick. "Josh Harris, Philadelphia 76ers Owner, Has Roots in Washington." *Washington Post*, May 7, 2012.

Neubeck, Kyle. "What Has Really Been Going on with Markelle Fultz?" PhillyVoice, February 2, 2018.

Noland, Terrance. "Jahlil Okafor Is on His Way Up." *Chicago* magazine, December 16, 2013.

O'Neil, Dana. "Mother's Memory Constant for Okafor." ESPN, November 12, 2014.

O'Shaughnessy, Patrick. "Data, Decisions and Basketball with Sam Hinkie." *Invest Like the Best* podcast, Investor's Field Guide, May 22, 2018.

Pompey, Keith. "Markelle Fultz Proved His Mettle at Famed DeMatha High School." *Philadelphia Inquirer*, June 24, 2017.

Rappaport, Max. "Sixers Owner Michael Rubin on Meek Mill, Bob Kraft...and That Chopper Ride." Bleacher Report, July 23, 2018.

Rys, Richard. "Jesus. What If Howard Eskin Was Your Dad?" *Philadelphia* magazine, April 26, 2013.

Sanchez, Robert. "From Bar Fights to On-Court Troubles, Jahlil Okafor Opens Up." ESPN, February 10, 2016.

Sharp, Andrew. "Life, Liberty, and the Pursuit of Crappiness." *Grantland*, March 3, 2015.

Shelburne, Ramona. "The Greatest Story Ever Trolled." ESPN, December 12, 2017.

Shelly, Jared. "Sixers CEO on Marketing the NBA's Most Radical Rebuilding Plan." *Philadelphia* magazine, October 26, 2015.

Smith, Gary. "How Allen Iverson, Larry Brown Learned to Live Together." *Sports Illustrated*, April 23, 2001.

Spears, Marc. "Jerry Colangelo Empathizes with Black Athletes in More Ways Than One." The Undefeated, July 22, 2016.

Spring, Joe. "17-Year-Old Takes All the Attention in Stride." *New York Times*, February 16, 2013.

Tinsley, Justin. "How Meek Mill Opened Sixers Owner Michael Rubin's—and So Many Others'—Eyes to a Broken Criminal Justice System." The Undefeated, May 10, 2018.

Torre, Pablo. "The 76ers' Plan to Win (Yes, Really)." ESPN, January 16, 2015.

Tramel, Berry. "How Sam Hinkie Went from Marlow to General Manager of the Philadelphia 76ers." *The Oklahoman*, March 5, 2014.

————. "Rocketing to the Top of the NBA." *Price Magazine*, Spring 2008.

Vorkunov, Mike. "Why Is an NBA Team Trying to Become Tech's Next Big Incubator?" *REDEF*, April 10, 2017.

Wang, Jennifer. "It All Started with Wrestling, Says Billionaire Owner of Philadelphia 76ers." *Forbes*, November 7, 2017.

Weiss, Jared, Derek Bodner, and Sam Amick. "Markelle Fultz Dealing with Wrist Ailment on Top of Shoulder Woes, Sources Say He Would Prefer a Move to New Team." The Athletic, November 21, 2018.

Wojnarowski, Adrian. "Brett Brown Joins Woj." *The Woj Pod*, April 12, 2017.

————. "Bryan Colangelo Joins The Vertical Podcast." *The Woj Pod*, September 21, 2016.

————. "Joel Embiid and Brett Brown Join Woj." *The Woj Pod*, November 11, 2016.

————. "76ers Coach Brett Brown." *The Woj Pod*, December 11, 2017.

Wolfe, Jason. "76ers GM Sam Hinkie Embraces Patience, Privacy in Rebuilding Effort." *USA Today*, July 20, 2014.

Young, Bob. "Son Is Shining." *Arizona Republic*, July 11, 1992.

Zumoff, Marc. "A Conversation with Brett Brown," *Zoo's Views*, NBC Sports, January 20, 2019.

Details and quotes pulled from other sources include, by chapter:

1. PURGATORY

12 *"I've never been done like that"*: Gary Smith, "How Allen Iverson, Larry Brown Learned to Live Together," *Sports Illustrated*, April 23, 2001.

12 *Inside, Iverson and Brown sat*: Kent Babb, *Not a Game: The Incredible Rise and Unthinkable Fall of Allen Iverson* (New York: Atria, 2015), 144.

13 *Three months later in Miami*: Ibid., 158.

13 *the deal fell through when Matt Geiger*: Marc Stein, "Geiger Really Kept Iverson a Sixer," ESPN, March 6, 2001.

16 *At 7:07...Iverson finally showed up*: Babb, *Not a Game*, 238.

16 *"I got a lot of fucking work to do"*: Ibid.

17 *"Do you want to be traded?"*: Ibid., 239.

19 *"Our organization is never"*: Richard Rys, "Ed Snider Killed the 76ers," *Philadelphia* magazine, October 29, 2010.

20 *"We have a good plan in place"*: "Stefanski Replaces King as 76ers' General Manager," Associated Press, December 5, 2007.

20 *Attendance had dipped*: ESPN.com.

22 *They ranked 23rd in home attendance in 2009*: Ibid.

22 *"I have to be honest with you"*: Rys, "Ed Snider Killed the 76ers."

2. THE BUYOUT

24 *Josh Harris had amassed*: Forbes.

24 *"Buying good companies with bad balance sheets"*: David Carey, "Apollo Fueled by $9.6 Billion Profit on Debt Beats Peers," Bloomberg, June 24, 2013.

25 *"They care about the future"*: Josh Kosman, *The Buyout of America: How Private Equity Will Cause the Next Great Credit Crisis* (New York: Portfolio, 2009), 15.

25 *spent $186 million*: Michael Corkery and Ben Protess, "How the Twinkie Made the Superrich Even Richer," *New York Times*, December 10, 2016.

26 *agreed to put down $17.1 billion*: Claire Hoffman, "Harrah's Agrees to $17.1-Billion Buyout Bid," *Los Angeles Times*, December 20, 2006.

26 *Harrah's was on the hook*: Sujeet Indap, "What Happens in Vegas...The Messy Bankruptcy of Caesars Entertainment," *Financial Times*, September 26, 2017.

27 *watched the 2014 Super Bowl*: Maggie Haberman and Kenneth P. Vogel, "Christie, Cuomo Chat," *Politico*, February 3, 2014.

27 *floated Kushner's real estate firm*: Jesse Drucker, Kate Kelly, and Ben Protess, "Kushner's Family Business Received Loans After White House Meetings," *New York Times*, March 1, 2018.

27 *reaching about $2 billion worth of investments*: Carey, "Apollo Fueled by $9.6 Billion Profit on Debt Beats Peers."

27 *at the time the largest private equity windfall ever*: Ibid.

27 *raised $565.4 million in its initial public offering*: "Apollo's Upsized IPO Raises $565.4 Million," Reuters, March 29, 2011.

29 *less than 14,751 fans a game*: ESPN.com.

29 *and were still losing money*: Forbes, January 26, 2011.

31 *The Sixers cost Harris and Blitzer*: Peter Latman, "Private Equity Princes Reach Deal for 76ers," *New York Times*, July 14, 2011.

32 *soared to 17,502 per game*: ESPN.com.

34 *Fifteen hundred fans showed up*: "Sixers Fans Show Up to Cheer Andrew Bynum at Introductory Press Conference," *Sports Business Daily*, August 16, 2012.

35 *"I had a little bit of a setback"*: "Andrew Bynum Had Setback," Associated Press, November 17, 2012.

36 *"I think it happened bowling"*: Brian Windhorst and Chris Broussard, "Andrew Bynum Hurt While Bowling," ESPN, November 19, 2012.

36 *"We made a huge deal"*: NBC Sports, February 26, 2013.

37 *"If I had to make that decision again"*: Derek Bodner, "Should We Trust the 76ers Ownership Group?" Liberty Ballers, April 24, 2013.

38 *decorated with business awards*: Carey, "Apollo Fueled by $9.6 Billion Profit on Debt Beats Peers."

3. "HE SPOKE STANFORD"

39 *an $8-a-night YMCA*: Greg Bishop, "Professor Casserly's Lessons Outline a Course for Life," *New York Times*, April 13, 2008.

41 *who had just moved in*: Jason Wolfe, "76ers GM Sam Hinkie Embraces Patience, Privacy in Rebuilding Effort," *USA Today*, July 20, 2014.

41 *at around 10:30 in the morning*: Official medical report.

41 *John Smith came by the Hinkie home*: Patrick O'Shaughnessy, "Data, Decisions, and Basketball with Sam Hinkie," *Invest Like the Best* podcast, Investor's Field Guide, May 22, 2018.

43 *flying from Stanford to Houston*: Wolfe, "76ers GM Sam Hinkie Embraces Patience, Privacy in Rebuilding Effort."

43 *"what it took to get to the top"*: Anna Simon and Ann Hampton, *Kimberly's Flight: The Story of Captain Kimberly Hampton, America's First Woman Combat Pilot Killed in Battle* (Havertown, PA: Casemate Publishers, 2012), 23.

43 *He was valedictorian*: Wolfe, "76ers GM Sam Hinkie Embraces Patience, Privacy in Rebuilding Effort."

43 *make him special tests*: Chris Ballard, "After The Process: Meet Sam Hinkie 2.0," *Sports Illustrated*, August 21, 2012.

44 *squating close to 500 pounds*: Tom Moore, "Sixers' Hinkie Wouldn't Trade High School 'Lessons for Anything,'" *Bucks County Courier Times*, March 31, 2016.

44 *"He couldn't have just walked out"*: Ibid.

44 *working out in Jumpsoles*: Ballard, "After The Process: Meet Sam Hinkie 2.0."

44 *"Basketball was a pretty important part of my life"*: Berry Tramel, "How Sam Hinkie Went from Marlow to General Manager of the Philadelphia 76ers," *The Oklahoman*, March 5, 2014.

44 *He kept a key to the high school gym*: Ibid.

44 *spending his life as a college coach*: John Gonzalez, "What's Next for Sam Hinkie?" The Ringer, March 5, 2018.

44 *all sorts of fancy committees*: Berry Tramel, "Rocketing to the Top of the NBA," *Price Magazine*, Spring 2008.

44 *"The reason I thought I wanted to marry her"*: O'Shaughnessy, "Data, Decisions, and Basketball with Sam Hinkie."

44 *proposed on a bench*: Wolfe, "76ers GM Sam Hinkie Embraces Patience, Privacy in Rebuilding Effort."

45 *"I come from a worldview"*: O'Shaughnessy, "Data, Decisions, and Basketball with Sam Hinkie."

46 *"I don't even care"*: Jason Friedman, "Higher Learning," NBA.com, August 21, 2012.

48 *arrived at the restaurant*: Pablo Torre, "The 76ers' Plan to Win (Yes, Really)," ESPN, January 16, 2015.

49 *"I suggested that if you really"*: Zach Lowe, "Sam Hinkie," *The Lowe Post* podcast, ESPN, April 5, 2016.

4. THE LONGEST LENS

53 *"We will not bat a thousand"*: Tony Manfred, "Sixers GM Gave the Best Explanation Yet for His Radical Tanking Plan," Business Insider, February 20, 2015.

57 *rehabbing eight hours a day*: Jared Zwerling, "Inside Nerlens Noel's Six Months of Rehab on Road Back to Philadelphia 76ers," Bleacher Report, January 20, 2014.

5. "WHO THE HELL IS BRETT BROWN?"

63 *Who required his students to wear hats*: Adrian Wojnarowski, "Brett Brown Joins Woj," *The Woj Pod*, April 12, 2017.

63 *"We ruined many of my mother's dinners"*: Gordie Jones, "Brett Brown's Dad Quietly Helps Him Dodge the Deluge," NBC Sports, April 9, 2017.

63 *he dated one at South Portland High School*: Ibid.

63 *pull the family car out*: Keith Pompey, "New Philadelphia 76ers Coach Brett Brown Hails from Revered Southern Maine Family," *Philadelphia Inquirer*, August 25, 2013.

64 *"He is a very intelligent backcourt player"*: "Commentators Talking About Brett Brown Boston University Career | Rick Pitino's Thoughts," The NBeye Official, YouTube, May 4, 2018.

65 *One time he showed up at 5:59 p.m.*: Rick Pitino, *The Pitino Press* podcast, October 30, 2018.

65 *Now he was clearing six figures*: Marc Zumoff, "A Conversation

with Brett Brown," *Zoo's Views* podcast, NBC Sports, January 20, 2019.

66 *"You just peel them off"*: Jonathan Gold, "Living in Australia, Brett Brown Once Stole Eggs from an Emu's Nest for an Omelet," ESPN, April 23, 2019.

66 *"I could have a laugh with her"*: Ibid.

66 *Brown convinced Pitino*: Zumoff, "A Conversation with Brett Brown."

66 *"I really didn't know what I was doing"*: Ibid.

66 *"I'll coach anybody that'll listen"*: Wojnarowski, "Brett Brown Joins Woj."

68 *a new 37,800-square-foot practice facility*: Johnny Ludde, "Practice Made Perfect," *San Antonio Express-News*, September 18, 2012.

68 *the team needed a coach*: Mike Monroe, "Player Development Falls to Spurs' Assistants," *San Antonio Express-News*, June 1, 2013.

69 *He asked Bruce Lindberg*: Wojnarowski, "Brett Brown Joins Woj."

69 *"I had heard good things"*: Jessica Camerato, "Brett Brown Still Has Lasting Effect on Gregg Popovich's Spurs," NBC Sports, February 9, 2017.

70 *"favorite people, not coaches"*: Ibid.

70 *"[He] reminded me"*: Wojnarowski, "Brett Brown Joins Woj."

71 *"I want to be talked to last"*: Ibid.

72 *"I was pretty candid with Brett"*: Max Rappaport, "The Definitive History of 'Trust the Process,'" Bleacher Report, August 23, 2017.

72 *while in a Chevy Suburban*: Pablo Torre, "The 76ers' Plan to Win (Yes, Really)," ESPN, January 16, 2015.

73 *"I needed to feel good and secure"*: Wojnarowski, "Brett Brown Joins Woj."

73 *He told Hinkie he needed a four-year deal*: Ibid.

73 *He called Popovich*: Ibid.

6. "EVERYONE IN THE CITY IS GOING TO HATE ME"

78 *"You have six NBA players"*: John Adair, "Brett Brown: Sixers Have Six NBA Players," TheSixersSense.com, October 23, 2013.

78 *"The challenge is harder"*: Tom Moore, "Brett Brown 'in the Right Place' with Sixers," *Bucks County Courier Times*, October 30, 2013.

82 *Players were given bracelets*: Zach Lowe, "The Ignored Evolution of the Sixers," *Grantland*, December 16, 2014.

84 *His parents rarely attended*: Pete Thamel, "Everybody Wants a Piece of Nerlens Noel," *New York Times*, March 10, 2012.

86 *"We knew it was going to be a circus"*: Michael Carter-Williams, "Don't Talk to Me About Tanking," The Players' Tribune, November 13, 2014.

86 *"Tell you the truth"*: Jeré Longman, "A 25-Game Skid, but All Is Not Lost for Sixers," *New York Times*, March 26, 2014.

86 *"If you're putting that roster on the floor"*: Eliot Shorr-Parks, "Stan Van Gundy Calls Sixers 'Embarrassing' and Says They Are Trying to Lose," NJ.com, March 1, 2014.

87 *"You don't like to see any team"*: Longman, "A 25-Game Skid, but All Is Not Lost for Sixers."

87 *"Play Hard, Smart, Together"*: Ibid.

7. THE RIGHTS TO RICKY SANCHEZ

91 *brought a Walkman into the delivery room*: Jeré Longman, "Too Close to Call?," *Philadelphia Inquirer*, April 23, 1989.

91 *One even tried choking him*: Ibid.

93 *"always intelligent, unbiased"*: Michael Levin, "Evan Turner Will Start Rest of Season, Not Be Traded Per Howard Eskin," Liberty Ballers, March 7, 2012.

8. THE SECOND COMING

102 *"I had never seen anything like that"*: Joel Embiid, "It's Story Time," The Players' Tribune, August 31, 2018.

102 *"Kobe!" he'd shout*: Ibid.

103 *After school he'd arrange*: Ibid.

105 *He spent the day at home*: Jackie MacMullan, "Cameroon Calling," ESPN, May 8, 2017.

105 *He hugged his family*: Jason King, "Meet Kansas' Joel Embiid, a Cameroon Native Blossoming into a Top NBA Prospect," Bleacher Report, December 17, 2013.

106 *"You laugh now"*: MacMullan, "Cameroon Calling."

106 *"White People Shooting 3 Pointers"*: Embiid, "It's Story Time."

106 *"I know it's a stereotype"*: Ibid.

110 *"It was crazy"*: King, "Meet Kansas' Joel Embiid."

111 *That night Joel recalled*: Embiid, "It's Story Time."

113 *"Americans have crazy ideas"*: Ibid.

114 *"One of the lights at the end of the tunnel"*: Patrick O'Shaughnessy, "Data, Decisions, and Basketball with Sam Hinkie," *Invest Like the Best* podcast, Investor's Field Guide, May 22, 2018.

9. TRUST THE PROCESS?

118 *"If you are going to invest"*: Zach Lowe, "Sam Hinkie," *The Lowe Post* podcast, ESPN, April 5, 2016.

118 *"It's a better option for me"*: ASAP Sports transcript.

120 *"You thought incrementally"*: Marc Zumoff, "A Conversation with Brett Brown," *Zoo's Views* podcast, NBC Sports, January 20, 2019.

121 *one to the University of Pennsylvania*: James Herbert, "Brett Brown's Process: How 76ers Coach Uses Schoolteacher Tactics with Young Team," CBS Sports, January 2, 2018.

122 *Joel Embiid was alone*: Jackie MacMullan, "Cameroon Calling," ESPN, May 8, 2017.

123 *He spent the night in his apartment*: Ibid.

123 *"That, for me, was one of the darkest"*: Adrian Wojnarowski, "Joel Embiid and Brett Brown Join Woj," *The Woj Pod*, November 11, 2016.

123 *"I was a vampire"*: Lee Jenkins, "76ers' Joel Embiid: I'm The Process," *Sports Illustrated*, October 16, 2016.

124 *The team tried filling the fridge*: Brian Geltzeiler, "Covert Dealings, Embiid's Attitude Are Undermining Philadelphia's 'Process,'" The Cauldron, October 25, 2015.

124 *"Joel has all the resources"*: Keith Pompey, "Embiid Staying at Home During West Coast Trip," *Philadelphia Inquirer*, December 27, 2014.

126 *He'd scored 1600 on his SATs*: Chris Ballard, "The Smartest Basketball Mind Outside the NBA," *Sports Illustrated*, March 8, 2018.

130 *"I was pretty up-to-speed"*: Keith Pompey, "Michael Carter-Williams Loves Former Teammates," *Philadelphia Inquirer*, February 25, 2015.

10: LOST UNICORNS

135 *"He won't get past No. 4"*: Adrian Wojnarowski, "The Unlikely Story of How Kristaps Porzingis Found His Way to the Knicks," Yahoo! Sports, January 29, 2016.

135 *"You said that I would get a meeting"*: Ibid.

138 *"He can shoot"*: Marc Berman, "Kevin Durant Fawns over Unique Porzingis as Free Agency Looms," *New York Post*, January 26, 2017.

140 *"literally almost ran all our bigs"*: Ramona Shelburne, "The Greatest Story Ever Trolled," ESPN, December 12, 2017.

141 *"I was in a dark place"*: Shams Charania, "Anxiety, Depression Had Jahlil

Okafor in a 'Dark Place,' but He's Come a Long Way," The Athletic, October 9, 2018.

141 *Okafor was sitting in the living room*: Reid Forgrave, "Duke's Jahlil Okafor, His Father Rose Together from Tragedy," Fox Sports, February 23, 2015.

141 *Benton gasped for air*: Ibid.

141 *Okafor laughed again*: Terrance Noland, "Jahlil Okafor Is on His Way Up," *Chicago* magazine, December 16, 2013.

141 *"I'm going to take your Oreos"*: Ibid.

141 *She kept wheezing*: Ibid.

141 *He and his half sister sprinted*: Ibid.

142 *"It happened right in front of me"*: Ibid.

142 *He helped steal cars*: Forgrave, "Duke's Jahlil Okafor, His Father Rose Together from Tragedy."

142 *He attended five high schools*: Ibid.

142 *a rim made from a coat hanger*: Joe Spring, "17-Year-Old Takes All the Attention in Stride," *New York Times*, February 16, 2013.

142 *a new bedroom basketball hoop*: Forgrave, "Duke's Jahlil Okafor, His Father Rose Together from Tragedy."

142 *run in weighted shoes*: Noland, "Jahlil Okafor Is on His Way Up."

142 *Tracy Webster, who offered him*: Joe Spring, "17-Year-Old Takes All the Attention in Stride."

143 *"My deepest fear"*: Noland, "Jahlil Okafor Is on His Way Up."

144 *At around 2 a.m.*: John Gonzalez, "Witness: Gun Pulled on Jahlil Okafor in October Old City Altercation," NBC Sports, November 27, 2015.

144 *"Look at me"*: A. J. Perez, "76ers' Jahlil Okafor Had Gun Pointed at Him," *USA Today*, December 24, 2015.

145 *"I remember just being upset"*: Jordan Brenner, "How the Process Failed Jahlil Okafor," SB Nation, October 11, 2017.

145 *His advances were rebuffed*: Boston Police Department statement, November 27, 2015.

146 *"I don't remember a lot of it"*: Brenner, "How the Process Failed Jahlil Okafor."

11. THE COUP

150 *"I wanted to be the boss"*: David Nguyen, "Scott O'Neil Carries Villanova Values to 76ers' Front Office," *The Villanovan*, April 30, 2019.

151 *with a ringing of a bell*: Jake Fischer, "Despite Tough On-Court Season, 76ers' Sales Staff Finds Success," *Sports Illustrated*, March 19, 2016.

151 *a Brett Brown–signed hard hat and championship belt*: Ibid.

151 *increase their season ticket sales*: Ibid.

151 *23,000 viewers per game*: Roy Burton, "Sixers' TV Ratings Are 'Embarrassing,'" Liberty Ballers, July 19, 2015.

154 *a house built by his Italian immigrant grandfather*: Marc Spears, "Jerry Colangelo Empathizes with Black Athletes in More Ways Than One," The Undefeated, July 22, 2016.

154 *"Jerry is the primary arbiter"*: Debroad Lake, "Our Hero," *Phoenix New Times*, March 26, 1988.

156 *"[We] talked about how it would help"*: Zach Lowe, "The Hinkie Chronicles' Latest Chapter," ESPN, December 11, 2015.

156 *"We had strong desires"*: Ibid.

157 *Brand spoke to Duke coach Mike Krzyzewski*: Ibid.

157 *he'd get a company credit card*: J.J. Redick, "Elton Brand on the Sterling-Era Clippers, His Path to GM, and Staying off Social Media," *The JJ Redick Podcast*, The Ringer, October 23, 2018.

157 *"Players didn't want to come"*: Zach Lowe, "Elton Brand, Sixers GM," *The Lowe Post* podcast, ESPN, September 26, 2018.

157 *"I'm going on a vacation"*: Ibid.

12. #HEDIEDFORYOURSINS

166 *moved with his wife and four kids*: Chris Ballard, "After The Process: Meet Sam Hinkie 2.0," *Sports Illustrated*, August 21, 2012.

167 *accompany his two oldest boys*: Ibid.

167 *"Why do we watch"*: Ibid.

167 *"My people"*: Ibid.

168 *"We wanted to go outside the box"*: Tom Haberstroh, "Trusting the Process: The Sixers' Plan to Get Joel Embiid Healthy," ESPN, March 10, 2016.

171 *"I wanted to establish"*: Bob Young, "Son Is Shining," *Arizona Republic*, July 11, 1992.

173 *"It was a little bit humbling"*: Adrian Wojnarowski, "Bryan Colangelo Joins The Vertical Podcast," *The Woj Pod*, September 21, 2016.

174 *to lobby on behalf of*: Zach Lowe, "Inside the Brooklyn Nets' Attempt to Rise from the Ashes," ESPN, August 3, 2017.

174 *Colangelo wore suits*: Eric Andrew-Gee, "Dunkonomics: How the Toronto Raptors' Bryan Colangelo Plans to Reinvent His Team," *Toronto Life*, November 16, 2012.

179 *"I had to go on the court in front of all these thousands of people"*:

Jordan Brenner, "How the Process Failed Jahlil Okafor," SB Nation, October 11, 2017.

13. "THIS IS NOT THE FUCKING KID WE DRAFTED"

185 *"Joel came up"*: Markelle Fultz, "What's Up, Philly?" The Players' Tribune, June 23, 2017.

186 *Ebony had spent years*: Pat Forde, "How Markelle Fultz Rose from Obscurity to Top NBA Draft Prospect (and Trick-Shot Expert)," Yahoo! Sports, November 2, 2016.

186 *"Sometimes things got tight"*: Ibid.

187 *filling a seventy-quart storage bin*: Kent Babb, "Markelle Fultz Never Forgets," *Washington Post*, June 22, 2017.

187 *Some schools got creative*: Ibid.

187 *"Coach, you are going to call me crazy"*: Keith Pompey, "Markelle Fultz Proved His Mettle at Famed DeMatha High School," *Philadelphia Inquirer*, June 24, 2017.

188 *Chillious and Romar made Fultz their primary target*: Ibid.

14. CONFETTI

199 *were outlined across thirty-five detailed pages*: Adrian Wojnarowski and Bobby Marks, "Joel Embiid's Deal Protects 76ers in Case of Contractually Specific Injury," ESPN, October 11, 2017.

203 *both of whom had cracked*: Kevin Arnovitz, "The Future Is Bright for the 76ers, but Was the Process Worth It?" ESPN, May 9, 2018.

203 *so had their local TV ratings*: Ibid.

203 *Rubin first met Meek Mill*: Max Rappaport, "Sixers Owner Michael Rubin on Meek Mill, Bob Kraft...and That Chopper Ride," Bleacher Report, July 23, 2018.

204 *"I didn't really know anything"*: Ibid.

204 *"Meek used to always say to me"*: Justin Tinsley, "How Meek Mill Opened Sixers Owner Michael Rubin's—and So Many Others'—Eyes to a Broken Criminal Justice System," The Undefeated, May 10, 2018.

204 *"I want him at the game tonight"*: Ben Baskin, "Philly Freedom: Behind the Scenes of Meek Mill's Release," *Sports Illustrated*, April 25, 2018.

208 *"My mindset was to make"*: J.J. Redick, "T.J. McConnell on Being an

Unlikely Hero, Bringing the Grit, and Player-Coach Relationships," *The JJ Redick Podcast*, The Ringer, February 1, 2018.

15. "UNKOWN" SOURCES

213 *with the help of editors*: The Rights to Ricky Sanchez, "The Ben Detrick Interview," August 8, 2018.

16. STAR HUNTING

221 *"I don't like the look of you"*: Chad Ford, "Jimmy Butler Finds a New Home, Hope," ESPN, June 18, 2011.

221 *He spent the next four years:* Lee Jenkins, "Don't Try to Change Jimmy Butler," *Sports Illustrated*, October 9, 2017.

221 *By the end of high school*: Ibid.

222 *"It was either"*: Sam Amick, "Jimmy Butler Opens Up on Difficult Relationship with Fred Hoiberg, Embracing Tom Thibodeau," *USA Today*, November 9, 2017.

224 *He tried prying Bob Myers*: Marc Stein, "Buss's Move," *New York Times*, April 16, 2019.

228 *"It's not like their games"*: Zach Lowe, "Brett Brown," *The Lowe Post* podcast, ESPN, March 14, 2019.

228 *"You're gonna be teammates"*: Ibid.

229 *"You fucking need me, Scott"*: Adrian Wojnarowski, "Jimmy Butler Rips into Wolves Front Office, Teammates During Practice," ESPN, October 11, 2018.

229 *"He can't do shit against me!"*: Chris Haynes, "Sources: Karl-Anthony Towns, Andrew Wiggins Primary Targets of Jimmy Butler's Practice Insults," Yahoo! Sports, October 10, 2018.

229 *"They ain't shit!"*: Ibid.

229 *skipping the group stretching period*: Ibid.

236 *Brown was pulled into a room*: Lowe, "Brett Brown."

237 *"The assets you give up"*: Ibid.

INDEX

ABOUT THE AUTHOR

Yaron Weitzman is an award-winning NBA writer for *Bleacher Report* and a former senior writer for the magazine *SLAM*. His work has also been published in *ESPN*, the *New Yorker*, *New York Magazine*, the *Ringer*, the *Athletic*, *SB Nation*, *Tablet Magazine*, and more.